AMERICAN PLACES

BOOKS BY WILLIAM ZINSSER

Any Old Place with You

Seen Any Good Movies Lately?

The City Dwellers

Weekend Guests

The Haircurl Papers

Pop Goes America

The Paradise Bit

The Lunacy Boom

On Writing Well

Writing with a Word Processor

Willie and Dwike

Writing to Learn

Spring Training

American Places

EDITOR

Extraordinary Lives: The Art and Craft of American Biography
Inventing the Truth: The Art and Craft of Memoir
Spiritual Quests: The Art and Craft of Religious Writing
Paths of Resistance: The Art and Craft of the Political Novel
Worlds of Childhood: The Art and Craft of Writing for Children
They Went: The Art and Craft of Travel Writing

AMERICAN PLACES

A WRITER'S PILGRIMAGE TO
15 OF THIS COUNTRY'S MOST
VISITED AND CHERISHED SITES

WILLIAM ZINSSER

HarperCollins*Publishers*

HarperCollins books may be purchased for educational, business, or sales promotional use. For information, please call or write: Special Markets Department, HarperCollins Publishers, Inc., 10 East 53rd Street, New York, NY 10022. Telephone: (212) 207-7528; Fax: (212) 207-7222.

FIRST EDITION

Designed by George J. McKeon

Library of Congress Cataloging-in-Publication Data

Zinsser, William Knowlton.
    American places : a writer's pilgrimage to 15 of this country's most visited and cherished sites / by William Zinsser.
        p. cm.
    Includes bibliographical references (p.).
    ISBN 0-06-016638-X (cloth)
    1. Monuments—United States. 2. Natural areas—United States. 3. Historic sites—United States. 4. United States—Description and travel—1981- . 5. Zinsser, William Knowlton—Journeys—United States.   I. Title.
E160.Z56 1992
917.3'04928—dc20   91-58381

92 93 94 95 96 ❖/HC 10 9 8 7 6 5 4 3 2 1

Contents

Many of these chapters first appeared in magazines, often in somewhat different form: *Condé Nast Traveler* ("Niagara Falls"), *National Geographic Traveler* ("Lexington & Concord," "Mount Vernon"), *Smithsonian* ("Montgomery," "Pearl Harbor") and *Travel Holiday* ("Abilene," "The Alamo," "Appomattox," "Chautauqua," "Hannibal," "Kitty Hawk," "Mount Rushmore," "Yellowstone Park").

Looking for America

I set out to look for America in the spring of 1990. The decade had turned, and suddenly the wind was blowing from a new direction. Love of country was back in fashion, replacing love of money, and so was patriotic travel. American families began to hit the road, going in search of the founding ideals they felt the country had lost during the '80s. I like the idea of pilgrimages, and I liked reading about the new pilgrims. One day I happened to go to Washington, and whatever was in the air must have been catching. I found myself walking over to the Capitol and into the Rotunda. I had never been there before.

While I was looking around, some tourists came through. Most of them were in family groups—it was school vacation time—and I remember them more vividly than I remember the Rotunda. They were enjoying being on vacation together, but what I thought they were mainly enjoying was the feeling that the building belonged to them. It didn't belong to the Senate, or to the House, or to any other branch of the government. *They* were the government. They were the truths that Thomas Jefferson held to be self-evident in the Constitution ("governments deriving their just powers from the consent of the governed") and that Abraham Lincoln reaffirmed at Gettysburg ("government of the people, by the people, and for the people"). Only in America, I thought, would the citizens be so unafraid of their governmental seat and so genuinely eager to drop in and look around. I wondered where those tourists would go next. Mount Vernon? Mount Rushmore? Independence Hall? Plymouth Rock? I had never been to any of those places either.

About an hour later an unpleasant voice in my head said, *"Why have you never been to Mount Vernon or Mount Rushmore or Independence Hall or Plymouth Rock? Or Concord bridge? Or Gettysburg? Or Niagara Falls? Or any of the big, cliché places that millions of other Americans visit every year?"* The question bothered me, and I fidgeted for an answer. It wasn't that I was a New York snob; I've traveled all over small-town America, assuming that I would find America's basic values there. The answer, when it came, was as unpleasant as the question. I think I took a certain pride in never having been to the big places—the places where everybody else went.

I also saw that I had had a deprived childhood. My three older sisters and I were never put in a car and hauled around America and shown the great monuments and parks that were our heritage. As old New Yorkers we were still tethered to the Old World, and the cultural tours that we did get taken on were "grand tours" of Europe. Nor did I attend schools that organized class trips to historic sites. Probably I would have resisted those well-meant excursions, being history-resistant. But at least they would have insinuated into my head the message: "These places are important. If they are clichés, they are clichés for the very good reason that they embody fundamental truths about America." Instead I've been history-illiterate, loving my country in principle but wanting to be spared the boring details. Maybe. . . was it possible? Maybe those details weren't so boring.

Suddenly I knew what I wanted to do next. I decided to write a very obvious book. I had looked for America long enough in its microcosmic places. This time I was going after the big ones.

I figured that 15 sites would be about right and that my pilgrimage would take a year and a half. (It did.) Right away I thought of eight places I knew I wanted to visit. Four were super-icons: Niagara Falls, Mount Rushmore, the Vietnam Memorial and Pearl Harbor. In the case of Pearl Harbor I felt an extra tug: the Japanese attack that pulled America into World War II also pulled me into the army and sent me overseas. The other four were places that embody a powerful idea about America: Hannibal, Missouri, the boyhood home of Mark Twain, which he used to create the potent myth of the Mississippi River and of an ideal childhood; Abilene, Kansas, the boyhood home of Dwight D. Eisenhower, which represents the values of small-town America; Kitty Hawk, the lonely dune off North Carolina where the Wright brothers invented flight, symbolic of America as a nation of genius-tinkerers; and Chautauqua, the little town in upstate New York that hatched some of America's biggest ideas about self-education and self-improvement.

So I set out, starting at Mount Rushmore, and the rest of my lineup fell into place as I told people what I was doing and listened to their ideas. Often those ideas were a revelation. The tenacious hold of the Alamo on the national psyche was news to me; obviously no book could be written about American icons that didn't include the old fort in San Antonio. Nor had I known about the strong grip of Yellowstone Park on the national imagination. I first glimpsed its power when a ranger in another park told me that during Yellowstone's disastrous fires in 1988, the park got letters from men, women and children all over the country offering to come and help. I wanted to see those letters—and the park that elicited them.

Diversity of region and theme was important to me—which meant, for instance, choosing George Washington's Mount Vernon over Jefferson's Monticello. I was also after America's beginnings, and Washington was the father of us all. For a New England site I chose Lexington and Concord, partly because the American Revolution started in those two towns, but also because Concord's Henry David Thoreau is one of my favorite American revolutionaries, another father of us all. For a Civil War site I first selected Gettysburg. But over the months I found myself drawn to Appomattox, where Lincoln's terrible war finally ended, just five days before he died. His peace interested me more than his war, and the reconciling Lincoln was the Lincoln I cared about.

Thinking about California, I first chose Sutter's Mill, where the 1849 gold rush started. As a child I knew about those forty-niners because I had one for a great-grandfather, a boy just over from Germany who went west in a covered wagon and lost both his mother and his sister along the way. But in the end I felt that the essence of the California dream is not gold but make-believe, and I flew, at a speed unimaginable to that German boy, to Disneyland. If it was a fake icon, it was no more fake than Mount Rushmore, a sculptor's creation, or Hannibal, a writer's creation. Thinking about New York, I thought first of the Statue of Liberty and Ellis Island. But America is also a nation of great cities, icons in themselves, and none has exerted such a magnetic pull as Manhattan. I ditched the lady in the harbor and her neighboring island and went to Rockefeller Center, New York's beacon for tourists of all seasons. Only one of my shrines was new: Maya Lin's memorial in Montgomery, Alabama, to the men, women and children who were killed in the civil rights movement in the South. When I heard about it I decided to trade one Maya Lin monument—her Vietnam Memorial—for another. I had been bothered by the absence of black American voices in my book, except as slaves. I wanted those voices.

My method at every site was to go to its custodians and ask them: Why do *you* think two million people a year come to Mount Rushmore? Or three million to the Alamo? Or one million to Concord's bridge and Mount Vernon, or a half million to Kitty Hawk, or a quarter million to Hannibal? What patriotic or psychic baggage are all these people bringing to this place? That method is the heart of the book. It's not a historian's book, though it contains enough history to enable a novice to understand what happened at each place; I know, because I had to learn that history myself—a scandalously late education. It's not a travel book—the words "bed and breakfast" will not be found in its pages—and it's not an essayist's book; these are not musings on democracy. It's a reporter's book about the ideas that shaped America. It's the book of a writer who caught a lot of planes and rented a lot of cars. My aim was to enter into the intention of each place: to attempt to find out what *it* was trying to be, not what *I* might have expected or wanted it to be.

By interviewing the custodians—park rangers, curators, librarians, scholars, town historians, merchants, ministers, old-timers, Daughters of the Republic of Texas, ladies of the Mount Vernon Ladies' Association—I tapped into the affection and the emotional equity that thoughtful people bring to the place where they have chosen to work, and their answers were rich and often eloquent. Writing down what they told me, I kept thinking: Isn't that wonderful! and when I got home and told people about some comment that had caught me with its insight or its beauty, they would say, "Weren't you lucky to be there on a day when that ranger was on duty?" I said it didn't matter: the luck of the draw is lucky on any given day. The eloquence of the so-called ordinary man or woman is the most extraordinary resource waiting for any writer who goes looking for America.

This is the story of the America I found.

1

Mount Rushmore

Idecided to start at Mount Rushmore, the "shrine of democracy" in the Black Hills of South Dakota that consists of gigantic heads of Washington, Jefferson, Lincoln and Theodore Roosevelt drilled out of a mountain. If I was looking for iconic places, nowhere had the nation's icons been so baldly foisted on the nation—four pharaohs in the sky. Nor was there another monument that so baldly displayed the traits of personality that got America cleared and settled and built: raw energy, brash confidence, love of size, crazy individualism. In such a country an immigrant's son could literally move mountains.

Beyond all that, I had a personal appointment to keep: Mount Rushmore and I grew up together. The carving of the four Presidents ran through my entire boyhood like an alternating current, stopping for long periods when the money ran out. I never quite took it seriously; it was another one of those Depression-era oddities, like the Dionne quintuplets. Somewhere out West, starting in 1927, a sculptor whose very name said "mad scientist"—Gutzon Borglum!—was blasting one of God's mountains and promising to bring forth four immense heads. Even when the project was broke he was often in the news, badgering Congress for more money or hounding current occupants of the White House to turn up for dedication ceremonies that P. T. Barnum would have admired for their showmanship—both Calvin Coolidge and Franklin D. Roosevelt made the long trip—and when he died in early 1941, at the age of 74, exhausted, having brought the promised heads almost to completion, he had forced his vision on the country. That autumn the work finally ended, and so did a part of my life. I put away Mount Rushmore and my boyhood and my baseball card collection and went off to war. By the time I came home, Mount Rushmore had crossed over into the American iconography.

I still didn't take it seriously. But I began to see that it wasn't going to get out of my life, or anybody else's. Hollywood had given the monument a final push into American myth—the image of Cary Grant hanging by his fingers from a presidential chin in Alfred Hitchcock's *North by Northwest* is stamped on the retina of every movie fan—and today Mount Rushmore is visited by two million tourists a year. Maybe Borglum and his mountain had something to say to me after all. I flew to Rapid City, rented a car and drove 20 miles to Keystone, Mount Rushmore's nearest tourist town.

Keystone is an old mining camp that still looks like an old mining camp, unencumbered by charm. I got there late in the day and was eager to catch an initial glimpse of the monument while some daylight was left. Earlier the day had been rainy, and the clouds were still low and gray. As I drove up the mountain I peered through the windshield to try to spot the familiar configuration of heads: Washington jutting forward, Jefferson and Roosevelt recessed behind him, and Lincoln at the far end of the curve, all of them pristine. What I finally made out were four dirty gray faces that looked like postage stamps side by side, their features as flattened as the statues on Easter Island, hardly separable from the rest of the mountain. They didn't even look particularly big. "Is *that* all?" I said to myself—or, more probably, to Borglum. My initial glimpse was a bust.

The next morning I could hardly believe what a difference a day made. I had forgotten one of the oldest truths in travel: good weather is crucial. The sky behind the Presidents was blue, and the sun had dried them out, leaving a granite surface that was stunningly pure. The play of sunlight and shadow on the features of the four men gave them an aliveness unusual in sculpture; Lincoln's eyes were particularly expressive. Together they were gods, all-powerful, and throughout the day I kept looking up to make sure they were still there.

Actually there wasn't much else to do. The site has few trails to walk and few exhibits to see; perhaps no other outdoor attraction in

America is so concentrated. What it says is: "Stop, look, and think about it." Obviously one question to think about is: "How was this thing done?" But the real question that Mount Rushmore puts to us is not "How?" but "Why?" Why are those four men up there? The longer I looked, the more I felt the question working on me, stirring patriotic juices that went back to the classrooms of my childhood. But I also felt my ignorance. Given a test—which, luckily, I wasn't—I'm not sure I could have said exactly what unifying idea about America those four Presidents embody that John Adams or James Madison, for instance, didn't also embody, or Polk. Assuming that there was such an idea, I was curious to know how it gets imparted to two million tourists a year.

"This isn't a monument to Presidents—it's a monument to America," said Jim Popovich, chief of interpretation for the National Park Service site, "and what we try to do with our exhibits and rangers' talks is to make that one point. Most people today don't even know who their grandparents were, much less how they fit into the history of their country. The four Presidents on Mount Rushmore represent the nation's finest ideals as they were shaped in our first 150 years and that we've lived by ever since. Washington of course represents the founding of the country and its democratic government. Jefferson represents stability, because he wrote the Declaration of Independence, and he also stands for expansion; he believed that there was a lot of land out West for people to live in, and he bought the Louisiana Territory and encouraged explorers like Zebulon Pike and Lewis & Clark. Lincoln preserved the Union and freed the slaves, and Theodore Roosevelt defended the rights of the common man against big business and opened the Panama Canal. He also stands for the belief that in America you can do whatever you want to do."

I remembered that not everybody had wanted Teddy Roosevelt on the mountain; he was a controversial latecomer to Borglum's plan. But I was glad to see him up there. No other President so personified America as the land of the "rugged individualist," and nobody was his more natural heir than Borglum. They were two of a kind. Borglum's idol among the Presidents was Lincoln, but he took his energy and his optimism from T.R.—traits, he argued, that enabled Roosevelt to be America's last empire-builder, completing the continental growth that

Jefferson began. No further candidates need apply. A feminist campaign for Susan B. Anthony was waged in 1936, and every modern occupant of the White House, including Ronald Reagan, has been proposed by grateful voters. The good news is that there is no more carvable rock.

"People come here with a real reverence," Jim Popovich told me. "In summer we get as many as twenty thousand a day—that trail sometimes looks like we're herding cattle—and yet the crowds are remarkably quiet and reflective. Many of them become very emotional. You see tears in their eyes when they stand out there on the terrace."

"What they take away from Mount Rushmore is what they bring to Mount Rushmore," said Dan Wenk, superintendent of the site. "Someone who fought in World War II brings something very different from someone who hardly knows there *was* a World War II. The veteran fought for the ideals that those Presidents stood for. Young people don't have time for that yet, but they will. They'll remember that they were here, and when their values begin to mature, Mount Rushmore will have a meaning for them. Some of the most patriotic people we get are motorcycle groups. They come in packs of two hundred fifty or three hundred, and they're extremely respectful of the mountain and of other people."

Assistant superintendent Jim Riggs, who was about to retire from the National Park Service, told me that he had spent part of his 35-year career at Gettysburg, and I asked him how the two sites compare. "They're very different," he said. "Here the feeling is one of inspiration. Anytime you look up at the work you're impressed, and you always find yourself thinking about the inspirational things of the country. At Gettysburg the feeling is one of division. There's a lot of sadness—you're thinking about the death of a great many young men. But you're also thinking about the re-creation of the United States after the war. If you didn't have that, you'd be too depressed."

Patriotism is a changing tide in American life, and nobody has observed its fluctuations at Mount Rushmore longer than Kay Steuerwald, who has been running the gift shop for 40 years. "When I came here in 1951," she said, "patriotism was at its peak, because World War II was still a fresh memory. Some visitors had lost relatives in the war, and for them it was a grief type of patriotism. But for everyone it was a time of great national pride." I remembered that time—I was home from the war myself. All of us were still high on love of country; America had saved the world and there was no limit on our future. "Today's visitors don't let their patriotism show as much," Steuerwald told me. "The mountain brings out their feeling for America and also a certain humility, but often these things surface without their recognizing them."

I wasn't surprised that today's tourists are less revealing of their patriotic emotions—too many Vietnams and Watergates have made us wary. Yet something was obviously still happening at Mount Rushmore, perhaps for just that reason. If the present is dark, at least the founding gods were noble, and the guarantees that they established for us are no less noble now. George Washington's face gives us that assurance. Poised higher and farther forward than the other three Presidents, more fully released from the surrounding rock, he seems to be gazing south across the nation as far as San Antonio and seeing nothing to fear.

"I'm struck by how many of the tourists have been here before," said Lori Weisser, a schoolteacher who spends her summers as a ranger at Mount Rushmore. "Why do they come back? It's not to see the Black Hills. I remember one older man who became very choked up when he talked to me about what he felt here. A few months later I saw him again, this time with one of his grandchildren, and when I said hello he was surprised that I remembered him. But those of us who work here aren't the only ones who stand out from the crowd. There are certain visitors who make an impression on *us*. It's not just the mountain that's impressive."

So dominating were the four Presidents, each one an American original, that for a while I couldn't think about anyone else. But then I became aware of a fifth man tugging at my sleeve, demanding equal time. Gutzon Borglum was no less an American original. "Americans harbor a special love for the impossible task," says the opening sentence of an orientation film that shows Borglum's crew blasting the stone around the emerging Presidents. One shot in particular sticks in my mind. The original plan put Jefferson at Washington's left (as seen from below), and by 1933 the workers had roughly carved his hair, his eyes and his nose. At that point Borglum began to run out of good rock and also encountered a large crack in the granite. He simply dynamited the half-finished Jefferson into the gorge and started a new head on Washington's other side. That's not a man suffering from a failure of nerve. Jefferson never did fully cooperate. Because Borglum carved him as he looked at 33, when he wrote the Declaration of Independence, he appears younger and also more feminine than the other Presidents, partly because of his wig. Many early visitors were disappointed. They said it wasn't a good likeness of Martha Washington.

Borglum was the son of an immigrant Dane, born in 1867 in Idaho, a product of the frontier in his view of America as a land of limitless opportunity. Like other aspiring artists of his generation, he went to Paris in the 1890s to study. There he met Auguste Rodin, who became his mentor. It was Rodin, apparently, who taught Borglum how to use light to animate the eyes in a sculptured head. At Mount Rushmore, what appears to be a pupil in the eyes of the Presidents is a protruding shaft of granite almost two feet long.

"In the early afternoon, when the sunlight throws the shadows into that socket," one of the rangers, Fred Banks, told me, "you feel that the eyes of those four men are looking right at you, no matter where you move. They're peering right into your *mind*, wondering what you're thinking, making you feel guilty: 'Are you doing your part?'"

Returning home in 1901, Borglum became one of America's most productive sculptors, creating, among many popular groups, the 12 apostles in the Cathedral of St. John the Divine in New York, the bronze equestrian statue of General Sheridan in Washington, and two figures that are probably his best-loved works: the marble bust of Lincoln in the Rotunda of the Capitol and the seated Lincoln in Newark, sometimes known as "the children's Lincoln" because children like to climb onto its lap. Borglum's feelings about America bordered on the religious, and they were harnessed to the American love of size, a religion in itself. Sculpture that claimed to celebrate what made the country great should dare to be gigantic, he often said, citing his admiration for the Colossus of Rhodes and the massive statues of ancient Egypt.

Thus he must have taken it as the voice of destiny when he was approached in 1915 by a group of Georgia citizens who wanted to create a monument to the Confederacy. Could Borglum carve the head of Robert E. Lee on the side of Stone Mountain near Atlanta? Arriving to view the site, Borglum found his hosts' idea paltry. Suddenly, as Gilbert C. Fite recalls the moment in his enjoyable and definitive book, *Mount Rushmore*, "a tremendous thought seized [Borglum]. Why not carve the legions of Lee on the march . . . a panorama of Southern military might trailing across the mountainside for more than a quarter of a mile of marching men, stamping horses and rolling guns? Lee, Jefferson Davis and Stonewall Jackson were to be the central and dominating figures. . . . No modern artist had conceived or executed so vast a design. Borglum's vision overshadowed anything accomplished by the ancients."

Duly approved, his project was stalled by World War I, and not until 1923 did he begin to grapple with the huge problems of engineering, safety and carving for which no modern precedent existed. Borglum later said that without the lessons learned at Stone Mountain he couldn't have undertaken Mount Rushmore. In any case, he learned them well enough to finish his head of Lee in 1924. What followed was less triumphant. The sculptor and his patrons fell to quarreling so violently over artistic control that he was finally fired. Warned that the people who fired him were about to seize his designs, Borglum went to his studio and smashed all his models. Then he went to the top of Stone Mountain and had Jackson's head and Lee's shoulders pushed over the side. So ended Borglum's first venture into mountain carving. As for the memorial to the Confederacy, it sputtered to a halt and wasn't resumed for almost 40 years, finally reaching completion in 1970.

Borglum was thus at a low ebb in his career—his best years perhaps over, his name dragged through newspapers as an artistic crank—when the call came from South Dakota that offered a second chance. The man behind the call was the state historian, Doane Robinson. Robinson envisioned huge heads carved on "the Needles," the Black Hills' distinctive stone spires, commemorating various Indian and white heroes of the Old West such as Red Cloud, Sacajawea, John Frémont and Jim Bridger. Borglum, invited to Rapid City, quickly let it be known that mere regional heroes were not worthy of his talents. Any heroes he would carve would be national heroes. He would carve George Washington and Abraham Lincoln, he said, and he drew a rough sketch of those two men perched on the Needles.

How the two sketched Presidents on the Needles turned into four carved Presidents on Mount Rushmore, a peak that was shown to Borglum when the Needles were deemed unsuitable, is a tangled story of political maneuvering, punctuated by strong opposition to the idea of defacing nature—a repugnance that has never entirely gone away; on some level Mount Rushmore will always be an arrogance and an affront. On the separate issue of Indian integrity—the fact that the Black Hills are sacred to the Sioux—nobody seems to have been particularly bothered at the time; not until the 1960s did Native American rights become a moral issue for the nation. (One response to the imposition of four white chiefs on an Indian mountain is being made near Custer, 10 miles away. A colossal statue of Crazy Horse is being wrested out of a hill, and I drove over to take a look. I was amazed by the chalk marks outlining the statue's eventual shape. Crazy Horse, seated "in the round" on his horse, will be so big that all four of the Presidents on Mount Rushmore could fit inside his head.)

Amid the political chaos, the personality that finally swept the cause of Mount Rushmore to approval was that of Borglum. More persuasive than any son of South Dakota, a darling of the press and a wizard at orchestrating its coverage, he charmed the normally immovable Calvin Coolidge into giving the speech, on August 10, 1927, that launched the work and generated the kind of national publicity that press agents less gifted than Borglum can only dream of. Coolidge, improbably dressed in cowboy boots and a 10-gallon hat, declared that future generations would flock to Mount Rushmore "to declare their continuing allegiance to independence, to self-government, to freedom and to economic justice." So saying, he handed Borglum a set of drills. No stranger to dramatic timing, Borglum jumped into a bucket and had himself hauled up the mountain, where, dangling by a cable, he began drilling the master "points" for George Washington's face.

That was the first of countless airborne trips that he would make, a familiar figure with a bushy mustache and a Stetson hat—and one whom the workmen tried to avoid because of his volatile moods. "I got along with him because I stayed out of his way," I was told by 83-year-old Howard Peterson, who put in 13 seasons on the mountain and is one of the project's few survivors. I found him living in Rapid City in a small house that had, among other mementoes, a framed photograph of himself hanging by a cable from Abraham Lincoln's nose. Howard's brother Merle wasn't as lucky—he was fired by Borglum eight times. Eventually, however, he became a master carver and, Howard said, "did all the work across George Washington's forehead." Most of the workmen were unskilled hard-rock miners, and one of the wonders of the project is that many of them became artisans, sensitive to the stone they were shaping and to Borglum's wishes.

Today their drills and winches are on display in the sculptor's studio, along with Borglum's model of Lincoln's head. The models for all four heads were 5 feet tall, and the heads on the mountain are 60 feet tall. Borglum's task was therefore to replicate his models at 12 times their size, which he did by placing reference points on the mountain to guide the workmen with their pneumatic drills. "There were hoses all over the place," Howard Peterson recalled. I was struck by the fact that the heads on the mountain are far better than the models. Not satisfied to simply reproduce his models on a scale never before achieved, Borglum continued to refine them—studying them from below with binoculars, watching the play of southern sun across the features of the four Presidents and then hurrying up to make corrections.

"He'd jump in that bucket and come up to where we were working," Peterson told me, "and he'd say 'five inches here, six inches there.' We always had a can of paint ready for him, and he'd take a brush and paint '5' or '6' or '7' on the stone. Then it was up to the driller to figure out what he meant." That Borglum continued to work as an individual artist on what was in fact a group feat of engineering is probably the secret of its potency. Foreign visitors—I noticed many Japanese tourists—see Mount Rushmore primarily as a work of art.

I asked Howard Peterson what it had been like to be part of such a historic project. He said that its importance never occurred to them. "We thought it was just a job. It paid fifty cents an hour, which was better than they were paying in the mines, and we were glad to get any kind of job. It was seasonal work, and we never did know how long it was going to last. In no way did we envision what that place was going to become. It wasn't until the 1960s, when they started holding Fourth of July celebrations up there, which were very emotional, that it dawned on us: By gosh, we really had been part of something."

From beginning to end Borglum drove everybody crazy. Gilbert Fite's *Mount Rushmore* should have been called *Mount Borglum*: it's the chronicle of a man who is impossible to satisfy. Year after year, the sculptor keeps up a bitter tirade—Stone Mountain revisited—against the administrators of the project, greeting their saintly efforts to accommodate him with rash charges of ingratitude and betrayal.

Nobody escapes—not Congress, not the government, not President Roosevelt. Yet through it all they never lose their affection for him; there was something about him that they couldn't help liking.

The final bill came to $982,992.32. Of this the federal government ended up paying $836,000; the remainder was coaxed out of corporations, small businesses and individual citizens. Borglum's attitude throughout was that he was doing South Dakota an enormous favor, and the decades have proved him right; largely because of Mount Rushmore, tourism has become the state's second industry, after agriculture. But during those Depression years, local merchants found it hard to share the sculptor's notion of gratitude as currency. I was surprised by how many old-timers made a point of telling me, more than a half century later, that Borglum "had a habit of not paying for things," especially things like meals and movies, or of even allowing the people who were with him to pay. "Hell, Korczak, just walk on in! I never pay to see a movie here," he said as his assistant, the sculptor Korczak Ziolkowski, got out his wallet at the Elks Theater in Rapid City.

One woman in her seventies, recalling her teenage summer job as cashier in the grill of the Alex Johnson Hotel, told me about a night when Borglum's credit and the manager's patience had both run out. "The grill closed at ten," she said, "and Borglum came in with his entourage at ten minutes to ten and ordered steaks for everybody. 'I'll sign the chit,' he said. I said, 'I've been instructed to say that it would be nice for you to pay cash.' He said, 'Do you know who I am?' I said, 'Of course I do.' In retrospect it's kind of comical. I guess maybe because he was such a genius and because of what he did for the area he should be forgiven." Such is Borglum's lingering power, however, that when I asked the woman if I could use her name she said she didn't think that would be wise.

For many tourists the climax of a visit to Mount Rushmore is the evening program held in an outdoor amphitheater at the foot of the mountain. It consists of a short talk by one of the rangers, followed by a 20-minute film explaining the historical importance of Washington, Jefferson, Lincoln and Roosevelt, narrated with due solemnity by Burgess Meredith. The film ends with "The Star-Spangled Banner," and at its conclusion Borglum's four Presidents are suddenly bathed in light. The tourists sit stunned, momentarily unable to contend with their feelings. Eyes are dabbed; noses are blown.

"When those lights click on at nine-thirty there's a lot happening out there," said Lori Weisser, who gave the talk on the night of my visit. "In my talks I always find my theme to be that no two people see things the same way," Weisser told me as the crowds picked up their emotions and began to leave. "Mount Rushmore will mean something different to everyone. During the year, I teach fourth grade at Pinedale School in Rapid City. I teach *all* subjects to a group of nine- and ten-year-olds, who relate to them in the same way, being from the same background. At Mount Rushmore it's just the opposite: I teach *one* subject to a group of people who are from totally different backgrounds. So I talk first about what Mount Rushmore means to me—how it's a real constant in my life, like an old childhood friend with whom you never lose touch. Every summer when I come back it represents the values that will always be important to me, no matter how many other things in my life have changed in the meantime. Then I challenge the audience to ask themselves the same question. I tell them, 'After the program tonight, before you move on to see something new, sit for a few minutes, look one more time, think about it. What do you want to get out of this? What do you want to remember? What does Mount Rushmore mean to you?' I'm not going to give them the answer, because then they won't get involved with the monument. I tell them just what I tell the kids in my class: '*You* figure it out.'"

2

Lexington & Concord

I'm a fourth-generation New Yorker, but I also have a lot of New England in my bones. My mother came from a long line of Maine and Connecticut Yankees, I went to boarding school in the historic Massachusetts village of Old Deerfield, and I taught for nine years at Yale, where, every spring, on Powderhouse Day, I was startled by the long and insistent booming of cannon on New Haven's historic green. It was, as I never managed to remember from one year to another, the annual reenactment of the episode in which Benedict Arnold turned over the keys to the powderhouse or somebody turned over the keys to him.

With so much exposure, I didn't need any reminding that New England has more than the usual allotment of iconic places, starting with Plymouth Rock. (My mother claimed that an ancestor of hers named Edmund Doty arrived there on the *Mayflower*, but since he seems to have been an indentured servant I assume that he got off the boat after everyone else.) Mount Rushmore had put me in a patriotic mood, and I began to think about the New England origins of the country that the four Presidents symbolized. Boston alone was a museum of colonial sites. Just as I was trying to decide which site to visit, somebody told me about the annual Patriots Day reenactment of the Battle of Lexington, which, on April 19, 1775, along with a skirmish later that morning in nearby Concord, launched the American Revolution and linked those two Massachusetts towns forever in the new nation's mythology. That settled it. If I wanted to understand how America was born, I thought I should start at the beginning.

I called Lexington to reserve a room for the preceding night at the Battle Green Inn, which sounded, if nothing else, convenient. Only then did I get the news that the battle is staged at 6:00 A.M. I'm not a morning person—the daily act of getting out of bed brings a daily twinge of self-pity. But I fought off my resentment at such strict historical fidelity, caught a plane to Boston, drove to the motel, went to bed, set my alarm for 5:15, got up, pulled on my clothes, and stumbled out into the street. The simulated British troops were due to reach Lexington Green at 6:00 to fire on the town's militiamen, and I wanted to be there early to get a good view; I knew the British would be punctual. It was one of those jarringly cold, damp mornings that New Englanders find so bracing.

What I never expected was that 12,000 people would be at Lexington Green ahead of me. (Later I heard they had started arriving at 4:00.) Except for its triangular shape, the green was a classic New England common, surrounded by stately old white houses and a white-steepled church, and the spectators were standing densely packed on all three sides. Many were parents with young children. I heard one mother ask a boy who was perched on her shoulders, "Can you see better than last year?"

Historically, the battle we were about to watch was rooted in the colonists' resentment of British taxes and other infringements on what they felt were their rights. To keep them pacified, the British sent some regiments to Boston in 1774. But their presence only aggravated the revolutionary spirit, and when the British commander, General Thomas Gage, learned that the colonists were stockpiling guns and ammunition in Concord, he decided to end the uprising before it could start. On April 18, a British military force started out for Concord—a distance of 18 miles—to confiscate the arms. Word got out, however, and two men, William Dawes and the silversmith Paul Revere, rode through the countryside to spread the alarm, reaching Lexington around midnight. (Dawes had the bad luck not to make it into Longfellow's immortalizing poem, perhaps because his name was not as euphonious.)

Thus on the following morning at dawn, 77 militiamen were assembled on Lexington Green when 200 redcoats led by Major John Pitcairn marched into town. The battle that ensued was both brief and accidental. Captain John Parker, seeing that his Americans were outnumbered, ordered them to disperse and not to fire, and Major Pitcairn also ordered his troops not to fire. But one shot rang out—nobody knows from where—and in the resulting panic the British soldiers fired into the backs of the retreating militiamen before their officers could regain control and continue on to Concord. Eight Americans lay dead and six wounded—the first casualties of what nobody yet knew was the American Revolution. Lexington's lone shot, however, was not the legendary "shot heard round the world"; that bullet would be fired several hours later, in Concord.

True to history's script, our reenacted battle lasted only a few minutes. The British grenadiers marched down the main street, saw the militiamen, and stopped to decide what to do next. Then I heard the crack of a single shot. Then I heard a flurry of musket fire—a series of loud BOOMS—and saw some puffs of white smoke rising over the green. Then it was all over. The British soldiers regrouped, and the Americans looked to their dead and wounded. One young father next to me, holding his daughter high in the air, asked, "Did you see it?" She was a perfect lady, two years old going on 40. "Yes," she said, "and I don't want to see any more!"

As the crowd broke up, I made my way onto the green, where women in period skirts and bonnets bent over their fallen husbands and sons. Colonial men carried the bloodstained militiamen off the battlefield. I realized that soldiers hadn't been the only actors in the drama; many people had turned up to play a noncombatant role. They were all practitioners of the hobby called "living history"—men and women who go around the country reenacting historic events. "We emulate what happened years ago," I was told by Charles Hatch, a white-haired gentleman who had come over before dawn from the town of Boxford with five fellow Minute Men. An optical engineer in real life, Mr. Hatch looked every inch a respected Boxford elder circa 1775. "In those days an alarm would go from town to town," he explained, "and the message was to assemble. For us that would have meant coming twenty-two or twenty-three miles across country to Lexington."

Elsewhere on the green, Minute Men whose Battle of Lexington was over for another year were holding ad hoc seminars for onlookers. Bob Childs, who later that morning would turn into a research physicist at MIT, was showing some 1991 boys how his 1767-model musket worked. Fishing a Revolutionary War bullet out of a historic-looking pair of pants, he demonstrated how lopsided it was—and therefore how unlikely to fly straight. "I got into this hobby," he told me, "because I'm interested in the military weapons of that time—in the artistic ability of those people to make guns—but I do it just for the love of history." Minute Man John McWeeney, who belongs to many reenactment groups, was explaining to some teenage girls the significance of what they had just seen. "War hadn't been declared yet," he said. "It was just a civil disturbance. But somebody panicked—like Kent State—and what happened started everybody thinking."

"Lexington is the birthplace of American liberty," said John Fitzgerald, chairman of the town's celebration committee and a tireless overseer of the day's events devoted to that proposition, including a sunrise youth parade, the arrival on horseback of Paul Revere, and various memorial services. Patriots Day is a holiday in Massachusetts, and patriots of all ages had descended on Lexington to revisit its hour of glory and to tour its Revolutionary landmarks. Many of them were wearing tricorn hats that they had bought from Lions Club vendors. The most evocative of the old houses was Buckman Tavern, a 1710 inn, where the Minute Men assembled in the early hours to wait for the British. I also visited the Hancock-Clarke House, a parsonage where Paul Revere stopped on his ride to warn the colonial agitators Samuel Adams and John Hancock. (A year later, Hancock would become the first signer of the Declaration of Independence.) The two men were staying overnight with the Reverend Jonas Clarke, who was known for his fervent sermons in support of the colonial cause, and a replica of the double bed where Adams and Hancock were sleeping, or trying to sleep, is in an upstairs bedroom.

How seriously Lexington takes its vows as liberty's shrine I found out when John Fitzgerald told me how the reenacters prepare for the battle. "They meet in February to assign parts," he said. "Somebody is assigned to play Captain Parker and somebody is assigned to play Sergeant Munroe, and everyone who gets a part goes to the library and reads up on what took place, and in March they have a written exam.

They don't fool around! Then in early April there's a rehearsal on the green. Lately there's been a terrific change in people's attitudes toward the American way of life. A few years ago you couldn't get a Boy Scout to turn out for these events. But today at the sunrise youth parade—you saw it for yourself—every troop was well represented."

I would have been glad to hang around Lexington all day and even wear a tricorn hat. But I had another town to see. If Lexington was the prologue to the American Revolution, Concord was Act One, and I wanted to know what happened when the British soldiers got there. I would also be keeping a rendezvous that went back to my school days. All those American Lit courses that finally busted out of New England to examine rougher diamonds like Mark Twain and Bret Harte were grounded in the intellect of writers who lived in Concord: Ralph Waldo Emerson and Henry David Thoreau, Nathaniel Hawthorne and Margaret Fuller, Bronson and Louisa May Alcott. To judge from their turn of mind, living in Concord bred an almost holy belief in individual freedom; how else did they become such early opponents of slavery and such fierce apostles of self-reliance? Thoreau's *Walden* was America's great permission-giving book, a bible for individualists, and as I drove toward his town I thought that those Concord writers were no less American Revolutionaries than the townsmen who asserted their resistance in 1775, when, in Emerson's near-mythic words:

> By the rude bridge that arched the flood,
> Their flag to April's breeze unfurled,
> Here once the embattled farmers stood,
> And fired the shot heard round the world.

How did that famous shot get fired? News of the killings at Lexington was brought by Samuel Prescott, a young Concord doctor who had been in town courting a Lexington girl. Meeting Revere and Dawes, he urged them to let him join them on their ride to Concord. Along the way they were intercepted by British troops, and only Prescott escaped to warn his hometown. As a result, more than 400 Concord Minute Men and militiamen were assembled at 8:00 A.M. on Punkatasset Hill, overlooking the North Bridge, which spans the Concord River one mile outside town. From the hill they saw smoke coming from Concord, where British troops were searching for ammunition and had set fire to some supplies.

"Will you let them burn the town down?" adjutant Joseph Hosmer asked his fellow officers. Their decision was to "march into the middle of town for its defense or die in the attempt," but not to shoot unless they were shot at. At the North Bridge, which was being held by three companies of British infantry, they were met by a volley of fire, and two men, Isaac Davis and Abner Hosmer, were killed. Seeing them fall, Major John Buttrick cried, "Fire, fellow soldiers, for God's sake, fire!"

That was the shot heard round the world, for it was the colonists' first deliberate attack on the Crown, and the tides it set in motion would never be reversed. The British retreated in disarray, back through Lexington and all the way to Boston, along a corridor known today as Battle Road, under constant guerrilla fire from militiamen who came from surrounding towns and sniped at the redcoats from behind houses and stone fences. At Menotomy (now Arlington), more than 5,000 men were involved in the fighting, and when the exhausted British troops finally staggered home to Boston, after dark, their losses were 73 dead, 174 wounded and 26 missing. American losses were 49 dead, 40 wounded and 5 missing. The Revolution had begun.

"One of our main functions here at the National Park Service is to reestablish the importance of Battle Road," said Lou Sideris, chief of interpretation at Minute Man National Historical Park, a narrow strip that extends from Concord's North Bridge almost to Lexington and includes many sites where militia from nearby towns joined the running battle. "Sometimes too much emphasis is put on Lexington Green and the Concord bridge. You have to look at the whole day: that whole long retreat that became the point of no return, when the colonists knew: 'The die is cast: we have a revolution.'"

But the emotional heart of Revolutionary Concord is the North Bridge. One million tourists walk across it every year. As a shrine the bridge is far from authentic—it's the fourth replacement, built in 1956, of the one that was fought over in 1775. But it looked almost authentic, its wooden planks starting to show some historic rot, and it made a moderate arch over the Concord River, which seemed almost motionless—hardly Emerson's flood. I sat by the bridge and took pleasure in its pastoral calm. It wasn't the first time I had been struck by the tendency of America's old battlefields to be places of unusual tranquillity.

Crossing the bridge, I came to Concord's most famous monument, the Minute Man statue by Daniel Chester French. Best known for his majestic seated figure of Abraham Lincoln in the Lincoln Memorial in Washington, French was an obscure young Concord sculptor when his Minute Man was unveiled in 1875, on the centennial of the battle, before a crowd of 4,000 that included President Grant. Today his Minute Man also does iconic work as the symbol of the National Guard, although the analogy, as Lou Sideris pointed out, is far from exact.

"The National Guard takes its orders from the state government," he said, "whereas the Minute Men were fighting for the right of *self*-government. You have that dramatic moment when they *decide* to march down there and face the British and take a stand: 'We will not be de-armed.' That idea—that the town is the center of self-government—is very much a part of the character of New England. I'm from California, and I'm tremendously struck by the town meeting as a New England institution. It's still alive in every town around here, and there's nothing else in the country like it. People always talk about how the Revolutionary War was a protest over taxes. But it was really about local control."

Lou Sideris and I were standing on Punkatasset Hill, where the Minute Men stood and looked down at the advancing redcoats. Around me I heard tourists speaking French, Italian and several languages I didn't recognize. "Words like liberty and freedom are poetic words," Sideris said, "and the million tourists who stand on that bridge every year project onto it whatever they're going through at the time. After the liberation of Eastern Europe in 1990 we began to get visitors who had been active in those revolutions, and for them the bridge represented the throwing off of tyranny. In the 1960s it was probably seen as the triumph of the little guy over the establishment. But however you interpret it, the notion of the shot heard round the world keeps being echoed."

The next day I went in search of literary Concord, starting at Sleepy Hollow cemetery, just outside town, where, on an elevation called Author's Ridge, the eminent Transcendentalists were at rest. Somebody had left a circle of pine cones around Louisa May Alcott's stone. Thoreau was in a modest family plot, Hawthorne was nearby, and

Emerson's grave was marked by a gigantic boulder; in death as in life, the sage of Concord loomed over his friends and acolytes. But later, in the town's bookstores, I got different news. "There's a steadily growing demand for Thoreau," said Susan Tucker, co-owner of Books with a Past, "and there's also a strong interest in Louisa May Alcott. Emerson is less in demand now, and so is Hawthorne."

Walking around Concord, I found it very familiar, partly because I've tagged along with Thoreau on so many of his rounds, but also because it was one of those New England towns that have a visibly deep sense of identity. Unlike Lexington, which looks post-World War II suburban, Concord is early-1800s solid: serene and graceful but not strenuously picturesque, with many well-aged houses. I wasn't surprised to learn that Concord's present residents include a high ratio of writers and academics—people as invigorated by ideas as the 19th-century men and women who lived in so many Concord houses and thereby made them historic. One was the Old Manse, built in 1749 by Emerson's grandfather, the Reverend William Emerson. Both Emerson and Hawthorne lived in it as younger men and were inspired by it, Hawthorne coming there with his bride, Sophia Peabody, in 1842. I also caught up with Hawthorne at the Wayside, probably the most engaging of Concord's homes for the succession of artisans, scientists and writers who occupied it.

But my main business was with Thoreau, and by midday some inner gravity had steered me to the Thoreau Lyceum, a run-down shingled house on a nondescript street, which is world headquarters for Thoreau scholarship, publishing two journals—*The Thoreau Society Bulletin* and *The Concord Saunterer*—and holding classes for students ranging in age from second grade to Elderhostel. "The idea behind the Lyceum was that there ought to be a place in Concord that people interested in Thoreau could visit besides Walden Pond," said Anne McGrath, its curator. Today such visitors include professors at colleges in the Middle West and Far West, who call and ask if they can bring their entire class. "We sit them on the floor and give them the word," McGrath said, "and *then* we take them out to Walden Pond."

A born-and-bred Concordian, McGrath told me that her father used to read some Thoreau every day, leading her as a child to believe that the two men knew each other. "He'd say, 'Henry walked to

Fairhaven one hundred years ago today,' and of course when you're a child a hundred years doesn't mean anything. I grew up surrounded by places connected to Thoreau, but when I got to high school, I didn't hear any more about him. He wasn't taken seriously." Even now the Lyceum hasn't entirely struggled free of Thoreau's local reputation as an idler, especially in contrast to the decorous Emerson.

"Concord people thought everything Mr. Emerson did was perfect," McGrath told me. "They liked him because he was famous and because he was polite—he behaved exactly the way a college-educated person should behave. You never saw Mr. Emerson walking around in the woods with a flute and a spyglass." Thoreau was no less a college graduate, and he would put his Harvard education to rich use in his writing and his political thinking; he just didn't look like a Harvard man.

"I hate the popular image of Thoreau as a hermit sitting by a pond eating nuts and leaves," McGrath said. "But things are improving. People are reading Thoreau, especially for the style. One teacher told me, 'My students will take Emerson in sentences but not in paragraphs.' What's striking about our visitors is that they're such a mixed bag. Many are interested in Thoreau because of his life as a naturalist. Others are interested in his strong antislavery stand; his mother's attic was a stop on the Underground Railroad. We also get a lot of foreign visitors—Tolstoy wondered why Americans were so interested in foreign authors when they had Thoreau right here—including many from Japan, which has its own Thoreau Society, and from India because of Gandhi, who was tremendously influenced by *Walden* and by the essay on civil disobedience. One night I was about to close up, when a very old Indian gentleman came to the door and introduced himself as a friend of Gandhi. He said Gandhi had always planned to make a pilgrimage to Concord and that he was making it for him."

Though small, the Thoreau Lyceum has a good collection of books, research materials and memorabilia, plus a replica, out in the backyard, of Thoreau's cabin at Walden Pond: a one-room brown-shingled shack, 15 feet long by 10 feet wide, with two windows, a brick chimney and fireplace, a caned bed, a small writing desk, and three plain chairs. The radical simplicity of the cabin reminded me that it was as a teacher that Thoreau first sprang his unorthodoxy on the town. After graduating from college in 1837, he took a job teaching in a local school but quit after two weeks because he refused to use corporal punishment. Instead he and his older brother, John, started a school of their own.

"He was a wonderful teacher," McGrath said, "and if the school had lasted it would have made a great impact on education. The idea was that children would learn better if they enjoyed what they were learning, which was of course directly counter to the ideas of the day. People thought that if children enjoyed a subject it would fly right out of their heads. Well, after three years the parents realized that the children *were* learning better, though they were a little nonplussed at the emphasis on the American Indian—Thoreau thought young Americans should know more about the first Americans—and also by the fact that the boys and girls were taken out-of-doors."

But John got tuberculosis, the disease that would kill Thoreau at 44, and doctors advised closing the school for a while. When John appeared to be recovering, he died of lockjaw from an infected cut. It was the central crisis of Thoreau's life. His zest for teaching was gone, and he fell into a three-year decline. What pulled him out was Emerson's offer of the use of an 11-acre tract at Walden Pond, where he could build a cabin and live and write. From the journals that Thoreau kept during his two-year stay he wrote the two works that would be published in his lifetime. One, *A Week on the Concord and Merrimack Rivers*, was relatively simple. The other, *Walden*, would take eight years and seven drafts to piece together—perhaps no classic of American literature was more painstakingly written and rewritten—and would become one of America's iconic books.

I left the Lyceum and drove out to Walden Pond, which is a little more than a mile from the center of town. Over the years I had heard that the area had gone tacky and commercial, but I found no such sacrilege. The pond lies within a state reservation, protected from development, and except for a small public bathhouse at one end, I saw no works of man along its shores. The once-huge summer crowds have been thinned, I was told, by limiting the number of spaces in the state parking lot, and several conservation groups have joined to try to stave off the encroachment of condominiums and offices on property adjoining the state's land.

The site of Thoreau's cabin is a 10-minute hike from the parking lot—the entire pond can be circled in a half hour—and I walked there on the well-worn trail, meeting many walkers and joggers along the way, and ate the sandwich I had brought from town, not unlike Thoreau himself, who, far from being a recluse, was in and out of Concord frequently, seeing his family and getting provisions. Today the pine-wooded slope where his cabin stood is marked by a simple sign and a cairn of stones that several generations of tourists have piled up. Otherwise the spot is unmemorable except for the memory of the man who was its tenant from 1845 to 1847.

Sitting on that spot almost 150 years later, I was glad to be there as a pilgrim, but I didn't romanticize the moment, in part because the pond itself was just a pond, with no distinguishing quirks of landscape. But mainly I didn't linger because I don't think that living in the woods was the point about Thoreau. He wasn't a woodsman; he was a writer. His stay at Walden Pond gave him a literary framework, enabling him to reshape two years of experience into one year of art. It also gave him the serenity to find out who he was and what he thought.

But where Thoreau speaks most passionately to Americans is not in the solitude of nature but in the crowded places where he rubs against people and their institutions—marveling, often with considerable humor, at the willingness of the mass of men to lead lives of quiet desperation. "I have traveled a good deal in Concord," he writes, "and everywhere, in shops, and offices, and fields, the inhabitants have appeared to me to be doing penance in a thousand remarkable ways." Politically, he was no less libertarian ("that government is best which governs least"), and in my own long, silent quarrel with the government over its military-industrial use of my tax money I often think of the night Thoreau spent in Concord jail for refusing to pay his own tax, claiming, as he later wrote, that "I do not care to trace the course of my dollar, if I could, till it buys a man, or a musket to shoot one with."

I wasn't quite through with Concord. There was one more American original I wanted to look up, and I drove back to town and went to Orchard House, where Louisa May Alcott and her parents and two of her sisters lived from 1857 to 1884 and where she wrote *Little Women*. (The fourth of the "little women," Elizabeth, had died earlier.) They were a family of highly advanced ideas. Bronson Alcott was a Transcendentalist writer and philosopher and a visionary educator. Abigail

Alcott, who had been one of the first paid social workers in Boston, was active in issues of women's rights, abolition and poverty, and their daughters, besides Louisa, included Anna, an actress, and May, an artist and an early teacher of Daniel Chester French. Today Orchard House is furnished with many of their belongings, and the family is strongly alive in its rooms because Louisa's book fixed them so vividly in the hearts of her readers.

"I see women crying—they become so moved that they're *here*, standing next to the desk where Louisa wrote *Little Women*," said Christine O'Connor, a young woman who, as a guide to the house, lives with the phenomenon of the book's lifelong grip on women who are now old. "Many of these women say they've read *Little Women* ten times—it's *the* book they modeled their life on—or they want me to know that they were named for one of the characters. 'I was named after Amy,' they tell me. The house is a shrine for all the women who dreamed when they were growing up of becoming the kind of woman Jo March was." Jo was the sister Louisa May Alcott based on herself.

"Jo was a radical character, totally unlike the heroines of other romantic novels of the day," O'Connor said. "She was nontraditional. She wanted to be able to lead her own life, so she embodies what every girl was feeling who also yearned to become independent and have a career, or who didn't have the right social graces. Jo doesn't have *any* social graces. On the other hand, there's something in the book for everybody; the other sisters provide different choices for a satisfying woman's life. Not every girl wants to be Jo."

Watching the older women who were touring the house, I wondered how many of them who once wanted to be Jo had actually grown up to be Jo. Not many, I suspected. They were from a generation of domesticated wives who seldom got to act out their dreams. No wonder Orchard House can bring them to tears. The writer who lived there—the woman who *was* Jo—was the closest connection they would make with the woman they had hoped to become.

But I also noticed many young girls in the crowd. "The fascinating thing about these girls—they're mostly under fifteen—is that they don't know *Little Women* but they know all about Louisa May Alcott," said librarian Lisa Marcinkowski. Interest in Alcott skipped her own generation, she said, but has bobbed up in a whole new set of young fans, beneficiaries of recent scholarship that has revealed Alcott as a woman of darkness and complexity, interested in adult and feminist themes, not the saint painted in a biography written soon after her death, called *The Children's Friend*.

The Louisa May Alcott who is emerging from these Victorian mists, as seen in new biographies and in her own letters and journals, was a woman whose first books, written under the pen name A. M. Ballard, were thrillers of murder and revenge—"blood and thunder tales," she called them—with titles such as *Behind the Mask*. Later she became a Civil War nurse, which, Marcinkowski told me, was a turning point. "She had grown up in a house with abolitionist parents, and now she was finally able to act on her ideals and go off on her own. Her book *Hospital Sketches* established her name and helped her to find her true style, and by the late 1870s she was the highest-paid author in the United States.

"She thought it was funny that people saw her differently—as the goody-goody 'children's friend'—from the way she saw herself. She had a bad temper, she didn't consider herself domestic, she was an active suffragette, and she was far more proud of the novels she wrote for adults—especially *Moods*, a love story about divorce and other themes that were taboo—than she was of her children's books. She regarded herself as a writer first of all and felt that she had to put her energy there and not into marriage. That's another thing that interests feminists: the fact that she was struggling a hundred years ago with the question of whether women could 'have it all.' I can tell by listening to the people who are coming through Orchard House today that Louis May Alcott is starting to have a big cultural impact."

The next day a literature class from a college in Arkansas was scheduled to visit. I didn't wait. Concord was in good hands, running on the same old current. Making a cultural impact had always been its specialty.

3

Niagara Falls

Walden Pond and the Concord writers got me thinking about America's great natural places, and I decided to visit Niagara Falls and Yellowstone Park next. I had been reminded that one of the most radical ideas that Emerson and Thoreau and the other Transcendentalists lobbed into the 19th-century American air was that nature was not an enemy to be feared and repelled, but a spiritual force that the people of a young nation should embrace and take nourishment from. The goal, as Thoreau put it in his essay "Walking," was to become "an inhabitant, or a part and parcel of Nature, rather than a member of society," and it occurred to me that the long and powerful hold of Niagara and Yellowstone on the American imagination had its roots in the gratifying news from Concord that nature was a prime source of uplift, improvement and the "higher" feelings.

Niagara Falls existed only in the attic of my mind where collective memory is stored: scraps of songs about honeymooning couples, vistas by painters who tried to get the plummeting waters to hold still, film clips of Marilyn Monroe running for her life in *Niagara*, odds and ends of lore about stuntmen who died going over the falls, and always, somewhere among the scraps, a boat called *Maid of the Mist*, which took tourists . . . where? Behind the falls? *Under* the falls? Death hovered at the edge of the images in my attic, or at least danger. But I had never thought of going to see the place itself. That was for other people. Now I wanted to be one of those other people.

One misconception I brought to Niagara Falls was that it consisted of two sets of falls, which had to be viewed separately. I would have to see the American falls first and then go over to the Canadian side to see *their* falls, which, everyone said, were better. But nature hadn't done anything so officious, as I found when the shuttle bus from the Buffalo airport stopped and I got out and walked, half running, down a path marked FALLS. The sign was hardly necessary; I could hear that I was going in the right direction.

Suddenly all the images of a lifetime snapped into place—all the paintings and watercolors and engravings and postcards and calendar lithographs. The river does indeed split into two cataracts, divided by a narrow island called Goat Island, but it was man who put a boundary between them. The eye can easily see them as one spectacle: first the straight line of the American falls, then the island, then the much larger, horseshoe-shaped curve of the Canadian falls. The American falls, 1,060 feet across, are majestic but relatively easy to process—water cascading over a ledge. The Canadian falls, 2,200 feet across, are elusive. Water hurtles over them in such volume that the spray ascends from their circular base as high as the falls themselves, 185 feet, hiding them at the heart of the horseshoe. If the Canadian falls are "better," it's not only because they are twice as big but because they have more mystery, curled in on themselves. Whatever is behind all that spray will remain their secret.

My vantage point for this first glimpse was a promenade that overlooks the falls on the American side—a pleasantly landscaped area that has the feeling of a national park; there was none of the souvenir-stand clutter I expected. My strongest emotion as I stood and tried to absorb the view was that I was very glad to be there. So *that's* what they look like! I stayed at the railing for a long time, enjoying the play of light on the tumbling waters; the colors, though the day was gray, were subtle and satisfying. My thoughts, such as they were, were banal—vaguely pantheistic, poor man's Wordsworth. My fellow sightseers were equally at ease, savoring nature with 19th-century serenity, taking pictures of each other against the cataracts. (More Kodak film is sold here than at any place except the Taj Mahal.) Quite a few of the tourists appeared to be honeymooners; many were parents with children; some were elementary school teachers with their classes. I heard some foreign accents, but on the whole it was—as it always has been—America-on-the-road. The old icon was still worth taking the kids to see. Today more people visit Niagara Falls than ever before: 10 million a year.

Far below, in the gorge where the river reassembles after its double descent, I saw a small boat bobbing in the turbulent water, its passengers bunched at the railing in blue slickers. Nobody had to tell me it was the *Maid of the Mist*—I heard it calling. I took the elevator down to the edge of the river. Even there, waiting at the dock, I could hardly believe that such a freakish trip was possible—or even prudent. What if the boat capsized? What if its engine stopped? What if . . . ? But when the *Maid of the Mist* arrived, there was no question of not getting on it. I was just one more statistic proving the falls' legendary pull—the force that has beckoned so many daredevils to their death and that compels so many suicides every year to jump.

On the boat, we all got blue raincoats and put them on with due seriousness. The *Maid of the Mist* headed out into the gorge and immediately sailed past the American falls. Because these falls have famously fallen apart over the years and dumped large chunks of rock at their base, the water glances off the rubble and doesn't churn up as much spray as a straight drop would generate. That gave us a good view of the falls from a fairly close range and got us only moderately wet.

Next we sailed past Goat Island. There I saw a scene so reminiscent of a Japanese movie in its gauzy colors and stylized composition that I could hardly believe it wasn't a Japanese movie. Filtered through the mist, a straggling line of tourists in yellow raincoats was threading its way down a series of wooden stairways and catwalks to reach the rocks in front of the American falls. They were on a tour called "Cave of the Winds," so named because in the 19th century it was possible to go behind the falls into various hollowed-out spaces that have since eroded. Even today nobody gets closer to the falls, or gets wetter, than these stair people. I watched them as I might watch a colony of ants: small yellow figures doggedly following a zigzag trail down a steep embankment to some ordained goal. The sight took me by surprise and was surprisingly beautiful.

Leaving the ants, we proceeded to the Canadian falls. Until then the *Maid of the Mist* had struck me as a normal excursion boat, the kind that might take sightseers around Manhattan. Suddenly it seemed very small. By now we had come within the outer circle of the horseshoe. On both sides of our boat, inconceivable amounts of water were rushing over the edge from the height of a 15-story building. I thought of the word I had seen in so many articles about Niagara's stuntmen: they were going to "conquer" the falls. Conquer! No such emanations were felt in our crowd. Spray was pelting our raincoats, and we peered out at each other from inside our hoods—eternal tourists bonded together by some outlandish event voluntarily entered into. (Am I really riding down the Grand Canyon on a burro? Am I really about to be charged by an African rhino?) The *Maid of the Mist* showed no sign of being afraid of the Canadian falls; it headed straight into the cloud of spray at the heart of the horseshoe. How much farther were we going to go? The boat began to rock in the eddying water. I felt a twinge of fear.

In the 19th-century literature of Niagara Falls, one adjective carries much of the baggage: "sublime." Today it's seldom heard, except in bad Protestant hymns. But for a young nation eager to feel emotions worthy of God's mightiest wonders, the word had a precise meaning— "a mixture of attraction and terror," as the historian Elizabeth McKinsey puts it. Tracing the theory of sublimity to mid-18th-century aestheticians such as Edmund Burke—in particular, to Burke's *Philosophical Enquiry into the Origin of Our Ideas of the Sublime and Beautiful*—Professor McKinsey says that the experience of early visitors to Niagara Falls called for a word that would go beyond mere awe and fear. "Sublime" was the perfect answer. It denoted "a new capacity to appreciate the beauty and grandeur of potentially terrifying natural objects." Anybody could use it, and everybody did.

Whether I was having sublime feelings as I looked up at the falls I will leave to some other aesthetician. By any name, however, I was thinking: This is an amazing place to be. I wasn't having a 19th-century rapture, but I also wasn't connected in any way to 20th-century thought. I was somewhere in a late-Victorian funk, the kind of romanticism that induced Hudson River School artists to paint a rainbow over Niagara Falls more often than they saw one there. Fortunately, in any group of Americans there will always be one pragmatist to bring us back to earth. Just as I was becoming edgy at the thought of being sucked into the vortex, the man next to me said that he had been measuring our progress by the sides of the gorge and we weren't making any progress at all. Even with its engines at full strength, the *Maid of the Mist* was barely holding its own. That was a sufficiently terrifying piece of news, and when the boat finally made a U-turn I didn't protest. A little sublime goes a long way.

The first *Maid of the Mist* took tourists to the base of the horseshoe falls in 1846. Now, as the mist enveloped our *Maid*, I liked the idea that I was in the same spot and was having what I assume were the same feelings that those travelers had almost 150 years ago. I liked the idea of a tourist attraction so pure that it doesn't have to be tricked out with improvements. The falls don't tug on our sense of history or on our national psyche. They don't have any intellectual content or take their meaning from what was achieved there. They just do what they do.

"When people sit in the front of that boat at the foot of the falls they get a little philosophical," said Christopher M. Glynn, marketing director of the Maid of the Mist Corporation. "They think: There's something bigger than I am that put *this* together. A lot of them have heard about the Seven Wonders of the World, and they ask, 'Is this one of them?'" Glynn's father, James V. Glynn, owner and president of the company, which has been owned by only two families since 1889, often has his lunch on the boat and talks with grandfathers and grandmothers who first visited Niagara on their honeymoon. "Usually," he told me, "they only saw the falls from above. Down here it's a totally different perspective, and they find the power of the water almost unbelievable. You're seeing one of God's great works when you're in that horseshoe."

Most Americans come to the falls as a family, said Ray H. Wigle of the Niagara Falls Visitors and Convention Bureau. "They wait until the kids are out of school to visit places like this and the Grand Canyon and Yellowstone. They say, 'This is part of your education—to see these stupendous works of nature.' On one level today's tourists are conscious of 'the environment,' and they're appreciative of the magnificence of the planet and the fact that something like this has a right to exist by itself—unlike early tourists, who felt that nature was savage and had to be tamed and utilized. But deep down there's still a primal response to uncivilized nature that doesn't change from one century to another. 'I never realized it was like this!' I hear tourists say all the time, and when they turn away from their first look at the falls—when they first connect again with another person—there's always a delighted smile on their face that's universal and childish."

I spent two days at Niagara, looking at the falls at different times of day and night, especially from the Canadian side, where the view of both cataracts across the gorge is the most stunning and—as so many artists have notified us—the most pictorial. Even when I wasn't looking at them, even when I was back in my hotel room, I was aware of them, a low rumble in the brain. They are always *there*. Some part of us, as Americans, has known that for a long time.

Sightseers began coming to Niagara in sizable numbers when the railroads made it easy for them to get there, starting in 1836 with the opening of the Lockport & Niagara Falls line, which brought families traveling on the Erie Canal. Later, workers came over from Rochester on Sunday afternoon after church, and passengers taking Lake Erie steamers came over for a few hours from Buffalo. To stroll in the park beside the falls was an acceptable Victorian thing to do. No other sublime experience of such magnitude was available. People might have heard of the Grand Canyon or the Rockies, but they couldn't get there; vacations were too short and transportation was too slow.

So uplifting were the falls deemed to be that they became a rallying point after the Civil War for religious leaders, educators, artists and scientists eager to preserve them as a sacred grove for the public. This meant wresting them back from the private owners who had bought the adjacent land from New York State, putting up mills, factories and tawdry souvenir shops, and charging admission for a view of God's handiwork through holes in the fence. That the state had sold off its land earlier was not all that surprising; before the Concord poets and philosophers suggested otherwise, the notion that nature should be left intact and simply appreciated was alien to the settler mentality. Land was meant to be cleared, civilized and put to productive use.

Two men in particular inspired the "Free Niagara!" movement: the painter Frederic Edwin Church and the landscape architect Frederick Law Olmsted, designer of New York's great Central Park. Church's seven-foot-long *Niagara*, which has been called the greatest American painting, drew such worshipful throngs when it was first exhibited in a Broadway showroom in 1857—thousands came every day—that it was sent on a tour of England, where it was unanimously praised by critics, including the sainted John Ruskin. If America could produce such a work, there was hope for the colonies after all. Back home, the painting made a triumphal tour of the South in 1858-59 and was reproduced and widely sold as a chromolithograph. More than any other image, it fixed the falls in the popular imagination as having powers both divine and patriotic: "an earthly manifestation of God's attributes" and a prophecy of "the nation's collective aspirations." Iconhood had arrived; Niagara Falls began to appear in posters and advertisements as the symbol of America. Only the Statue of Liberty would dislodge it.

Olmsted, the other man who shaped Niagara's aesthetic, proposed the heretical idea of a public park next to the falls and on the neighboring islands, in which nature would be left alone. This was counter to the prevailing European concept of a park as a formal arrangement of paths and plantings. In the 1870s Olmsted and a coalition of zealous Eastern intellectuals launched a campaign of public meetings, pamphlets, articles and petitions urging state officials to buy back the land and raze everything that man had put on it. Massive political opposition greeted their effort. Not only were the owners of the land rich and influential; many citizens felt that the government in a free society had no right to say, "In the public interest we're taking this land back." The fight lasted 15 years and was narrowly won in 1885 with the creation of the Niagara Reservation, America's first state park. (One hundred thousand people came on opening day.) Olmsted's hands-off landscaping, which preserved the natural character of the area and kept essential roads and buildings unobtrusive, became a model for parks in many other parts of the country.

Gradually, however, the adjacent hotels and commercial enterprises began to go to seed, as aging resorts will, and in the early 1960s Mayor E. Dent Lackey of Niagara Falls, New York, decided that only a sharp upgrading of the American side would enable his city to attract enough tourists to keep it healthy. Sublimity was no longer the only option for honeymooners; they could fly to Bermuda as easily as they could fly to Buffalo. Mayor Lackey, riding the 1960s' almost religious belief in urban renewal, tore down much of the "falls area." Like so much '60s renewal, the tearing down far outraced the building back up, but today the new pieces are finally in place: a geological museum, an aquarium, a Native American arts and crafts center, a glass-enclosed botanical garden with 7,000 tropical specimens, an "Artpark," a shopping mall and other such placid amenities. Even the new Burger King is tasteful. The emphasis is on history, culture, education and scenery.

By contrast, over on the Canadian side, a dense thoroughfare called Clifton Hill offers a Circus World, a Ripley's Believe It or Not Museum, a House of Frankenstein, a Guinness Book of Records Museum, several wax museums, a Ferris wheel, a miniature golf course and other such amusements. The result of Mayor Lackey's faith that Americans still want to feel the higher feelings is that tourism has increased steadily ever since he got the call.

> Niag'ra Falls, I'm falling for you,
> Niag'ra Falls, with your rainbow hue,
> Oh, the Maid of the Mist
> Has never been kissed,
> Niag'ra, I'm falling for you.

This terrible song is typical of the objects I found in the local-history section of the Niagara Falls Public Library, along with 20,000 picture postcards, 15,000 stereopticon slides, books by writers as diverse as Jules Verne and William Dean Howells, and thousands of newspaper and magazine articles. Together, for two centuries, they have sent America the message WISH YOU WERE HERE!, sparing no superlative. Howells, in his novel *Their Wedding Journey*, in 1882, wrote: "As the train stopped, Isabel's heart beat with a child-like exultation, as I believe everyone's heart must who is worthy to arrive at Niagara." Describing the place where Isabel and Basil got off the train as a "sublime destination," Howells says: "Niagara deserves almost to rank with Rome, the metropolis of history and religion; with Venice, the chief city of sentiment and fantasy. In either you are at once made at home by a perception of its greatness . . . and you gratefully accept its sublimity as a fact in no way contrasting with your own insignificance."

What the library gets asked about most often, however, is the "stunts and stunters," according to Donald E. Loker, its local-history specialist. "Just yesterday," he told me, "I got a call from an advertising agency that wanted to use Annie Taylor in an ad campaign." Mrs. Taylor was a schoolteacher who went over the falls in a barrel on October 4, 1901, and survived the plunge, unlike her cat, which she had previously sent over in her barrel for a trial run. Thereby she became the first person to conquer the falls—and also one of the last. Most of the other conquerors tried their luck once too often. Today there is a ban on stunts, but not on ghosts. "Didn't somebody tightrope over this?" is one question that tour guides always get. "People want to see the scene," one of the guides told me. "They want to know: 'How did he do it?'"

Of all those glory-seekers, the most glorious was Jean François Gravelet, known as the great Blondin. A Frenchman trained in the European circus, he came to America in 1859 under the promotional arm of P. T. Barnum and announced that he would cross the Niagara gorge on a tightrope on June 30, 1859. "Blondin was too good a show-man to make the trip appear easy," Philip Mason writes in a booklet called "Niagara and the Daredevils." "His hesitations and swayings began to build a tension that soon had the huge crowd gripped in suspense." In the middle he stopped, lowered a rope to the *Maid of the Mist*, pulled up a bottle and sat down to have a drink. Continuing toward the Canadian shore, "he paused, steadied the balancing pole and suddenly executed a back somersault. Men screamed, women fainted. Those near the rope wept and begged him to come in. . . . For the rest of the fabulous summer of 1859 he continued to provide thrills for the huge crowds that flocked to Niagara to see him. Never content to merely to repeat his last performance, Blondin crossed his rope on a bicycle, walked it blindfolded, pushed a wheelbarrow, cooked an omelet in the center, and made the trip with his hands and feet mana-cled."

I left the library and went back to the falls for a final look. Far below and far away I saw a tiny boat with a cluster of blue raincoats on its upper deck, vanishing into a tall cloud of mist at the center of the horseshoe falls. Then I didn't see it any more. Would it ever come back out? Historical records going back to 1846 said that it would.

4

Yellowstone Park

I drove to the north entrance of Yellowstone Park from the airport in Bozeman, Montana—an instant immersion in the grandeur of the American West—and had no trouble recognizing it when I got there. The entrance was a massive stone arch with the words FOR THE BENEFIT AND ENJOYMENT OF THE PEOPLE inscribed across the top. It wasn't a thing of grace or beauty, like most triumphal arches, but it had its own rough integrity, perfectly symbolizing the idea that it was put there to celebrate. Yellowstone was America's—and the world's—first national park, created by an act of Congress in 1872, and no American idea has been more of a triumph. It became the model for all other national parks and prompted the birth of the National Park Service, which was established in 1912 to take care of it. Sixty million tourists have visited Yellowstone since it opened.

That was a long line of pilgrims, and I thought of them as I drove in. Why had we all come? It wasn't just to see Old Faithful. I suspected that it had something to do with ownership. Of all the places that Americans regard as a shrine, probably none has such a high percentage of repeaters: men and women who were first brought to Yellowstone as children and who come back with children and grandchildren of their own. The park is a family possession—to be handed on, cared for, and, as happened during the fires of 1988, worried about.

I chose the north entrance because I wanted to start at park headquarters, which is at Mammoth Springs, just over the border from Montana. (The park occupies the northwestern corner of Wyoming.) I didn't know much about Yellowstone except that it was some kind of geological freak show, and Mammoth Springs was a crash education in that fact. Nature was visibly hard at work. Water boiled and bubbled up from pools and basins, plumes of steam rose from fissures and drifted across the landscape, and terraces of pink travertine formed a backdrop that looked like dripping candle wax—a Dali painting come to life, or a Monet.

From all the turbulence I assumed that I was somewhere in the vicinity of Old Faithful. Only when I checked in at the Mammoth Springs Hotel and bought some books did I realize the magnitude of my misconception about the magnitude of the park. Yellowstone covers 2.2 million acres and is larger than Rhode Island and Delaware combined. Old Faithful was 51 miles to the south. In the center of the park the wonders are mainly volcanic, the result of a violent eruption 600,000 years ago that caused the core of what is now the park to collapse, forming a caldera, or basin, 47 miles long and 28 miles wide. Heat from the molten rock in that caldera has kept the park in a turmoil of boiling water and steam ever since, activating its thousands of geysers, hot springs, mud pots and fumaroles, or steam vents. Elsewhere the park's spectacular sights include the Grand Canyon of the Yellowstone River and its two waterfalls, the largest mountain lake in North America, and a multitude of wild animals.

News of these marvels was first brought out to a disbelieving nation in the 1830s by trappers like Jim Bridger, whose reputation for tall tales made their accounts easy to disbelieve. Not until after the Civil War was the park visited by two expeditions of such credibility that Americans awoke to the miracle in their midst. One, the Washburn Expedition of 1870, had among its members a 20-year-old former bank clerk, Nathaniel P. Langford, who kept a journal describing not only the park itself but the emotions it aroused. In an entry composed at a point overlooking the Grand Canyon of the Yellowstone, he writes:

> We are all overwhelmed with astonishment and wonder at what we have seen, and we feel that we have been near the very presence of the Almighty. . . . These two great cataracts are but one feature in a scene composed of so many of the elements of grandeur and sublimi-

ty, that I almost despair of giving to those who on our return home will listen to a recital of our adventures, the faintest conception of it. The immense cañon . . . is calculated to fill the observer with feelings of mingled awe and terror.

Turning scientific, Langford provides a profile of the canyon: its length and depth, the height of the two waterfalls, and other gargantuan details. But God continues to crowd science out of his thoughts:

As I took in this scene, I realized my own littleness, my helplessness, my dread exposure to destruction, my inability to cope with or even comprehend the mighty architecture of nature. I felt as never before my entire dependence upon that Almighty Power who had wrought these wonders.

Upon his return Langford presented a lecture to a small audience in Washington, D.C., which included Ferdinand V. Hayden, head of the U.S. Geological Survey. The conjunction of speaker and listener couldn't have been more opportune. Langford's talk inspired Hayden to ask Congress for funds to make an official exploration; the public had begun to take an interest in the Yellowstone region, and the idea of creating a "Yellowstone National Park", was in the air. Congress agreed, and Hayden assembled a group of scientists and scholars who spent the summer of 1871 studying the park: topographers and meteorologists, botanists and mineralogists, entomologists and zoologists. But he was salesman enough to know that mere words could never capture Yellowstone, and he also took along a photographer, William H. Jackson, and an almost unknown artist, Thomas Moran, who would later become known as the dean of American landscape painters. To this day Moran's watercolors and sketches of Yellowstone hold their great beauty and appeal.

That winter Hayden arranged a display of Moran's sketches, Jackson's photographs and some Yellowstone specimens in the Rotunda of the Capitol. He also saw that every congressman got a copy of a recent. article by Langford on "The Wonders of Yellowstone." Thus lubricated, the congressional machinery cranked out the first bill setting aside wild lands "for the benefit and enjoyment of the people" under the management of the federal government, and on March 1, 1872, President Grant signed it into law.

Neglect, however, was the park's early fate. Poorly supervised, Yellowstone was in danger of expiring before it could be properly born. Poachers slaughtered the great animals, and tourists chipped off the mineral formations. Finally, as Hollywood has so often certified, the cavalry came to the rescue. In 1886, Yellowstone was turned over to the army, which administered it for 30 years with a sensitivity that it has seldom been accused of since. Military governance ended with the creation of the National Park Service, but its imprint remained, partly because a number of soldiers quit the army, joined the Park Service and became lifelong rangers, having developed an affection for Yellowtone and for the vocation of protecting it. Another reminder of their stay is the military post at Mammoth Springs, which was built to house them. Arrayed along a parade ground, the great stone officers' quarters that once were Fort Yellowstone are as frozen in time as an old engraving. I half expected to hear a bugle call and to see a colonel who looked like Henry Fonda smoking a cigar on the porch after dinner and listening for Apaches.

Today those buildings are the park's headquarters, and to bring my story into the present I called on Yellowstone's chief of interpretation, George B. Robinson, a second-generation ranger, who says he has had the National Park Service in his blood for 50 years.

"Almost three million people a year come to Yellowstone Park," Robinson told me. "They come for certain obvious reasons. The first one is that it's part of their culture. Visiting national parks is an American family tradition, and the one park that everybody has heard about from an early age is Yellowstone. But there's also a hidden reason. I think people have an innate need to reconnect with the places from which they have evolved. One of the closest bonds I've noticed here is the bond between the very young and the very old: they're nearer to their origins. Most Americans are urban or suburban—they live in a synthetically built world that tends toward uniformity. But health is in diversity. People sense that; there's a longing to get away from the sameness and to recapture our relation to the planet—how we came to be what we are. That's where the Park Service's role comes in: to help people see that Yellowstone is not just black bears and Old Faithful but a spiritual and emotional experience.

"In this great park, too often we're dealing with superlatives: the

2.2 million acres; the canyon; the falls; the lake; the geothermal features, especially Old Faithful, which is the one spot that *all* American and foreign tourists visit; and (as one of our naturalists calls them) 'the charismatic mega-fauna': grizzly bear, black bear, bison, elk, moose, bighorn sheep, mule deer and pronghorn antelope. But Yellowstone is a highly complex and interrelated natural system, and its diversity is amazing—not only the number of different species and processes but the number of life forms within those species. For example, there are 30,000 individual elk. It's important that there be on the planet a reservoir of biological diversity from which we can learn what the process of nature is all about. Yellowstone is relatively unaltered by the onslaught of time and technology and society, so it's a place where we can renew our values and can experience the world on a fundamental sensory level. The things we learn best and remember longest are those that we've come in physical contact with."

The next day I set out to make contact with the park myself. First I boned up on its tourist rules and admonitions, starting with a flier that said:

WARNING

MANY VISITORS HAVE BEEN

GORED BY BUFFALO

Buffalo can weigh 2000 pounds

and can sprint at 30 mph,

three times faster than you can run

"Bears may appear tolerant of people," another notice said, "but are known to attack without warning. Odors attract bears! Store all food and cooking utensils in a secure place such as (1) the trunk of your car, or (2) suspended 10 feet above the ground and 4 feet horizontally from a tree or post." A third item, headed "Scalding water can ruin your vacation," said: "Scalding water underlies thin, breakable crusts; pools are near or above boiling temperatures. Each year, visitors off trail in thermal areas have been seriously burned, and people have died in the scalding water."

Never having tried to suspend food 10 feet above the ground, I was glad I wasn't a camper and wouldn't have to try. Otherwise I was sobered by the warnings; probably I had assumed that I could out-sprint a buffalo. But I also felt fresh admiration for the grand experiment that Yellowstone's 19th-century founders had the audacity to think would work. If 60 million tourists have been enabled to view America's great animals in their habitat, that was a considerable gift to the American people.

How deeply the viewing urge is encoded in the national DNA I learned on my first drive. (Yellowstone has only one sightseeing road, which makes a figure-8 loop through the park.) What I learned was that at the sight of a real or a rumored animal, all the rules of driving conduct get suspended. Cars ahead of me would suddenly just stop. Traffic jams formed and dissolved at unexpected points along the road. One was just breaking up as I arrived; tourists with cameras were climbing back into their cars, and I asked one woman what everyone was looking at. "There was a big bull moose," she said, "but he's gone on." Gone on about his moose business.

Afterward I watched a herd of elk trying to coax their two-week-old calves across a stream. The elk, I was told by a man in a camper, had come down from the mountains, where they had spent the winter, and were moving into the lower park. The calves didn't want to go— they hadn't bargained on crossing water—and the drama played itself out for an hour, the mothers calling to their young in high chirps. I had never seen or heard such a drama before, and as I watched I felt a surge of gratitude. How did I get so lucky?

For sheer sublimity—the word I first encountered at Niagara Falls—nothing in the park was more beautiful and terrifying than the Grand Canyon of the Yellowstone, which I visited that afternoon, getting out of my car at various lookout points along the 8,000-foot-high rim and peering, not always willingly, down. I recalled that Nathaniel Langford also used "sublimity" to avoid having to pin down such a primordial place: a 20-mile gorge with garish ocher walls—the source of the Yellowstone River's name—and two lofty waterfalls. The air was altitude-thin, and the wind had a threatening chill. I felt the same "mingled awe and terror" that Langford felt, and I didn't hang around. Nature had worked on a scale too vast for me, and that night, back at my hotel, I fell asleep counting baby elk.

The next day I made Old Faithful my goal and took the road that meanders down the western part of the park, bringing tourists past five geyser basins. More diversity! Yesterday's canyon had been a finished job, fixed in its present appearance 10,000 years ago. Today nothing was finished; on the contrary, I soon began to accept as normal the sight of escaping steam and the hovering smell of sulfur. I didn't even want to think about what the steam was escaping from. Not only was the landscape too grotesque; it was also too close to the traditional renditions of Hell as a geothermal theme park.

No such theological naggings troubled the naturalist John Muir. The park, he wrote, was a chance "to see nature at work as chemist or cook, cunningly compounding an infinite variety of mineral messes . . . making the most beautiful mud in the world, and distilling the most ethereal essences," and I tried to remember those words as I stopped at three geyser basins—Norris, Midway and Upper Geyser—on my way to Old Faithful. "You have entered the hottest, most volatile thermal area on this continent, if not in the world," said the brochure that I got at Norris Basin, which guided me past such volatile performers as Emerald Spring, Vixen Geyser, Phillip's Caldron, Green Dragon Spring and Arch Steam Vent and across a large lunar expanse called Porcelain Basin, a masterpiece by John Muir's chemist, tinted in delicate pastel colors. I didn't wait for Steamboat Geyser, which in a major eruption is the world's tallest geyser, reaching 300 feet. The problem for tourists is its schedule. Typically, it had 23 major eruptions in 1954, 12 in 1983, five in 1984, and none again until 1989. I needed a geyser that was more constant.

I had reserved a room at the Old Faithful Inn, and when I first saw it across a landscape of gusting steam it was as quirky an apparition as anything else: a high, steep-roofed rustic hotel—mutant Lincoln Logs. It is said to be the largest log structure in the world, and who would argue? Designed in 1903 by a 29-year-old architect from the East, Robert C. Reamer, it has a lobby that soars upward with all its balconies and structural logs exposed, anticipating by at least 60 years the modern hotel "atrium." Its gigantic stone chimney passes through the ridge 85 feet above the floor. Reamer wisely chose to be a vernacular architect, not an Eastern aesthete, and for his materials he just looked around him. His loggers were obviously told to bring back every log they saw that was twisted or bent in a fanciful shape, and he found a spot for everything they collected—in railings and banisters and drinking fountains. The lobby is a fantasia of crooked lines.

Tourists were in Yellowstone long before Reamer built his wooden birdcage. They started arriving soon after the park opened, gladly submitting to its many frontier hardships and dangers. One young couple, Mr. and Mrs. George Cowan, came down from Montana in the summer of 1877 in a party of nine that included Mrs. Cowan's 12-year-old sister. At Upper Geyser Basin they found themselves in the path of the famous retreat of Chief Joseph and his 600 Nez Perce Indians, who had entered the park from Idaho, pursued by the United States Army. Chief Joseph had provoked the army's attack and his tribe's poignant flight by refusing to sign an unlawful treaty ceding the Nez Perce land to white settlers. In a later memoir of that meeting, Mrs. Cowan described how her husband was shot in the head and left for dead in a scuffle with an Indian and how she was brought at nightfall to Chief Joseph's camp:

> The chief sat by the fire, somber and silent, foreseeing in his gloomy meditations possibly the unhappy ending of his campaign. The "noble red man" we read of was more nearly impersonated in this Indian than in any I have ever met. Grave and dignified, he looked a chief.

Mr. Cowan, however, regained consciousness, crawled to safety, and was ultimately reunited with his wife. They were a well-matched pair, resilient and uncomplaining—a trait that Yellowstone's pioneer tourists would need as they dealt with crude roads and lodgings. Their lot improved in the late 19th century with the coming of the railroads, which, having been barred from the park, deposited hordes of tourists at stations just outside, where they were met by stagecoaches. "Some idea of the magnitude of the problem," Aubrey L. Haines writes in his fine two-volume history, *The Yellowstone Story*, "can be had from a listing of the vehicles and stock used by the three transportation companies in 1909. There were six large Concord coaches of the six-horse, 29-passenger type known locally as a tally-ho; 165 four-horse Concord coaches seating 11 passengers, 79 two-horse surreys, 14 'formation wagons' and 129 mountain spring-wagons—the total drawn by 1,372 horses."

The passengers, judging by old photographs in Haines's book, were cheerful young men and women swathed in Victorian clothing, the women wearing long skirts and linen dusters and Gibson Girl hats, the men in hat, coat, tie and, quite often, tennis flannels, for, as befitted their mode of travel, most of them were members of the carriage trade—old-money or nouveau-riche Easterners, for whom, until then, "tourist resort" had meant Saratoga or Newport and "grand tour" had meant Europe. Not until cars were allowed, in 1915, did the park shed its identity as "a semi-exclusive haunt of middle- and upper-class vacationers." The automobile put all of America on the road, and the one sight that every car-borne American had to see was Old Faithful.

Like those millions, I wanted to know as soon as I checked in at the hotel when the geyser would go off. All my life I had carried as an American truth the fact that Old Faithful erupts with clocklike regularity; every 57 minutes was the figure I had in my head. Now, looking around Reamer's cavernous lobby, I saw a sign that said the geyser's next eruption was "predicted" for 3:42. Not only was that well over an hour away; I was surprised that it was a mere prediction, and I asked a Park Service ranger, Orville Bach, about it.

"The regularity of Old Faithful is a myth," he told me. "The time between eruptions has always varied, and over the years it has lengthened because of earthquakes and other changes under the ground. Today the average interval is 76 minutes. Our staff can only predict the eruptions one at a time." I asked him how they did this, and he handed me a sheet that said:

YOU TOO CAN PREDICT OLD FAITHFUL

In 1938 a ranger discovered a correlation between Old Faithful's duration and its subsequent interval. While the specific numbers have changed, we still use this principle to predict Old Faithful today. You can, too! Here's how:

1. Take note of the time that the water comes out and *stays out* of the cone.
2. Time the length of the eruption until absolutely no more water is splashing out of the cone.
3.

If the eruption lasts:	To the starting time add:
1.5 minutes	51 minutes
2.0 minutes	57 minutes
2.5 minutes	62 minutes
3.0 minutes	68 minutes
3.5 minutes	75 minutes
4.0 minutes	83 minutes
4.5 minutes	89 minutes
5.0 minutes	92 minutes

As you can see, the time between eruptions is based on the length of the eruption. Example: Old Faithful erupts at 10:07. The eruption lasts 4.5 minutes. So to 10:07 you add 89 minutes (one hour and 29 minutes) and the prediction will be about 11:36, plus or minus 10 minutes.

It was now 3:30, and I walked out toward Old Faithful to catch its predicted 3:42 show. Several thousand people were already sitting in the spectator area or were on their way, coming either from the hotel, where they were staying, or from the parking lot, where they had left their cars or tour buses to make the pilgrimage to Yellowstone's true shrine. "Most visitors to the park don't get out of the car a whole lot," Bach had told me, "but at two places they get out for sure: the Lower Falls in the Grand Canyon, and Old Faithful."

We pilgrims sat on logs that formed a semicircle around Old Faithful's cone, which was a slight elevation in the ground. As we waited I was struck by the simplicity of what we were waiting for. If the hidden reason for going to Yellowstone is "to recapture our relation to the planet," all of us had made a compact to let nature entertain us in its own good time and with its own elements. I thought of all the areas of daily life where Americans are assumed to be unable to enjoy themselves without electronic help. At ballparks the organist and the scoreboard tell us when to cheer; on television the laugh track tells us when to laugh; on planes and in cars and on walks, the movie and the tape deck and the Walkman divert us from having to look at the scenery or hear the birds or think our own thoughts. Yet here at Old Faithful we were waiting for a show whose only component was hot water. There was no impatience in the crowd. Even small children seemed to know we had signed up for something you can't buy at the mall.

Old Faithful kept us waiting ten minutes, and when it went off, gathering momentum after a few fitful spurts, everybody clapped. The eruption lasted only two or three minutes and wasn't very high, and I felt a twinge of disappointment. But it had a beauty that no photograph could convey, the water and the spray rising and falling and catching the sun and drifting away in instantly shifting patterns. When it was over, the motorized tourists went back to their vehicles and the rest of us went back to our hotel. Old Faithful, however, didn't let us alone. It continued to assert its presence in the lobby and the dining room, and for the rest of the day, whenever its predicted moment drew near, we all stopped what we were doing and walked out to watch. The geyser was duly faithful to us, and I was rewarded for my own fidelity by several eruptions of exceptional length and height and beauty, especially one in which the dancing waters were silhouetted against the setting sun.

"There are five hundred geysers on the planet, and three hundred of them are in Yellowstone Park," Orville Bach told me, "and one hundred and sixty of *those* are in this one little valley, the Upper Geyser Basin, which is only a mile and a half long. Other geysers come and go—they're active or they're dormant—but Old Faithful is reliable. I don't know what would happen if it ever stopped erupting. A lot fewer people would come to Yellowstone. Probably they would insist on some kind of artificial substitute."

The next day I left geyserland and swung east. Once again the park changed landscape on me—it became high forest, the road twice crossing the Continental Divide—and again I thought about its diversity. Unlike other national parks, which have one distinguishing strength—in Glacier it's mountains, in Sequoia it's trees—Yellowstone never quits. I continued to see buffalo and other big animals, the buffalo often standing in the classic profile that long adorned the nickel and that Western artists like Frederic Remington caught in their paintings of the huge herds that populated the Great Plains before hunters made them almost extinct. Yellowstone's 3,000 protected buffalo are one of the last remnants of those herds.

I didn't, however, see any bears—Yellowstone's other big tourist attraction, as President Theodore Roosevelt noted as early as 1903, when he went camping in the park with the naturalist John Burroughs:

> The effect of protection upon bear life [here] has been one of the phenomena of natural history. Not only have they grown to realize they are safe, but, being natural scavengers and foul feeders, they have come to recognize the garbage heaps of the hotels as their special sources of food supply. . . . They have now taken their place among the recognized sights of the park, and the tourists are nearly as much interested in them as in the geysers.

But over the years such proximity got many tourists killed or hurt and also came to be regarded as not good for the bears. In the early 1970s the Park Service closed the garbage dumps, thereby imposing a behavior modification program on the bears to wean them from dependence on human food and send them back into the wild. The program, though still controversial, has largely succeeded; the bears, back on a natural diet, are healthier, though they continue to meet tourists in certain places where their eating, sleeping and fishing interests coincide. One dissenter, Frank Craighead, author of *The Track of the Grizzly*, who feels that the withdrawal of food was too abrupt and that some dumps should be kept open, said, "You can't manage the park as a primeval area when it gets several million visitors a year." But I admired the Park Service for trying to do just that, and although I felt mildly deprived of my bear rights, I found it satisfying that Congress's 19th-century mandate to preserve Yellowstone in its natural state was still being honored as the 21st century approached.

I had made Fishing Bridge my last destination because it was a name I had heard all my married life; my wife worked in its store during one of her college summers, selling wind-up bears and keeping them wound up. First I stopped at the nearby Lake Hotel, the oldest and most elegant of the park's great tourist edifices, dating from 1891, and it was there that the park sprang its last big surprise on me. As I looked across Yellowstone Lake to the snow-topped Grand Tetons, I thought for a moment that I was in northern Italy; the lake and its setting had that Alpine majesty. I could hardly believe that my country had a lake of such scale—8,000 feet up, 110 miles of shoreline—that I never knew existed.

Because the lake is within a normal spectrum of vacation sites, unlike the bizarre geysers and the awesome canyon, it has long been popular with tourists of outdoor bent, many of whom first came there as children on family camping trips. "They're making a pilgrimage back to the memory of their childhood experience," ranger Mona Divine, supervisor of the lake district, told me.

At Fishing Bridge I heard the same echoes of continuity. "The names in Yellowstone are so evocative," said ranger Harlan Kredit. "Fishing Bridge! Old Faithful! It seems to be a tradition in this country that people want to recreate the things they did with their parents. It gives them an anchor in a rootless society. People say, 'I remember standing on that bridge when I was six.' Or they come in with a scrapbook and say, 'Where's this campground?' Americans have bought into the ownership of Yellowstone Park even more than into their city park back home. They demand to know why something has been changed, and you'd better be able to explain it. One big change, of course, is that bears are much less of a shrine: people are starting to get the message that there's more to Yellowstone Park than bears. A big educational effort has helped people to understand what *normal* bear behavior is, and normal behavior is not begging for potato chips along the park road.

"There's a philosophical aspect to the Yellowstone experience that brings people back year after year," said Kredit, who sees the same groups of hikers and fishermen at Fishing Bridge every summer. I asked him why those tourists couldn't do their hiking and fishing closer to home. "It's not the same," he said. "Here they're right in the middle of the oldest national park in the world, and there's magic in that. And the essence of the place has never changed. If you walk off the road one hundred feet in any direction, it's the same as it was when John Colter walked in here." Colter, a Virginian who had been a trapper with the Lewis & Clark expedition, was the first white man to discover what is now Yellowstone Park, in 1807.

"This is my summer school," said Kredit, who is a wintertime high school science teacher in Linden, Washington. "The place just grabs you. Most people in America live at sea level. But up here the air is so clear that you find yourself listening for the sounds of the park. It renews people to get away from the noise of everyday life. It reacquaints them with all their senses."

Of course it's not true that nothing has changed. During the summer of 1988 an epidemic of fires burned across 900,000 acres, or almost 40 percent, of the park—a minor event in nature's long calendar but not in the heart and soul of Yellowstone's once and future tourists. Like them, I had followed the news reports with dismay, and when I visited the park I expected to find much of it blackened. Instead I hardly gave the charred trees and ground a second thought.

To some extent that was a matter of denial: my tendency is to think all is well. It was also part claustrophobia—I'm not a motorist who thrills at the sign ENTERING NATIONAL FOREST, and I welcomed the thinning out of Yellowstone's dense, overgrown stands of lodgepole pine. But even as a reporter I didn't find the burned areas intruding on my enjoyment; most of the damage is in backcountry areas that tourists never see. Mainly what I wanted to find out was how fires of such ferocity started and why they were allowed to burn so long, and on my final day I went back to park headquarters and looked through the fire records.

In 1973 it became federal park policy to let any fire burn that starts from a natural cause, provided that no life or property is threatened. The theory is that fire is a necessary purifying element in the life cycle of a forest, clearing the ground for regeneration, and in 15 years of that policy only 34,000 acres of Yellowstone had burned. Thus when lightning touched off the "Shoshone" fire in the southern part of the park on June 23, 1988, rangers monitored its slow progress. Several other spontaneous fires were also watched and allowed to burn.

On July 22 two incidents gravely altered the scenario. The Shoshone fire, which had burned only 160 acres in a month, exploded overnight into a fire that covered 4,500 acres and began to race toward the tourist complex of Grant Village. Simultaneously, just outside the park's western boundary, in Idaho, a man-made spark started the "North Fork" blaze, which quickly spread into the park and became the most devastating of the summer's fires. At that point a decision was made to fight all the fires in Yellowstone as aggressively as possible. By then, however, several of the blazes had merged, and two unique conditions combined to put all of them beyond human control. One was the lack of rain and moisture; 1988 was the driest summer in Yellowstone's recorded history. The other condition was wind. Freakishly high winds, often gusting to 70 miles per hour, propelled the fires as much as 10 miles a day. They also blew embers ahead for distances that firefighters had never previously experienced—across fire lines and roads and rivers and even across the Grand Canyon of the Yellowstone—and started new fires.

By mid-August the park resembled a war zone and had become an international media happening, complete with fact-finding cabinet members and second-guessing politicians. At its height the $120 million effort involved 9,500 civilian and army firefighters, more than 100 fire engines, which came from as far away as Connecticut, more than 100 helicopters and aerial tankers, which dropped almost 1.5 million gallons of retardant, and all the latest technologies. None of it did any good. The infernos hurtled through the park, narrowly missing many tourist settlements—one came within a quarter mile of the Old Faithful Inn, whose 700 guests were evacuated—and a thick blanket of smoke hung in the daily air and eyes and lungs. Not until mid-September did nature put out its own conflagration with cool air, fall storms and light snow.

No less hard to extinguish was the hostility, some of it remarkably personal, directed at park superintendent Robert Barbee (WELCOME TO THE BARBEE-QUE, said a motel sign outside the park) and his rangers for allowing America's favorite park to burn. Fortunately, the fall storms also blew away the summer's worst fears. When the smoke lifted, autumn foliage brought bright colors to newly opened vistas, and in the spring, long-smothered wildflowers bloomed profusely where none had been seen before. The animal population was not harmed, and the tourist population has since gone steadily up.

Reading about the fires, I realized that I also now thought of Yellowstone as my park. I had joined the vast legion of co-owners from all over America. If I needed any final proof of their sense of ownership, I got it when I looked up the hundreds of letters that park officials received during the calamitous summer. Some of them contained technical advice:

> Am writing this after seeing pictures of the burning trees near the Old Faithful houses. I feel that these fires could be put out with liquid nitrogen and liquid carbon dioxide in large amounts. Have you heard this? If not, please try.

Some contained offers of help:

> My son Ryan and I would like to volunteer a few weeks of our time and energy. We had planned a vacation to Canada and already have reservations. We will be happy to cancel these, however, if you can use our help. Ryan is 15 years old and I am 44. We are both in excellent health and share a love and concern for our environment.

Some were in the handwriting of very young children:

> Dear Mr. Park Ranger:
> I am very sorry that your trees burned down. So I am sending you these 4 pine cone trees for you to plant. I hope they grow big and tall.

Some congratulated the Park Service for its handling of the fires ("Thank you for your efforts on behalf of the American people") and added moral support:

> I know you have received criticism on every side by those who have taken time out of their busy jobs of legislating, mayoring, ranching, etc., to tell you how a park should be run. I am only an ordinary citizen and a lover of Yellowstone Park. Nevertheless I have great faith that nature is self-renewing. . . . We have visited Yellowstone Park every year since 1975. In my eyes, it is an island of wilderness on our continent. It is the only place on earth to see 2 million acres left to nature. It is the only place on earth to see such a concentration of geysers and hot springs in such a huge caldera. Now it is the only place on earth to see a 1-million-acre aftermath of a forest fire. I can hardly wait! I want to take my children every year to see how the park renews itself.

5

Hannibal

I spent three days in Hannibal, Missouri, and didn't have one original thought about it. Everything that went through my head was put there by Mark Twain. In his book *Life on the Mississippi*, the writer who was born Samuel Clemens described the place where he spent most of his boyhood—from 1839, when he was four, to 1853, when he left at the age of seventeen—as a "white town drowsing in the sunshine of a summer's morning," and nothing had changed when I got there. The temperature was 100 and the town was still drowsing. I had purposely gone in summer because in my imagination Hannibal has no other season. It's a place where school is always out, or almost out, and where the Mississippi is always waiting to oblige a boy with a raft and a sudden need to slip off the chains of civilization.

I'm a pushover for the idea of the Mississippi and always have been. It's my Niagara and my Yellowstone, a mighty force of nature out in the middle of America, impossibly romantic, and when I started on my travels it was the place I heard calling to me loudest. As to which part of the Mississippi I should visit, that was no contest. Long before jazz came up the river from New Orleans and gave it a new cargo of legends to carry, Mark Twain lifted it above reality and made it an American icon. I wanted to see where he created that transfiguring myth and what was still left of it. I flew to St. Louis, rented a car and drove two hours north on Route 61 to Hannibal.

The first thing I did when I arrived was to go and look at the river, which is more than a half mile wide at that point, with a strong and muddy current. I sat on the riverbank and watched some tugs pushing barges south to St. Louis and Memphis and New Orleans. Except for a 1950s grain elevator and a 1930s bridge going over to Illinois, I felt that I knew what it was like to be the boy Sam Clemens looking at that view. Though he never went back to Hannibal to live after he moved away, he never forgot what it was like to grow up there. In *The Adventures of Tom Sawyer* and *Huckleberry Finn* he not only froze his own idealized childhood; he created one for everybody else. Today 250,000 tourists a year come to Hannibal to look for that childhood.

It doesn't matter that the people they have come to look for can't be found. I got my first intimation of that fact when I noticed a historical marker near where I was sitting and walked over to read it. It said:

> TOM SAWYER'S ISLAND
> IS SOUTHEAST FROM HERE
> ONE MILE DOWN THE RIVER.
> HERE HUCK FINN AND JIM
> STOPPED FOR A FEW DAYS
> ON THEIR WAY DOWN
> THE MISSISSIPPI.

I looked downriver and saw a dense mass of foliage over on the Illinois side. That would be it: Jackson's Island. For a moment I thought I saw a ferocious thunderstorm playing over the island and, somewhere in its interior, three boys, who earlier in the day had been fearless pirates, huddling for shelter against the bolts of lightning that were knocking down huge sycamores.

I walked up into the town and found its main historic block. I knew it was a historic block because it was paved with bricks and had "attractive" flower barrels at each end to keep cars out. The obvious focus of the block was a small white house that had a historical marker out on the sidewalk identifying it as Samuel Clemens's boyhood home. Attached to the house was a white fence, which also had a historical marker. It said:

> TOM SAWYER'S FENCE

> HERE STOOD THE BOARD
> FENCE WHICH TOM SAWYER

PERSUADED HIS GANG TO
PAY HIM FOR THE PRIVILEGE
OF WHITEWASHING. TOM
SAT BY AND SAW THAT IT
WAS WELL DONE.

Directly across the street was another old building with a historical marker. It said that the building had been the law office of Samuel Clemens's father, John Marshall Clemens; the words J. M. CLEMENS, JUSTICE OF THE PEACE were painted across its facade. Next to the law office was a pleasant white house with green shutters, which also had a historical marker. It said:

BECKY THATCHER'S HOME

THIS WAS THE HOME OF BECKY
THATCHER, TOM SAWYER'S FIRST
SWEETHEART IN MARK TWAIN'S
BOOK "TOM SAWYER." TOM THOUGHT
BECKY TO BE THE ESSENCE OF
ALL THAT IS CHARMING IN WOMANHOOD.

By now my head was beginning to swim. I went into Becky Thatcher's house, which is open to the public, and found that it was actually Laura Hawkins's house. Laura Hawkins was the girl Mark Twain used as a model for Becky Thatcher; as an older woman she recalled that young Sam Clemens "showed off" for her, as Tom Sawyer showed off for Becky, when she and her family moved in across the street. Inside the house I picked up a brochure for Mark Twain Cave, one mile south of town. Tourists could take a one-hour walk in its labyrinthine passageways. It was the cave, the brochure said, where Tom and Becky got lost.

That was when I hit the wall—or the fence. What kind of chump did these people take me for? *I* know Tom and Becky didn't get lost in that cave. *I* know Huck and Jim didn't stop on that island. I was annoyed that the town thought I would fall for such claptrap. But then a stronger idea began to tug at me, and I thought: This is some writer! I was in the presence of a powerful literary force. Was there any other American writer whose characters are so alive that tourists come from all over the country to see where those characters lived and had their adventures?

I walked back across the street to the small Mark Twain Museum and introduced myself to its curator, Henry H. Sweets III. One of the rooms in the museum had two sets of paintings by Norman Rockwell—eight paintings illustrating scenes from *Tom Sawyer* and eight illustrating scenes from *Huckleberry Finn*—and I had noticed a group of tourists studying them intently. "I watch families going around the museum," Sweets told me, "and they spend a long time under those pictures. In the *Huckleberry Finn* pictures they only recognize one or two of the episodes, but in the case of *Tom Sawyer* they know every character and every situation, and they even know the words Mark Twain used. They'll say, 'There's Tom taking the pain-killer medicine'—which is a term nobody uses today."

Hannibal's tourists come in all sizes and ages, starting in late spring, when swarms of schoolchildren descend on the town, brought by their teachers, fresh from reading *Tom Sawyer*. In July and August the sightseers are mostly parents vacationing with their kids, and after that hordes of older and retired people arrive, having waited for September and October's cooler weather and smaller crowds. Whatever their age, they are all there on the same quest: the quest for an idyllic growing up.

"Young boys simply *become* Tom Sawyer while they're here," said Ila May Dimmitt, owner since 1968 of the Show Me Antiques & Gifts shop on Main Street, who says she is the oldest merchant in the area. "They buy a straw hat and a corncob pipe and they walk all over town looking for adventure."

Tom's fence is the most potent icon in town. "All summer I see parents posing their children in front of that fence," Sweets told me. "Where else does something as simple as a fence become a focal point for pictures?" He thinks the fence derives its power from the timelessness of the book in which it is such a memorable character. "Nobody has been sent out to whitewash a fence for a long time," he said. "But the idea of getting other people to do our work for us—and to pay us for doing it—is an idea that all of us love to think about. *Tom Sawyer* reminds us of all the things we wish *we* had done when we were young."

Visitors often ask Sweets how old Tom Sawyer is. "I can't answer that," he said, "because to me, Tom ages dramatically in the course of the book. In the early chapters he's a boy of maybe eleven or twelve, but near the end, when he's in the cave, he's very mature in his treatment of Becky. Most tourists don't care one way or the other; they say, 'It's just childhood.' Looking back, people remember *Tom Sawyer* as a book where life is mostly good—the weather is good, there's no winter—even though many bad things happen in it. But that's how our minds temper things."

No such erasing of hard truth occurs with *Huckleberry Finn*. The book is remembered as much for its darkness as for its light, mainly because it was written by a Mark Twain who was nine years older and wiser and was trying to come to grips with the trauma of race, but also, as Sweets pointed out, because people encounter the two books in two different ways. They read *Tom Sawyer* when they're young, often as early as fourth grade, usually for fun. They read *Huckleberry Finn* in high school or college, where it's taught as one of the great American novels and is analyzed with due academic solemnity. In another nine years, with *Pudd'nhead Wilson*, a satire on slavery, Mark Twain would outdarken *Huckleberry Finn*, putting his Hannibal boyhood to its last and least arcadian use and wrestling the issue of race to an honorable fall.

Of these later artistic struggles most American visitors to Hannibal don't know—or want to know—anything. "Their perception is that Mark Twain lived here all his life, wrote about it, and died here," Sweets said. Proof of Hannibal's centrality in American myth is that the grandiose mansion Mark Twain built in Hartford in the 1870s, at the height of his international fame and fortune—a house open to the public, widely promoted and easily reached—draws only half as many tourists as the small town on the Mississippi that isn't on anybody's way to anywhere and makes little effort to publicize its celebrated son.

Beyond America the view is more spacious. "The farther they are from Hannibal, the more they know about Mark Twain," Ila May Dimmitt said about the tourists who come into her shop, "especially tourists from Europe and Japan. Their education is deeper than ours, and they ask such informed questions about Mark Twain's life and work that I often have to send them over to the museum to get a scholarly answer. Many of them are young Asian students, traveling in America or going to school here."

Her statement would have surprised me if I hadn't already seen one of Hannibal's most striking sights: a display case in the museum containing a sample of books by Mark Twain that has been translated into other languages, including Afrikaans, Czech, Danish, Dutch, Estonian, Finnish, Greek, Japanese, Icelandic, Korean, Norwegian, Polish, Telugu, Turkish and Ukrainian. I saw a *Tom Sawyer* in Latvian, a *Prince and the Pauper* in Lithuanian, a *Life on the Mississippi* in Russian, and a short-story collection in Urdu. Altogether, I learned, Mark Twain's works have been translated into more than 60 languages, often soon after they first came out. *Tom Sawyer* was translated into German within a few years of its publication and has never been out of print in Germany since.

"There are a lot of people in Hannibal who don't like Mark Twain at all and wouldn't even consider picking up one of his books," said Drex Rothweiler, who owns B.J.'s Tavern, the oldest tavern in town. I had gone into B.J.'s to look for the real Hannibal because until then I had found no such place; I had only found the tourists' Hannibal. The tourists' Hannibal can only be seen if you bring along what you want to see: memories, associations, wishes, dreams, regrets, and vague longings for a simpler America, all instilled by one writer. But if you drove into Hannibal never having heard of Mark Twain, you would see an ordinary Mississippi River town of no particular charm. It hasn't been beautified or restored, and it hasn't gone cute; I didn't see a single boutique. Except for its historic district, the only allusions to its larger fame are a few commercial enterprises with names such as the Mark Twain Dinette, the Hotel Clemens and the Huck Finn Shopping Center.

"Hannibal has an identity crisis," several townspeople had told me, and in B.J.'s I caught up with the problem. The tavern maintains an old-time decor to attract sightseers who are "interested in the way the town might have been," Rothweiler said, and it does especially good business when the *Delta Queen* and the *Mississippi Queen* put in. Tourists off the two *Queen*s don't take long to find their way to B.J.'s, which is strategically located on Main Street, not far from the pier. There they settle down for a beer or a sandwich and savor what they persuade themselves is the same atmosphere they would have found if they had stepped off a steamboat in young Sam Clemens's day.

But such customers are no part of the town's identity. "Very few people in Hannibal are historically minded," Rothweiler said, "or Mark Twain-minded, and of course religious people have *no* use for him." I glanced around at the midday regulars having lunch in B.J.'s, bantering with each other across the tables in an old and easy affection. They had the look of farmers and factory hands, and I had a hunch that Tom Sawyer and his creator were not uppermost in their thoughts. "People cash their pension checks here who cashed their first paychecks here," Rothweiler told me. I wanted to know what kind of jobs those checks had paid them for doing. I suspected that Hannibal had been a tougher place all along than the utopia Mark Twain remembered when he looked back on it from far-off Hartford and the comforts of an affluent middle age.

I needed some social history, and to obtain it I called on Orland W. Yates, a retired clothier and an old Hannibal hand. A genial man of 77, Yates is a former president of the Hannibal Chamber of Commerce, like his father before him, and his family has lived in the area since the 1830s.

"This was a shoe-factory town," he told me. "Every little town in Missouri and Illinois and Arkansas had a shoe factory, but the biggest one was here. It was the main plant of the International Shoe Company, and it employed three thousand workers. Then, in the 1960s, the shoe industry left the Midwest to go abroad, just as the textile industry left the Northeast to go South, so all those jobs were lost. There was also a big cement factory down by the river—I always heard that it made all the cement for the Panama Canal—and a big machine shop that built the cars for the Burlington Railroad. They're gone now too."

Not only has the riverfront lost those factories; it has also lost the buildings that once stood on the two streets nearest the river—victims of the Mississippi's periodic floods. Today those blocks are vacant lots of dirt and cinders, a useful reminder that the Mississippi hasn't always been a benign god smiling on boyhood larks. In 1990 the town finally faced its old nemesis and began to construct a levee to hold the waters back. Its hope is that merchants will then return to the area and develop it with new stores. If such a revival takes place it will upgrade a part of Hannibal that was never up in the first place. "It was always a pretty tough neighborhood," Orland Yates told me. "Riverfront towns attracted that."

I asked Yates whether he and his friends had been strongly aware of Mark Twain as a local hero when they were growing up. He said they never gave it a thought. "I lived four blocks from Samuel Clemens's boyhood home and passed it every day. To me it was just another house. There was an old nearby box factory that was a lot more interesting. You could take the old lumber they put outside and make kites out of it."

Not until he went overseas in World War II did Yates realize what the local boy had done for the town. "Wherever I went, it was hard to meet anyone who hadn't heard of Hannibal," he said. "But even when the war was over, no attempt was made to cash in on Mark Twain's name. It was another fifteen years before people began to see the possibility of tourist traffic. A tourist board was formed, some advertising was done, and suddenly . . . here come the tourists! You can't stop 'em once they start. The word gets around."

The interest that Americans began to take in Hannibal was prompted by the interest they began to take in their past, starting in the 1960s. "That never used to be a national trait," Yates said. "Americans always loved things that were new—they'd go anywhere to see a new plane or a new tractor. Today there's nothing more sacred than an old tractor that's got iron wheels on it. People are hunting. The Midwest has got to find its past. There's glamour in the old Gary steel mills and the Kansas City stockyards. We can never go back to those industries or get them back here, but we need to have something to live for. That's what Mark Twain has done for this town. There's nothing to attract people to Hannibal except him. But because of him this place is almost a shrine."

With heavy industry gone, Hannibal's demographic portrait is changing, like the rest of America, from blue collar to white, from labor to "skills" such as electronics and computer services, bringing with it a population that is more educated—American Cyanamid is the town's big new plant—and more impatient with the idea of time standing still. Several times, in fact, I thought I was back in New York. Poking up and down the drowsing streets in my rented car at 15 miles an hour, craning my neck for any signal from an earlier time—some dowager empress of Victorian architecture, some alley where Tom and Huck might have meowed to each other at midnight—I was blasted by the car horn of a Hannibal resident who had been stuck behind one too many dreamers looking for a town that never was.

* * *

Amid so many shifting levels of truth and fiction I finally saw that there was only one reality in Hannibal, and that was the Mississippi River. There had to be a Mississippi before there could be a *Tom Sawyer* or a *Huckleberry Finn*, and there would be no telling it to go away; it would forever be part of the town's consciousness, levee or no levee. Driving north and south of Hannibal on roads that ran near or alongside or above the river, I kept being startled by its sudden presence and its beauty—a vast highway running down the center of America. I had to get out on that river myself, and I went back to where I had begun my visit and bought a ticket on a tourist riverboat called the *Mark Twain*.

I found a chair on the upper deck and sat there in the sunshine of a summer's morning for an hour while the boat slipped downstream and circled back up to Hannibal. I was in a state of contentment: the river was so majestic, so absolute in its flow to the Gulf. It flowed south without a bend as far as I could see—seven miles, the pilot told me— and again I found myself seeing it through the eyes of the boy who would grow up to write about it. What was beyond those seven miles? Where were all those steamboats and all those barges and all those people going? It must have driven the boy half crazy to find out, and when at last he did go forth into the world, he saw more of it than any other 19th-century American writer, fashioning from his early voyages two books—*The Innocents Abroad* and *Following the Equator*—that are still classics of travel literature.

But the waters that gave life to Mark Twain's writing were the waters of the Mississippi, and as I felt its current beneath our boat, I remembered a story that Henry Sweets, the museum curator, had told me. One day in 1982, he said, he got a letter telling him that Jorge Luis Borges, the great Argentinian writer, was coming to Hannibal. Borges had been invited to give a lecture on Walt Whitman at Washington University, in St. Louis, and had accepted on one condition: that his hosts would also take him to Hannibal. *Huckleberry Finn*, he explained, was a book he had read when he was a boy.

Borges was duly brought to Hannibal, an aging lion of letters, 83 years old and in frail health. "He walked with a cane," Sweets recalled, "and he was almost blind. In the museum, when I pointed to the Norman Rockwell paintings on the wall, his eyes didn't follow my arm. We went to lunch, and when lunch was over, Borges said, 'The Mississippi

River is the source of Mark Twain's strength. I want to touch the river.'

"I took him down to Front Street and led him across the cinders to where some cobblestones go down to the Mississippi. He squatted so that he could reach the river, and he leaned over and let the water run through his hands. Then he said, 'Now my journey is complete.'"

6

The Alamo

Hannibal made me aware of the tremendous power of myth. I saw that at any place that embodies a strong American idea or an American longing, as Hannibal makes us long for an idyllic childhood, there would be a gradual merging of fact and legend into a larger truth, one that people wanted and needed to believe. But I had no conception of the potency of myth as an altering force until I went to the Alamo.

Originally I hadn't intended to go there. The Alamo was just some Texas fort where all the defenders including Davy Crockett died in an assault by a Mexican general. But why it was worth defending with such holy fervor, and who those defenders were—soldiers? frontiersmen? homesteaders?—was one of those blurry episodes of territorial expansion in the Southwest that I didn't pay much attention to, growing up in the Northeast.

How badly I had missed the point about that Texas fort I realized when I started my travels and began telling people about my book. "Of course you'll include the Alamo," they always said. It was never a question; it was an assumption, and it shook me up. I was guilty of Eastism. I telephoned the Alamo to ask for an appointment with its custodians. The curator, Wallace Saage, said he couldn't talk to me unless he got permission from his bosses—the people who run the Alamo. Who were they? I asked. He said they were the Daughters of the Republic of

Texas. I said I would also want to talk to them. Would that be possible? He said he didn't know—the Daughters were very protective of their monument. I should write a letter explaining my intentions.

I wrote the letter, put on my best Yankee manners, and flew to San Antonio.

The cry "Remember the Alamo!" was first uttered in 1836, and Americans have been remembering the Alamo ever since. Novelists, poets and playwrights endlessly remembered it in the 19th century; movies and TV programs have endlessly remembered it in the 20th century, and now that I've been there I don't see any end to the remembering in the century to come. I was amazed by the size of the crowds. Three million tourists a year, including hordes of children, troop through the old fort. Whether they quite understand what happened there, or why it happened, or what it all meant, I wouldn't bet on. For a while I couldn't make head or tail of it myself—the story comes wrapped in too many layers of regional history and coated in too many layers of Hollywood paint. But on another level none of that matters. Alamo fact and Alamo myth have long since mingled.

Coming on the Alamo cold, I got two surprises. One was how small it was. The other was that it was right in downtown San Antonio—a sudden apparition around an ordinary street corner. Its humpbacked facade was instantly familiar to me, an iconic American shape evidently printed on my memory. Its history, however, took longer to disentangle. The Alamo was built in 1718 as a walled Spanish mission called San Antonio de Valera. By 1793 most of the Indians who were its intended Christian converts had died of disease, and the mission was closed. So began its second life—as a military fort prized for its strategic location, especially after Mexico won its independence in 1821 and claimed all Spanish land in the area, including the province known as Texas. The fort had also been given a new name: Spanish cavalry troops stationed there in the early 1800s called it Pueblo del Alamo. *Álamo* is the Spanish word for cottonwood, a tree that grows along the San Antonio River.

Mexican rule was at first benign. The new nation adopted a constitution based on that of the United States and opened Texas for colonization, luring settlers from the East and from many parts of Europe with offers of cheap land. But democracy ended in 1833 when the ambitious General Antonio López de Santa Anna was elected president of Mexico. Seizing power as a dictator, he passed tough laws that violated the settlers' freedoms, and by 1835 they began to threaten to revolt. Santa Anna sent his brother-in-law General Martín Perfecto de Cos to the Alamo, where he armed the fort and further suppressed the Texas colonists. They retaliated by sending a force of 300 men to attack General Cos, who surrendered and went home to Mexico, promising to stay there. Santa Anna, however, took the defeat less equably. It was an outrage to Mexican pride, and he vowed to lead an army to San Antonio to win the Alamo back.

Here the unremarkable story takes on the element of perversity or pride that makes it remarkable and gives it its continuing mystery. For the Texans' suicidal decision to hold the Alamo wasn't even militarily sound. Sam Houston, commander of the Texas army, felt that the fort was far too isolated an outpost for his troops to maintain, and he sent Colonel James Bowie there with 30 men to destroy it and withdraw the garrison. That Bowie couldn't bring himself to carry out the order, and that all but one of the 190 men who assembled there elected to stay, though no relief was coming and Santa Anna was on the march with more than 4,000 soldiers, is the psychodrama that tourists are plunged into and expected to grasp when they enter the Alamo.

The tourists are a patient lot. In summer the waiting line stretches for an entire block, as far as the historic Menger Hotel, itself an immersion in San Antonio's picaresque past. Teddy Roosevelt recruited his "Rough Riders" there for the Spanish-American War; its 19th-century guests included every itinerant dignitary from Ulysses S. Grant to Oscar Wilde, and its bar, according to a plaque beside the door, was "the site of more cattle deals than any other place in Texas." I joined the line and was surprised to find that there was no admission charge at the Alamo's door; the Daughters of the Republic of Texas maintain it with proceeds from the adjacent gift shop. They refer to the Alamo as the "shrine" and insist that all who enter are on sacred ground.

Architecturally, that notion was easy to fall in with. I had the feeling that I was in a small Romanesque church in Spain or southern France: stone walls, cool interior, pale light. Incised panels on the walls, not unlike the ones that describe the lives of saints in a Roman Catholic nave, recounted the exploits of various Alamo martyrs, and guards holding signs saying THIS IS A SHRINE reminded tourists to behave accordingly. Sinners were admonished to take off their hats, put away their cameras or cigarettes, and otherwise show respect.

But the story told in the shrine didn't add up—it was too fragmentary—and I went next door to the museum, which occupies the only other surviving structure from the siege of 1836, called the Long Barracks. Again, I was struck by the modesty of scale. The Alamo complex consists of only the shrine, the small museum and the gift shop, and many a visitor is back out in the street almost before you can say Antonio López de Santa Anna. In the museum, a brief video was being shown, and I started with that. It was hilariously unhelpful—one of those fact-laden scripts that omit the one necessary fact. It spoke stirringly of the "Texians." Who were the Texians? It spoke stirringly of "the revolution." What revolution? Obscure names of Mexican-sounding but actually American patriots (José Antonio Navarro) merged with names of obscure peripheral battles (Bexar, Gonzales). The only event I understood was the fall of the Alamo—the one I knew about when I went in.

The museum's exhibits were far richer in information, and from them I began to get a sense of what kind of people those early Texans were. They were men who were drawn to the frontier by the promise of land and a chance to start a new life—men who didn't like to be tied down. The initials GTT ("gone to Texas"), painted on the front door of a house back East, were often their way of saying goodbye, and when they arrived they wrote letters home describing the bounty of the land in a language of superlatives that was to become an organic part of Texas speech. Wives would find it less lovable; as one pioneer wrote, Texas was "a heaven for men and dogs, but a hell for women and oxen." Still, I could see how all of them would develop a fierce attachment to their new home and to the liberties that went with it—the kind of loyalty that can turn overnight into a mystique.

The museum also introduced me to the central figure in the Alamo story: Colonel William Barrett Travis. I had always thought Davy Crockett (of the coonskin cap) and Jim Bowie (of the Bowie knife) were the arch-heroes of the siege, and I had never heard of Travis. But it was Travis who commanded the defenders and inspired them to stay to the end. A 26-year-old lawyer who had become caught up in the colonists' quarrel with Mexico, he joined the volunteers and was

ordered by the governor to lead 30 men to reinforce Bowie's men at
the Alamo. Resenting the assignment to such a remote post, he became
a convert to its defense as soon as he got there, on February 3. "It is
more important to occupy this post than I imagined when I last saw
you," he wrote the governor. "It is the key to Texas." On March 6, the
thirteenth day of Santa Anna's assault, he died for that belief.

To try to bring these distant men and events more vividly to life, I left
the Alamo grounds and went to the nearby IMAX Theater to see a 45-
minute commercial film called *Alamo . . . The Price of Freedom*, which,
judging by the size of the crowds, is almost as obligatory a stop as the
shrine itself. I sat in an ocean of parents and children, all of them pre-
sumably as eager as I was for clarification. We were not disappointed;
clarification was not only clear but loud. Explaining that IMAX's
screen is the third largest in the world, six stories high, our host said,
"We're also going to surround you with sound. When you see a cannon fired in this film, you're going to feel the concussion of the blast."
He was pleased to be able to offer us this brush with combat. My visit
happened to coincide with the aftermath of the Gulf War, and more
than once I found myself musing on the link between modern America's macho love of weapons and its macho frontier past.

The movie, duly concussive, was an excellent re-creation of who
the Alamo's defenders were and how they died. Colonel David Crockett arrives with his Tennessee Mounted Volunteers and is warmly welcomed as a celebrity. He gives the crowd a few of his patented yarns
and reminds them of what he told the Tennessee voters after his defeat
for reelection as a fourth-term congressman: they could go to Hell,
and he would go to Texas. Turning orotund, he says: "I have come to
your country . . . to aid you all that I can in your noble cause. I shall
identify myself with your interests, and all the honor that I desire is
that of defending, as a high private, in common with my fellow citizens, the liberties of our common country."

But it is Travis who controls the drama. Inheriting full command
of the Alamo when his co-leader, Jim Bowie, falls gravely ill, he continues to hope that reinforcements will arrive, and at one point he takes
up his pen to write a letter for a courier to carry out of the fort after
dark. He addresses it "To the people of Texas & all Americans in the
world."

Fellow citizens & compatriots—I am besieged, by a thousand or more of the Mexicans under Santa Anna—I have sustained a continual Bombardment & cannonade for 24 hours & have not lost a man— The enemy has demanded a surrender at discretion, otherwise, the garrison are to be put to the sword, if the fort is taken—I have answered the demand with a cannon shot, & our flag still waves proudly from the walls—*I shall never surrender or retreat*. Then, I call on you in the name of Liberty, of patriotism & everything dear to the American character, to come to our aid, with all dispatch—The enemy is receiving reinforcements daily & will no doubt increase to three or four thousand in four or five days. If this call is neglected, I am determined to sustain myself as long as possible & die like a soldier who never forgets what is due to his own honor and that of his country—VICTORY OR DEATH.

But it becomes apparent that no relief will arrive, and Travis assembles his men. He tells them that if they remain they will all die. He says that he himself will stay: "This I will do even if you leave me alone." He then takes his sword and draws a line in the sand between himself and his men. "Freedom finally rests on those who are willing to die for it," he says. He asks every man who chooses to stay to cross the line and join him.

Historians still dispute whether an actual line was drawn. It hardly matters; what matters is the moment itself. Travis's line—visible in the sand or merely spoken—has come down as a metaphor for the willingness of Americans to die for freedom; during the Gulf War President Bush was frequently said to have drawn a line in the sand. Whatever the truth, Travis's proposition is an amazing moment in the film. When I heard it I asked myself, "Would *I* cross that line?" I thought I surely wouldn't. True, I was 155 years removed from frontier Texas, looking back over a century that has seen countless Americans die in wars that might have been settled by negotiation or that they shouldn't have been asked to fight.

But that wasn't finally the point. The point is that in any century, in any year, on any day, nobody wants to die, and the collective decision of 189 men to die for an idea, as I watched it being reenacted on the IMAX screen, was of a higher order of mysteriousness than one man's decision to die for an idea—a Nathan Hale saying "Give me liberty or give me death!" Individual martyrs are an old story; group martyrs are a rarer phenomenon, and I suddenly understood why the Alamo's dead occupy a unique niche in American mythology. I wondered whether any brotherhood of Americans would die for an idea today. I thought the only sensible person in the film was Louis Rose, a French mercenary who had survived the Napoleonic Wars and thought that wars were to be survived. "I am not prepared to die," he tells Travis in the film, after all the other men have crossed the line. That night Rose slipped over the wall, thereby giving history an eyewitness account of the fort's last days and giving the story the one element that rememberers of the Alamo would rather not remember.

The final 20 minutes of the movie are an orgy of bombardment and slaughter as Santa Anna's troops scale the walls and overwhelm the Texans, who nevertheless kill many Mexicans before falling to their own gallant deaths. Travis is one of the first to die. Santa Anna, walking among the corpses at the end, orders all the bodies of the defenders to be burned. "It was a great victory, Excellency," says one of his aides. "It was a small affair," the general replies.

That it was not a small affair is the moral of the film—and of the Alamo story, for, as the script explains, the 17-day resistance "bought precious time for Sam Houston to rally his army." Seven weeks later, galvanized by the cry "Remember the Alamo!", Houston's troops defeated Santa Anna at the Battle of San Jacinto and put Mexico out of their life forever. The Republic of Texas was born—a free nation that even had its own navy and didn't join the United States until 1846. I was grateful for the cathartic news that the defense of the Alamo actually did serve a purpose and help to win liberty for Texas. It wasn't just an exercise in male bonding; it was some kind of backwoods Thermopylae.

Returning to the Alamo, I dropped in on the gift shop. It was packed with tourists buying Alamo-related items: ashtrays, belts, bookmarks, books, buckles, bumper stickers, buttons, charms, Christmas ornaments, coins, cookie cutters, coonskin caps, cups, dolls, domino sets, flags, glassware, jewelry, jigsaw puzzles, knives, letter openers, lockets, magnets, maps, money clips, mugs, patches, pencils, pendants, pewter "mini-Alamos," pitchers, place mats, plates, playing cards, posters, pottery, powder horns, purses, puzzles, rings, salt and pepper shakers, spoons, sunglasses, T-shirts, tote bags, toy guns and yo-yos. I was impressed that one small martial shrine could lend its imagery to such a multitude of domestic uses. The items all appeared to be of a certain quality, above kitsch, and I walked around the display counters and racks taking notes. As I was finishing, a very tall security guard accosted me and told me to "step outside." I followed him out the door, my heartbeat accelerating ("*I'm being arrested in the Alamo!*") to a rate that I associate with the moment of sighting a cop in the rearview mirror.

"We saw you writing in there," the guard said. I asked him if he arrested everyone he saw writing in the gift shop. He said they couldn't be too careful. "We didn't know you were coming," he explained. I told him that I had made a point of applying to the Alamo in advance and that I had an appointment with Mrs. Diana Lindsay of the Daughters of the Republic of Texas. "That's not the proper hierarchy of clearance," he told me. He got out his walkie-talkie and said he would have to call his superintendent. The superintendent arrived as if summoned out of a bottle—he was there instantly. He had the look and manner of a sheriff and wanted no part of my attempt to explain that I had tried to observe the journalistic courtesies. I was some kind of troublemaker, possibly a Bolshevik.

He and the other guard hustled me upstairs into the presence of Mrs. Fern Dillard, manager of the gift shop. Mrs. Dillard said she couldn't be too careful about what got written about her shop. She wanted me to know that everything in the shop had to be related to Texas, to the Alamo or to the bluebonnet, the beloved spring flower of the Texas countryside. "Bluebonnet items sell very well during the bluebonnet season, when people driving around the state have seen them along the highway," she explained. "The rest of the year, nobody knows what they are." One best-seller that knows no season is the Texas flag. Another is children's merchandise. "You just know that grandmothers are going to demand that you have something they can take home for the grandchildren," Mrs. Dillard said, alluding to her "Kids' Corner," which features dolls dressed Texas-style and stuffed animals wearing Alamo T-shirts.

Mrs. Dillard further wanted me to know that the Alamo gets no public money—from the federal, state or city government—and that its revenue comes mainly from gift shop sales, along with some private donations. "We're sure proud that we can make it on our own without having to ask for help from the government," she said. "Taxpayers have enough problems. I always say, 'The Alamo is not on any taxpayers' dole.'"

My audience ended, to the relief of the superintendent, who had sat eyeing me suspiciously throughout. Later that afternoon I saw a guard interrogating a scholarly-looking man who was standing near one of the Alamo's outer walls, and afterward I asked the perpetrator what he had been doing. He said he was an archaeologist and had been measuring some bricks. The guard had told him, "We saw you using a ruler."

Diana Lindsay, who presides over an information desk in the shrine as official hostess for the Daughters of the Republic of Texas, was as open with me as the watchdogs of the gift shop had been wary. She is, as the rules of the job require, a Daughter, descended from a settler who lived in Texas before 1836, when it was still part of Mexico. (*That's* who the Texians were.) She is the first port of call for tourists who have a question, especially people who think they may be related to one of the Alamo's defenders, and she keeps handy a book called *The Alamo Heroes and Their Revolutionary Ancestors*, which contains as much biographical and genealogical information as is known about the 189 men who died. Several ancestor-seekers stopped at the desk while I was there and were given the book to consult.

"That man thought he might be a descendant," Lindsay said after one seeker came and went, "because he has the same last name as one of the heroes and because his family also came from England. But the facts in the book were too sparse. When that happens I often suggest that people look in the records of land grants. Texas was about land. You can usually trace those grants a long way back, and you're much more likely to find someone that way than through military records, which tend to be transient."

Tourists who sign the visitors' book come from every part of America and from many countries—a diversity that surprised me until I learned how many states and countries the Alamo defenders were born in. In addition to 9 Texians, 33 men were from Tennessee, 13 from Virginia, 12 from Kentucky, 10 from Pennsylvania, 7 each from New York, North Carolina and South Carolina, and 5 each from Georgia, Massachusetts and Missouri. The rest were from Alabama,

Arkansas, Connecticut, Illinois, Louisiana, Maryland, Mississippi, New Jersey, Ohio, Rhode Island and Vermont, plus 12 from England, 12 from Ireland, and another 8 from Denmark, Germany, Scotland and Wales. Twenty were of unknown origin, though the search goes on.

"If you read any letters from the period, it must have been a phenomenal place to come to," Lindsay said. "The country was fertile and beautiful, and the Mexican government made a very attractive offer of land and self-government, so it was natural for immigrants to want to come here to settle their families. Also, many men thought nothing of leaving their wives and coming out here to look for adventure. That was the beginning of the 'Go West!' movement, just before the gold rush. Texas was a 'happening' place to be, and when men start bonding in a war situation it's like a religious fervor, and it becomes even more of a happening place. To this day, Texans are the last of the macho men." San Antonio, she reminded me, has always been a military town and today has five major military bases—one of the steadiest suppliers of Alamo tourists.

"One of our goals is to provide a reverent atmosphere," Lindsay said, but with the size of the crowds that's no longer easy. "People want to say they've been here—it's the thing to do now, regardless of whether they understand it. The Alamo is a hit-or-miss experience for tourists; you have to be a museumgoer to get something out of it. You have to work at it. I suppose it could be argued that a site that gets so many children shouldn't be idealizing war. But at least the children are being taught things about freedom and democracy and other values that are important. The fact is, those men died for a cause—they gave their lives—and I think children should learn about that."

I asked Lindsay what was responsible for the huge popularity of the Alamo. "The movies," she said. "They had a lot to do with molding the myth." Her remark took me back to 1955, when suddenly, one day, every kid in America was wearing a coonskin cap and playing Alamo in the streets and singing "Davy, Davy Crockett, king of the wild frontier!" City kids and suburban kids and rural kids were all instant Crocketts, caught up in a craze that has seldom been matched in the cultural history of a nation that loves cultural crazes. What launched it was Walt Disney's three-part TV series and subsequent movie, *Davy Crockett, King of the Wild Frontier*, starring Fess Parker. Even Disney was amazed by what he had wrought; the American need for a frontier myth ran deeper than anyone had suspected. Crockett was more accessible than Daniel Boone, who had previously held the franchise as prototype pioneer and has hardly been heard of since.

Final canonizing came five years later when John Wayne made *The Alamo*, directing it himself and playing—who else?—Davy Crockett. "That's the movie that really did it," Lindsay told me. "It's not historically accurate, but it's the picture that everybody who comes here remembers, whether they're an Alamo buff or not." The news that Wayne's *Alamo* was less than authentic didn't surprise me; Hollywood has never been finicky in that regard. Why, for instance, didn't Wayne play the heroic Travis instead of the late-arriving bumpkin from Tennessee? Come to think of it, Disney's *King of the Wild Frontier* wouldn't win any awards for truth-in-history either. I began to wonder to what extent the image that Americans bring to the Alamo has been formed by successive waves of popular entertainment. I did some reading and got some revealing answers.

From the beginning, the molders of the myth molded it to suit their patriotic or political needs, stereotyping the Alamo heroes as exemplars of lily-white Anglo-Saxon virtue and the Mexicans as forces of evil: dark-skinned, brutal and, perhaps most ominous of all, Catholic. One form that this racism took in Alamo novels, including juvenile novels, was the use "on nearly every page" of the epithet "greaser" for all Mexicans ("Santa Anna and his army of greasers"), according to Don Graham, professor of English at the University of Texas, writing in *Southwestern Historical Quarterly*. "Mexican treachery was but one degree removed from savage barbarity," a typical novel told its readers. Another, describing the Mexican army, said that its "savage legions were given to every kind of horrible excesses and [their] arms were deeply stained with the blood of helpless old men, feeble women and innocent children." As for their leader, Santa Anna was "an opium user, tyrant and ravisher of fair Anglo-Saxon womanhood."

With the advent of the 20th century a new medium took up the theme and gave it cinematic vividness, starting in 1915 with *The Martyrs of the Alamo*, a film supervised by D. W. Griffith, whose *Birth of a Nation* it resembled in its facile bigotry. Like the novels that had gone before, Graham writes, *Martyrs* "offers a simple racial paradigm: the Alamo defenders are upright Anglo-Saxon heroes, and the Mexicans are craven outragers of everything that is good, pure and decent. Once the battle begins, the racist interpretation is sustained on every level. Mexican soldiers are portrayed as cowards. . . . The most sensational vilification occurs in the mopping-up actions, when a Mexican soldier hurls a little blonde Anglo-Saxon girl against a wall, killing her instantaneously."

Seen in the troubled political context of 1915, however, *The Martyrs of the Alamo* was just the latest in a long series of uses of the Alamo to symbolize free people united against a foreign despot. "The threat to American democracy by the German Kaiser," Brian Huberman and Ed Hugetz write in *Southwest Media Review*, "is clearly encoded in the costume and performance of Santa Anna and his army; the historical Santa Anna had modeled himself and his army on another European tyrant, Napoleon." The writers point out that since the birth of the film industry at least one Alamo movie per decade has been made, each one using the model of the Alamo to respond to a specific threat to American liberties, and each one interpreting the story differently.

For John Wayne the specific threat was the cold war, and producing *The Alamo* at the end of the 1950s became a near-religious crusade. Spurned by every major Hollywood studio because he wanted to direct the movie as well as star in it, he formed his own company and made it himself, at a high cost in money, time and health. The Alamo, he told one interviewer, "was not a story that belongs only to Texas; it belongs to people everywhere who have an interest in a thing called freedom. I think we are all in danger and have been for a long time of going soft, of taking things for granted; neglecting to have an objective about the things for which we stand and forgetting the things that made this a great nation." Stating his political agenda more bluntly, he told the columnist Louella Parsons, "These are perilous times. The eyes of the world are on us. We must sell America to countries threatened with Communist domination."

In making that sale, Wayne was no more constrained by the probable truth of what happened at the Alamo than any of his predecessors were. On the contrary, as Frank Thompson writes in his book *Alamo Movies*, "*The Alamo* is a stirring, heartfelt epic, but it maintains virtually no contact with the facts. In fact, there is not a single instant or incident in *The Alamo* that corresponds with the actual historical moment." Thompson's book, a thorough and affectionate review of almost 80 years' worth of Alamo movies, finds all of them guilty of distortion and make-believe. "Confusing history with myth is, of course, what the Alamo movies do best; in the struggle, myth always wins out," he writes. Confirming this outcome, George A. McAlister, producer of the IMAX film that I admired, *Alamo . . . The Price of Freedom*, is quoted as saying that "some of the Alamo's events are just too muddled or controversial or both. When given a choice between two versions of the same incident, we came down on the side of heroism every time."

The result is that the 189 martyrs of the Alamo have descended through time unbesmirched, immune to the virus of revisionism that sooner or later disfigures even the noblest heroes and saints. Hollywood has always been one of the main revisers, Frank Thompson writes, noting that George Armstrong Custer was depicted as a hero in *They Died with Their Boots On*, as a fascist in *Tonka* and as a madman in *Little Big Man*. Of the Alamo defenders, however, he says that no captious word has been breathed on the screen; "their motives are always of the purest, highest caliber." That 189 such paragons were gathered in one fort in frontier Texas would seem to run counter to what is known about the kind of men who settled the West, not to mention what is known about human nature. There is even evidence that some of the defenders, including Davy Crockett, surrendered to Santa Anna and were executed by him when the battle was over.

After two days I rented a car and drove through the Hill Country, the distinctive region west of San Antonio and Austin that stretches up to Lyndon Johnson territory. I wanted to see what kind of land had drawn and bred this race of larger-than-life Americans. The trip left me exhilarated. I liked the deceptively simple beauty of the landscape: the blue of the bluebonnets, the subtle gray-greens of the rising and falling countryside, the longhorns standing by the fences, and the enormous sky—a sky that went on forever. Stopping in small towns, I caught a rodeo and a livestock fair and some country fiddling. The town of Bandera was holding its annual spring "money-raiser" for local beautification: all the beans and tortillas you could eat and all the beer you could drink for a donation of $1.

What struck me about the people was how much they laughed, and how easily. They seemed to have been born laughing—life was to be enjoyed and not worried about unduly. If these were the great-grandsons and great-granddaughters of those early Texians who got so up in arms about freedom, they had a pleasant way of life to be up in arms about, and as I headed back to San Antonio I thought that a little ancestral myth-making never hurt anybody. Night had fallen when I reached the city, and for the first time I saw the Alamo after dark. It caught me off guard with its dignity and its repose. The old stone facade was lit by floodlights, and it seemed to exist apart in time and space from the busy modern metropolis. It looked like—well, like a shrine.

"Because the Alamo today is in the middle of San Antonio," said its curator, Wallace Saage, when I went back the next morning, "it's hard for tourists to visualize what it was like at the time of the siege—how isolated it was. The next settlement was seventy miles away. The forest began right out the back door, and there were frequent Comanche attacks. All those movies have given people an image of the Alamo's size that is dispelled as soon as they get here. The comment I hear most often from tourists is, 'It's so small.' They're just overawed that the men decided to stay and fight against those odds."

I mentioned that the Alamo massacre as I saw and heard it and felt its concussions in the IMAX film struck me as a heavy dose of blood-shed to inflict on an audience, especially one that includes so many children. The film is not part of Saage's curatorial domain, but his reply answered many of the questions I had been wrestling with.

"We live in a society that has become much more realistic about violence," he said, "and maybe it's a good thing for people to see how things really were at the Alamo: to see that it was not a romantic ver-sion of war à la John Wayne, but that life out here was hard and that our freedoms were gained with that kind of violence—and that *that's* why Texans are proud of the stand those men made."

7

Appomattox

I'm not a Civil War buff. I've never heard the old battlefields like Gettysburg and Chickamauga calling to me to come and walk over them and reenact what happened there; the story is just too sad. When I watched Ken Burns's 13-week television series, I wondered how Civil War scholars can stand such a relentless diet of carnage and blundering—more than 620,000 men killed in four years—and I periodically switched to a ball game to get a few innings of relief.

But as a larger historical event, the Civil War is baggage that I'm stuck with: America's enduring trauma. I continue to lug around its unfinished business, especially the freeing of the slaves, and no President crowds into my mind as often as Abraham Lincoln. His second inaugural address, delivered only five weeks before his consuming war finally ended and six weeks before he himself was killed, moves me more than any American document—a continuing astonishment in its wisdom and compassion, in its plea for a reconciliation that would have charity for all, and in the Biblical grandeur of its language. Of all American writers, Lincoln is the one I most marvel at.

Therefore the Civil War site that kept beckoning to me as I traveled around the country was not one where the armies fought but the one where they stopped fighting. Appomattox was both a longed-for end and a longed-for beginning; America could get on with the business of being a nation. "Before 1861," James M. McPherson writes in his Pulitzer Prize-winning *Battle Cry of Freedom*, "the two words 'United States' were generally rendered as a plural noun: 'the United States *are* a republic.' The war marked a transition of the United States to a singular noun. . . . In [Lincoln's] First Inaugural address he used the word 'Union' twenty times and the word 'nation' not once. . . . In his address at Gettysburg [in 1863] the President did not refer to the 'Union' at all but used the word 'nation' five times to invoke a new birth of freedom and nationalism for the United States. And in his Second Inaugural address, looking back over the events of the past four years, Lincoln spoke of one side seeking to dissolve the *Union* in 1861 and the other accepting the challenge of war to preserve the *nation*." Appomattox was the birthplace of that nation, and I wanted to see it.

I flew to Richmond and drove west across southern Virginia, choosing that route because it would take me over terrain that General Robert E. Lee covered with his army in its last week—a week that ended with his surrender to General Ulysses S. Grant, on April 9, 1865, in a tiny village that just happened to be handy when the dream of the Confederacy finally unraveled. Picking up Lee's trail, I saw some historical markers, just beyond the town of Amelia, that told me how desperate his situation had become.

LEE'S RETREAT

SHERIDAN REACHED HERE ON APRIL 4, 1865,
WITH THE CAVALRY AND WAS ENTRENCHED. HE WAS
THUS SQUARELY ACROSS LEE'S LINE OF RETREAT
TO DANVILLE. ON APRIL 5, GRANT AND MEADE
ARRIVED FROM THE EAST WITH THE SECOND CORPS
AND THE SIXTH CORPS.

For nine months Lee's 55,000-man Army of Northern Virginia had been dug in near Petersburg. The railroad was its only source of supply. On April 1, General Philip Sheridan had seized the railroad town of Five Forks, severing the army's lifeline. On April 2, Lee ordered his army to retreat, hoping either to reach Lynchburg in the west or to turn south to join General Joseph E. Johnston's army in North Carolina. Grant, however, was in close pursuit:

FROM HERE UNION CAVALRY MOVED NORTH ON APRIL 5,
1865, TO ASCERTAIN LEE'S WHEREABOUTS. ON THE
MORNING OF APRIL 6, THE SECOND, FIFTH AND
SIXTH CORPS OF GRANT'S ARMY ADVANCED FROM
JETERSVILLE TOWARD AMELIA COURT HOUSE
TO ATTACK LEE.

By then Lee had already come and gone, finding that the rations he expected in the town of Amelia Court House hadn't arrived and that he couldn't wait for them. With the road to the south blocked by Sheridan,

... HE THEN TURNED WESTWARD BY WAY OF
AMELIA SPRINGS, HOPING TO REACH THE SOUTHSIDE
(NORFOLK & WESTERN) RAILROAD.

Three days later it was all over. On April 6, Union troops cut off and routed almost a third of Lee's army at Sayler's Creek, destroyed its supplies and took 6,000 prisoners. Hearing the news, Lee said, "My God! Has the army been dissolved?" It largely had. Pushed beyond their limit by hunger and exhaustion, huge numbers of soldiers had dropped out, and the army was down to some 28,000 men on April 7, when Lee, hurrying west, received a note from Grant calling on him to surrender.

Heavily outnumbered and almost encircled, Lee considered his dwindling options. One of his officers suggested that the troops could disperse and carry on the Confederate fight as guerrillas. Lee rejected the idea. The guerrillas, he said, "would become mere bands of marauders," hunted down by Union cavalry—an outcome that would bring needless agony to regions of Virginia that had escaped the havoc of war, which the country would take years to recover from. "There is nothing left for me to do but go and see General Grant," Lee said, "and I would rather die a thousand deaths." On April 9 he sent a note to Grant offering to surrender and sent his aide, Colonel Charles Marshall, into the village called Appomattox Court House to find a suitable place for the two men to meet.

* * *

Two hours' drive from Richmond, I came to Appomattox, not knowing anything about it except that it was where Lee surrendered to Grant. My schoolboy memory was that they met in a courthouse, but how long they talked and what terms were offered I had no idea. As it turned out when I got there, I was even wrong about the courthouse. In 19th-century southern Virginia, certain towns that served as the county seat had the words "court house" appended to their name. Appomattox Court House was such a town, and thus the image of the two generals conducting their formalities in a courthouse has come down through the years to schoolboys like me.

But in fact when Colonel Marshall rode into town looking for a surrender site it was Palm Sunday, and the courthouse was closed. Nor was much else stirring. The village had only about 100 people, some of whom were slaves, and most of the white home-owners, hearing the rumble of armies, had left to wait out the storm somewhere else. One person still in town was a merchant named Wilmer McLean, who, if he didn't already have a sense of irony, undoubtedly developed one that day. McLean was a refugee from northern Virginia, where his home had been used as a Confederate headquarters during the first major battle of the Civil War, near Manassas; a Yankee shell had landed in his living room. When a second battle took place at Manassas a year later, McLean, seeking an oasis where the war would never visit him again, moved his family to Appomattox Court House and bought its only imposing residence, a two-story red-brick dwelling. When Colonel Marshall inquired about a place where Grant and Lee could meet, McLean took him to a decrepit home that had no furniture. Marshall told him it wouldn't do. "Maybe my house will do," McLean said, reluctantly bowing to his destiny. So it came about that the man whose home was damaged in the earliest battle of the Civil War was the host for the talk that would bring it to a close.

Lee arrived first, wearing full-dress uniform with a sash and a jeweled sword. Grant, who had outraced his own supply wagon in his rush to seal off Lee's army, was in his customary private's blouse, with muddy trousers tucked into muddy boots. Seated in McLean's parlor, the two men chatted amiably for a while about their army days in the Mexican War, when Lee had been a colonel and Grant a captain. Finally Lee brought up "the object of our present meeting" and asked Grant to write out the terms "under which you would receive the surrender of my army." Grant took out a pen, wrote rapidly at a small wooden table, and handed the paper to Lee. It said:

> General: I propose to receive the surrender of the Army of Northern Virginia on the following terms, to wit: Rolls of all the officers and men to be made in duplicate, one copy to be given to an officer to be designated by me, the other to be retained by such officer or officers as you may designate. The officers to give their individual paroles not to take up arms against the Government of the United States until properly exchanged, and each company or regimental comman-der to sign a like parole for the men of their commands. The arms, artillery and public property to be parked and stacked, and turned over to the officers appointed by me to receive them. This will not embrace the side-arms of the officers, nor their private horses or bag-gage. This done, each officer and man will be allowed to return to his home, not to be disturbed by the United States authorities so long as they observe their paroles and the laws in force wherever they may reside.
>
> > Very respectfully,
> > U. S. Grant,
> > Lieutenant-General.

"This will have a very happy effect on my army," Lee said after reading the terms, which, far from hounding the Southerners with reprisals, simply let them all go home. Grant asked Lee if he had any-thing to add. Lee mentioned that his officers weren't the only horse-owners in his army; the soldiers in his cavalry and artillery also owned their horses. Could those horses be kept? Grant instantly agreed. He said he assumed that most of the men were small farmers and because "the country has been so raided by the two armies" he doubted that they could put in a crop to get through the next winter if they didn't take their horses home. (The soldiers hadn't been paid in more than a year.) "This will have the best possible effect upon the men," Lee said. "It will do much toward conciliating our people."

In parting, Lee told Grant that he would be returning some Union prisoners because he didn't have any provisions for them—or, in fact, for his own men. Grant said he would send three days' rations to Lee's army. Lee then rode back through the lines—the two armies were camped within sight of each other—and when word of the surrender reached Union headquarters, it touched off a spree of cannon firing. Grant put an end to it. "The war is over," he told his staff. "The rebels are our countrymen again, and the best sign of rejoicing will be to abstain from all demonstrations in the field." Victory had left him feeling "sad and depressed." He couldn't exult, he said, in "the downfall of a foe who had fought so long and valiantly." Catching the clemency of the moment, the Union soldiers decided not to wait for the official delivery of food to the defeated enemy. They went over to the Confederate camps and emptied their haversacks of beef, bacon, sugar and other such delicacies that the rebels had long gone without.

Grant ordered a printing press brought to the Clover Hill Tavern, and 28,231 parole passes for the Southern soldiers were printed by April 12. On that morning, four years to the day after the attack on Fort Sumter that started the war, the formal surrender was signed and the Confederate troops walked into the village and stacked their arms. Here the final act of healing that runs through the whole Appomattox story took place, set in motion by the man who, after Grant and Lee, was perhaps the most remarkable of the mighty captains assembled in the village that day. Joshua L. Chamberlain, the Union general designated to receive the surrender, had been a Bowdoin College professor. Requesting a leave of absence to study in Europe, he instead joined the army, won a battlefield commission for repeated feats of bravery and leadership, and was twice wounded, once so severely that his death was announced by the army doctor who attended him. After the war he became a four-term governor of Maine and a twelve-year president of Bowdoin.

Now, with his soldiers standing at attention, General Chamberlain watched the first of the ragged Southern regiments coming up the road—the remnants of the Stonewall Jackson Brigade, led by General John B. Gordon. "The momentous meaning of this occasion impressed me deeply," Chamberlain later wrote in his eloquent book, *The Passing of the Armies*.

> I resolved to mark it by some token of recognition, which could be no other than a salute of arms. [I was] well aware of the criticisms that would follow. . . . My main reason, however, was one for which I sought no authority nor asked forgiveness. Before us in proud humiliation stood the embodiment of manhood: men whom neither toils and sufferings, nor the fact of death, nor disaster, nor hopelessness

could bend from their resolve; standing before us now, thin, worn and famished, but erect, and with eyes looking level into ours, waking memories that bound us together as no other bond;—was not such manhood to be welcomed back into a Union so tested and assured?

Responding to his command,

instantly our whole line from right to left, regiment by regiment in succession, gives the soldier's salutation, from the "order arms" to the old "carry"—the marching salute. Gordon, at the head of the column, riding with heavy spirit and downcast face, catches the sound of shifting arms, looks up, and, taking the meaning, wheels superbly, making with himself and his horse one uplifted figure, with profound salutation as he drops the point of his sword to the boot toe; then facing to his own command, gives word for his successive brigades to pass us with the same position of the manual,—honor answering honor. On our part not a sound of trumpet more, nor roll of drum; not a cheer, nor word nor whisper of vain-glorying, but an awed stillness rather, and breath-holding, as if it were the passing of the dead!

From early morning until early afternoon the saluting Southern soldiers marched past the saluting Union soldiers, stacked their rifles and their tattered Confederate flags, and started for home. Home was anywhere from a hundred to a thousand miles away. Counting the Union troops, almost 100,000 men were in Appomattox Court House that day. Seventy-two hours later they were all gone again.

"Even before the surrender, this village had been bypassed by the railroad," said Ron Wilson, historian of Appomattox Court House, which is now a National Park Service site, "and after the surrender it went right back into its cocoon. Civil War veterans never came back here for a reunion or put up any kind of commemorative marker."

We were sitting on the porch of the Clover Hill Tavern, looking across a vista of overwhelming stillness. Off to the east, the old Richmond-Lynchburg stage road—the road that the surrendering rebels took into the village—climbed across a countryside so recognizable to me from 19th-century landscape paintings that I almost expected to see the rebels coming down the road again. No newfangled sights or sounds disturbed the air—no plane flying overhead, no far-off whine of power tools. The word "stillness" was in my mind because of Bruce

Catton's book *A Stillness at Appomattox*, a title perfectly evoking the sudden silence that the two clashing armies found there, and Catton may have taken it from the "awed stillness" that Joshua Chamberlain said he felt as he watched the conquered soldiers troop into town.

In any case, "stillness" is no less the perfect word for Appomattox Court House today. The town's vital signs, already faint, flickered out in 1892, when the courthouse burned down and the county seat was moved to the nearby railroad town of Appomattox. A year later the McLean house, which the luckless Wilmer McLean had long since sold, its parlor furniture and bric-a-brac having been carried off by souvenir hunters after Grant and Lee left, was dismantled by a subsequent owner, who intended to have it moved to Washington as a historic exhibit. The project ran out of money, however, and McLean's house survived only as a pile of rotting boards and bricks. Thus stripped of the only building that performed a civic function and the only house that had national importance, the village fell into decay.

Congress saved it from oblivion in the mid-1930s by making it a historic site, but the actual rescue was delayed by World War II, and not until the war was over could the Park Service get on with the work of putting the village back together. The McLean house was reconstructed from old photographs and records. So was the courthouse, whose interior now serves as the visitors center, thereby hiding what would have been an intrusive tourist facility. About 20 other long-neglected structures were repaired and restored: the tavern and its guesthouse and kitchen, the county jail, Meeks' Store, the Woodson Law Office, four private homes, and various small kitchens, servants' quarters, smokehouses and stables. Together, along with stately old trees and tidy yards and picket fences and split-rail fences, they make a village that's as pretty as a picture—almost too pretty; no town ever looked this spruce. Ordinarily I can take just so much *ex post facto* quaintness, and an entirely fake town like Colonial Williamsburg, peddling colonial authenticity, makes me little short of hostile. But at Appomattox Court House I felt contented and grateful. Though the village has been heavily patched and painted, it has the integrity of all those historic American places, like Harpers Ferry, where period buildings have been faithfully salvaged from near ruin and the original look of the streets is still intact.

"When visitors come here they expect to find a courthouse and nothing else," Ron Wilson told me. "They want to see where all those men who struggled for so long brought things to a conclusion. But then they find that they're in a village, walking on old roads, smelling country smells, looking at cows in the fields, slowing down to a different pace. We've gotten them out of the automobile and back to an earlier time. We try to bring about a contemplative feeling: to get people to reflect on where this nation has been and what it has come from, to realize that after the Civil War it could never have gone back to the way it was before. It had been pushed forward."

I was glad to be gotten out of the automobile and doing some reflecting. I had thought I was only going to see where the war ended. Now, as I talked with the rangers and looked at the exhibits and browsed in the bookstore (housed in the former tavern kitchen), I saw that the point of Appomattox Court House was that it was not an end but a beginning—the beginning of the America I knew. The country that the soldiers went home to in 1865 was fundamentally different from the one that had gone to war in 1861. Summing up this "second American revolution" in the epilogue of *Battle Cry of Freedom*, James McPherson writes:

> The old federal republic in which the national government had rarely touched the average citizen except through the post-office gave way to a more centralized polity that taxed the people directly and created an internal revenue bureau to collect these taxes, drafted men into the army, expanded the jurisdiction of federal courts, created a national currency and a national banking system, and established the first national agency for social welfare—the Freedmen's Bureau. Eleven of the first twelve amendments to the Constitution had limited the powers of the national government; six of the next seven, beginning with the Thirteenth Amendment in 1865, vastly expanded those powers at the expense of the states.

One major result of these changes was a shift of political power from the South to the North. Before the Civil War the great majority of Presidents, Supreme Court justices and Speakers of the House came from slaveholding states. After the war that imbalance was reversed, and a century would pass before a Southerner became President again.

"Most people come to Appomattox Court House because they

really want to—it's totally off the usual path," said Jon B. Montgomery, superintendent of the site, which gets roughly 110,000 tourists a year. "They're looking for inspiration. The story we try to tell is not the final battle. It's the reconciliation of the country and the generous terms offered by Grant. He didn't try to play the conquering hero. We want people to get a sense of the sacredness of the area."

The question that tourists most frequently ask, however, is of a lowlier order: Is the furniture in the McLean house original? "We don't want them to get off on a tangent about furniture and forget what happened here," Montgomery said. "We try to keep this place just the way it was. There's nothing commercial about it—you won't find any wax museums. At most Civil War sites you're so surrounded by the twentieth century that you can't block it out; when you go to Gettysburg it's hard to find the battlefield. But this is still just a quiet village." The absence of hucksterism had even struck me out on the highway that runs through the modern town of Appomattox, a strip consisting of such tourist amenities as a Burger King, a McDonald's, a Pizza Hut and a Super 8 motel. I saw no exploitation of the fact that a major historic site was just three miles down the road. Nobody had opened a Robert E. Lee Laundromat.

But through the stillness of the area one theme kept booming in my ears: forgiveness and rebirth. "Grant and Lee had to look far into the future," Ron Wilson said. "They knew that the energies that had been given to divisions for so many years would have to be devoted to rebuilding the country. Their meeting wasn't one of those peace conferences that plant the seeds of another war. There was no vindictiveness. The terms that Grant offered at Appomattox set the tone for the other three surrenders by Confederate units. They accepted exactly the same terms that Grant offered Lee."

Again, like the courthouse that the two generals didn't meet in, I saw that I had brought along a second misconception: that the Civil War ended at Appomattox. In fact, it was not until April 26 that Johnston surrendered to Sherman, near Durham, North Carolina, and not until early June that the last of the rebel units surrendered in ceremonies at Mobile and Galveston. "After Appomattox," park ranger Joe Williams reminded me, "there were still 200,000 Confederate troops fighting, and they wouldn't have laid down their arms if Grant had taken a hard line with Lee. The potential for long-term bitterness was there. Grant's surrender terms gave the rest of the Southern soldiers a good reason to go home."

Unfortunately, that largeness of spirit—the brotherhood that the soldiers of both sides had long since come to feel for one another—didn't spill over into civilian conduct. "If the soldiers could have handled the Reconstruction it would have been much less abusive of the South," Jon Montgomery told me. "And of course it would also have made a big difference if Lincoln had lived. Instead the politicians prolonged the agony. They wanted their pound of flesh."

But at Appomattox Court House such pettiness was still ahead—no part of its brief chronicle. The village, I felt, existed in a cul-de-sac of history, above politics and almost outside time, as if it had been brought to life for just one event. Only three people were strongly alive to me there. Two of them, Lee and Grant, continued to radiate powerful qualities that Americans still value and honor: one symbolizing nobility and the aristocratic tradition of the old South, the other symbolizing the self-made common man of the new North, Midwest and West.

The third person was the inescapable Lincoln. The man would never get out of my life. Appomattox was, finally, his show. I could almost see him standing over the little table in the parlor of the McLean house, where Grant sat scribbling the surrender terms. I knew that Lincoln had often spoken of wanting a merciful peace, but I didn't know whether he and Grant had found time to discuss it, and I asked Ron Wilson when the two men had last met. He said they had met on April 1 at City Point—on the *River Queen*, in the James River—and had talked at length about the rapidly approaching end of the war and the civil disarray it was bound to bring.

"You just know," Wilson told me, "that Lincoln said, 'Let 'em down easy.'"

8

Montgomery

Not long after I got back from Appomattox, with its best hopes and dreams still on my mind, I happened to meet Maya Lin, who designed the Vietnam Memorial in Washington when she was a 21-year-old Yale senior and who is now an architect in New York. I asked her about her recent work, and she told me about her Civil Rights Memorial in Montgomery, Alabama, which was dedicated in the fall of 1989. The monument, she said, is of black granite and takes as its text a paraphrase of a verse in the Book of Amos that was spoken on two historic occasions by Martin Luther King, Jr.: "We will not be satisfied until justice rolls down like waters and righteousness like a mighty stream." Its central idea is that water flows over those words and also over the names—incised in the stone—of 40 men, women and children who were killed during the civil rights movement. Like her Vietnam Memorial, it invites visitors to touch the names and thereby bring some part of themselves to the act of honoring the dead and of not forgetting that they died.

I had never heard of the memorial or of the organization that commissioned it, the Southern Poverty Law Center. Nor had I ever stopped to think that in a land strewn with heroic statuary there had been no statue commemorating the heroism of the struggle for civil rights. Montgomery was the inevitable site—a place waiting for a monument to happen. It was not only where Rosa Parks, by refusing to give up her seat in the "whites only" section of a bus, inspired the 13-month Montgomery bus boycott that gave the civil rights movement its irreversible momentum. It was also where an old Negro congregation and its new young pastor—the Dexter Avenue Baptist Church and Martin Luther King, Jr.—together fashioned a program of nonviolent activism that neither of them could have created alone and that grounded their cause in the oldest Christian teachings. If I wanted to see the new memorial, I also wanted to see the old church. Granite or brick, they were cut from the same stone.

"In the spring of 1988," Maya Lin recalled, "the Southern Poverty Law Center contacted me and asked me if I'd be interested in designing a civil rights memorial. I thought surely one had already been done. But there had only been very specific monuments to specific people; no memorial existed that encompassed the movement itself and caught what that whole era was about. It had been very much a people's movement—many people gave their lives for it, and that had been largely forgotten."

The center sent Lin some books and tapes about the civil rights era and about the Ku Klux Klan and other hate groups that had reemerged in the South. "I didn't know what the center was," she recalled, "until I started to read these stories—especially the story of Michael Donald, a black teenager who was lynched by the Klan in 1981. I found out that the center had brought a suit that not only convicted two men of murder but broke the entire Klan chapter, making the point that the group is responsible for the actions of the individual. So I admired what they were doing and I agreed to design the memorial, which would occupy the plaza in front of their building. I was horrified to realize that many of these murders had taken place during my lifetime and that I didn't know about them; it hadn't been taught to me in school—the case of Samuel Younge, Jr., for instance, a student who was killed in 1966 for using a 'whites only' bathroom. And I thought: If you stop remembering, you can quickly slide backward into prejudicial ways."

Lin spent several months doing research and just thinking about the civil rights movement, "waiting for a form to show up" and often despairing that it would. "The discipline is to not jump too fast," she said. "If you jump to a form too quickly, it won't have the understood meaning that you want for it." Finally the day came for her to fly to

Montgomery to inspect the site, which she hadn't yet seen, and it was on the plane, reading a book called *Eyes on the Prize*, that she encountered the phrase about justice rolling down like waters.

"The minute I hit that quote I knew that the whole piece had to be about water," she told me. "I learned that King had used the phrase not only in his famous 'I have a dream' speech at the Washington civil rights march in 1963 but at the start of the bus boycott in Montgomery eight years earlier, so it had been his rallying cry for the entire movement. Suddenly the whole form took shape, and half an hour later I was in a restaurant in Montgomery with the people from the Center, sketching it on a paper napkin. I realized that I wanted to create a time line: a chronological listing of the movement's major events and its individual deaths, which together would show how people's lives influenced history and how their deaths made things better."

What she didn't anticipate was the power that words joined with water would generate. "At the dedication ceremony," she said, "I was surprised and moved when people started to cry. Emmett Till's mother was touching his name beneath the water and crying, and I realized that her tears were becoming part of the memorial."

Morris S. Dees, cofounder and executive director of the Southern Poverty Law Center, who conceived the memorial, is a rangy man of 55 with curly brown hair and amused eyes, and when I met him at the center's new building in downtown Montgomery—its previous building was burned down by the Klan—I wasn't surprised to learn that he had been the subject of a made-for-television movie called *Line of Fire: The Morris Dees Story*, with Corbin Bernsen of "L.A. Law" in the role of the crusading attorney. I recognized him as a familiar American type—the maverick idealist—from dozens of Hollywood movies made in a more guileless era. He was Jimmy Stewart cleaning up the mess on Capitol Hill in *Mr. Smith Goes to Washington*. He was Gary Cooper in *High Noon* and Joel McCrea in *Sullivan's Travels*.

Dees is from a family that has farmed in Montgomery County since before the Civil War. His parents owned a small cotton farm. "They treated blacks differently from the way most white people around here did," he said. "They weren't liberals or integrationists; they were just fair-minded folks. I had several racist uncles—which was an extreme contrast to my parents—and their attitude also shaped my early views."

As a sideline in college, Dees formed a book publishing company, which became so prosperous that he later sold it to the Times Mirror Company in Los Angeles, thus becoming financially independent, and when he graduated from the University of Alabama Law School he began to take cases brought to him by blacks who were excluded from jobs because of their color. One case, in 1961, involved a man who wanted to become a state trooper but wasn't permitted to apply. Dees's suit resulted in the integration of Alabama's state trooper system— "one of the first hiring ratios in public service in the United States," he says. Another suit brought about the integration of Montgomery's YMCA.

In 1971, Dees and his partner, Joseph J. Levin, Jr., changed the sign on their law office from "Levin & Dees" to "Southern Poverty Law Center," incorporating themselves as a nonprofit entity. "The name is misleading," Dees said, "and we're now in the process of changing it to the Southern Center for Justice. But at that time it expressed our purpose exactly. We wanted to concentrate on customs, practices and laws that harmed people because of their poverty." As Klan killings and violence intensified in the late '70s, Dees began to represent the victims or their survivors. He also formed a unit of the center called Klanwatch, which monitors white supremacist groups. In this role Dees took the case of Michael Donald, a 19-year-old black boy who, in 1981, was on his way to a store when Klansmen abducted him, beat him, cut his throat and hanged him from a tree on a residential street in Mobile. Dees's suit led to one verdict of murder, one indictment of a Klansman, who is awaiting trial, and a $7 million jury award in 1987 that put one entire faction of the Klan out of business.

"The real thrust of our work is educational," Dees told me. "It's not just lawsuits. We want to stop the problem by educating people, especially young people. After that jury award I was invited to address the NAACP convention in Mobile, and I said that one day people would speak the names not only of Martin Luther King and Medgar Evers but of Emmett Till and Viola Liuzzo and Jimmie Lee Jackson and many other martyrs of the movement. Afterward a black teenage boy came up to me and said, 'We heard you talk about those people who died for freedom, and we know about Dr. King, and we know about those four little girls in that church in Birmingham. But who was Emmett Till? And who was Medgar Evers? And who were those other people?'

"I turned to the boys who were with him, and I said, 'Can any of you tell me who Medgar Evers was? Or Viola Liuzzo?' Not a single one of them knew. As I drove home I made a vow that I would do research to find out who had died and that we would build a monument to them. Back at the center, everybody liked the idea, and someone said, 'If we're going to do it, let's get a first-rate architect.' And Ed Ashworth, one of our board members, said 'Let's get Maya Lin.' So we called every Lin in the New York telephone book until the right one answered."

"As soon as you talk about putting names in granite, you create a lot of problems," said Sara Bullard, the center's director of research and author of its book, *Free at Last: A History of the Civil Rights Movement and Those Who Died in the Struggle*, which was sent to 55,000 junior and senior high schools. The book is a model of clear writing, taking its power from the simple recitation of events almost too terrible to believe: beatings, bombings, burnings, ambushings, shootings and lynchings.

"We needed some guidelines to help us choose the people who would go on the memorial," Bullard said, "and we finally decided that we would start with the 1954 Supreme Court decision *Brown v. Board of Education*, which banned segregation in public schools, and end with the assassination of Martin Luther King in 1968—realizing, of course, that the movement didn't have that clean a beginning or an end. In fact, as I started my research I realized that there were many significant deaths that fell outside our boundaries."

Her research didn't start well. "I went to Tuskegee Institute and looked through its lynching files," Bullard recalled. "We figured that a resource that big and famous would have everything we needed to know about who should be on the memorial. Well, it turned out that those files included all blacks who had ever been executed under capital punishment laws. That would have put us in the position of deciding who was innocent or guilty, because there was almost never enough information about the circumstances of the death or the motive of the killer: why these people were killed and who they were killed by.

"In the end we established three criteria for including people on the memorial. One was that they were killed because of their own nonviolent civil rights activism. Typically, these were men and women like Vernon Dahmer, a black businessman in Hattiesburg, Mississippi, who offered to pay the poll tax for anyone who couldn't afford the voting fee—he was killed when his home was firebombed—or Viola Liuzzo, a white housewife and mother from Detroit who was shot by Klansmen for driving freedom marchers back to Selma from Montgomery.

"Our second criterion was people who were killed by agitators trying to stir up opposition to the movement or throw some obstacle in its path. These tend to be the lesser-known victims—for example, Virgil Ware, a thirteen-year-old Birmingham boy who was shot while riding on the handlebars of his brother's bicycle by white teenagers coming back from a segregationist rally, or Ben Chester White, a caretaker in Natchez who was shot by Klansmen who wanted to divert attention from a civil rights march, or the four young girls—Addie Mae Collins, Denise McNair, Carole Robertson and Cynthia Wesley—who were killed by the bomb that exploded in the Sixteenth Street Baptist Church in Birmingham, which had been a center for civil rights meetings.

"The third criterion was people whose death created momentum for the movement—whose death was used by civil rights groups as a tool to show the nation the conditions that Southern blacks lived under and the injustices they suffered. The death of Emmett Till, for instance—a fourteen-year-old boy killed for speaking to a white woman in Mississippi—was the first death that brought wide support for the movement from outside the South. Or Jimmie Lee Jackson, who was shot by Alabama state troopers for trying to protect his mother and his grandfather from a trooper attack on civil rights marchers. His death changed the entire course of the movement. It inspired the Selma-to-Montgomery march and eventually led to the passage of the Voting Rights Act."

But finding the names wasn't easy. "A big problem was that newspapers in the South didn't cover these deaths," Bullard said, "so it wouldn't do me any good to go to Jackson and look in the Mississippi state archives. My best source turned out to be the Southern Regional

Council, in Atlanta, a group that does research and education on issues of poverty and civil rights. One of its categories was 'Violence and Intimidation.' The cardboard cartons containing those files had been stored in the basement, under a Korean grocery store—a filthy place, with a lot of dripping water. I spent a week in that basement and would come out at the end of the day totally black. But I found names that hadn't turned up anywhere else, and one name led to another—people like Clarence Triggs, a bricklayer who was shot by the roadside for having attended meetings sponsored by the Congress of Racial Equality, or Bruce Klunder, a white minister who tried to block the construction of a segregated school in Cleveland."

After much debate, 40 names were chosen for the memorial. "We all ended up feeling comfortable with the list," Bullard said, and the only painful residue is an occasional letter or phone call from a relative of a victim protesting the omission of a name. "I feel badly when that happens," Bullard said, "but the message that we try to convey is simply: 'This memorial represents the sacrifices of ordinary people during the civil rights movement. Here are some of those people.'"

The Civil Rights Memorial was designed to serve as the entrance plaza for the Southern Poverty Law Center's new headquarters, a small building with a handsome interplay of angles and glass. The memorial has two component parts, both of black Canadian granite. The first part is a nine-foot-high wall, on the face of which are carved the words:

... UNTIL JUSTICE ROLLS DOWN LIKE WATERS
AND RIGHTEOUSNESS LIKE A MIGHTY STREAM

MARTIN LUTHER KING, JR.

Water spills down the wall at waterfall speed, quite fast. Although the passage from the prophet Amos, here attributed to the prophet King, actually begins with "We will not be satisfied," Maya Lin told me that she started where she did because the word "until" catches the second purpose of the monument. "Unlike the Vietnam Memorial, which covers a specific period of time that's over," she said, "I wanted the Civil Rights Memorial to deal not only with the past but with the future—with how far we still have to go in a continuing struggle."

The second part of the memorial, resting on an asymmetrical pedestal nearby, is a circular tabletop, almost 12 feet in diameter, around whose perimeter, incised in the stone, somewhat in the manner of a sundial, are 53 brief entries, chronologically arranged. Twenty of them report landmark events in the movement:

13 NOV 1956   SUPREME COURT BANS SEGREGATED
               SEATING ON MONTGOMERY BUSES

30 SEP 1962   RIOTS ERUPT WHEN JAMES MEREDITH,
               A BLACK STUDENT, ENROLLS AT OLE MISS

28 AUG 1963   250,000 AMERICANS MARCH ON WASHING-
               TON FOR CIVIL RIGHTS

20 JUN 1964   FREEDOM SUMMER BRINGS 1,000 YOUNG
               CIVIL RIGHTS VOLUNTEERS TO MISSISSIPPI

The other entries describe 40 individual deaths:

7 MAY   1955   REV. GEORGE LEE. KILLED FOR LEADING
               VOTER REGISTRATION DRIVE. BELZONI, MS

21 JUN 1964   JAMES CHANEY. ANDREW GOODMAN.
               MICHAEL SCHWERNER. CIVIL RIGHTS
               WORKERS ABDUCTED AND SLAIN BY KLAN.
               PHILADELPHIA, MS

20 AUG 1965   JONATHAN DANIELS. SEMINARY STUDENT
               KILLED BY DEPUTY. HAYNEVILLE, AL

27 FEB 1967   WHARLEST JACKSON. CIVIL RIGHTS
               LEADER KILLED AFTER PROMOTION TO
               'WHITE' JOB. NATCHEZ, MS

4 APR   1968   DR. MARTIN LUTHER KING, JR.
               ASSASSINATED. MEMPHIS, TN

Extra space after King's entry shows that this is where the story ends. The story begins on 17 May 1954, the Supreme Court's *Brown* decision, and that's where most visitors start their visit, walking slowly around the table and touching the names beneath the water, which arises from a hole in the tabletop and flows over it evenly. The table is only 31 inches high, intentionally accessible to children.

"The water is as slow as I could get it," Maya Lin told me. "It remains very still until you touch it. Your hand causes ripples, which transform and alter the piece, just as reading the words completes the piece. The sound of the water is also very calming. Sound is important to me as an architect. At the Vietnam Memorial, the fact that the wall is below the surface of the earth buffers people from the noise of Washington traffic; crowds of schoolchildren arriving there become very quiet. You're setting the stage for a sacred experience."

Installing the Civil Rights Memorial put the contractor, Ken Upchurch, through some unusual moments. "Morris Dees explained the idea to me," he recalled, "and said, 'Can you do it?' I told him, 'We've never done anything like this before.' He said, 'Nobody has.' All along we were concerned about vandalism—feelings about Morris run high in this city—so we put a white construction fence around the site. But not a single mark was ever put on that fence. Morris said from the beginning that the memorial was a teaching tool, and in the case of my men he was right: it has already achieved that goal. Though all of us grew up in Montgomery, we learned more about the civil rights movement by doing this job than we did by growing up here. Everyone on the crew saw that their problems were minor compared to the problems of the people named on the table."

Ken Upchurch's company was founded by his grandparents in 1930. "My grandfather built our business on doing jobs that nobody else was willing to do because they were too risky. He prided himself on that, and *I've* always been proud that in sixty years we've never finished a job late." That record appeared to be in trouble as the granite fabricator up North kept fussing with the tabletop. Finally word came that the piece would arrive on a Saturday morning in November, just two weeks before the dedication. Nobody knew whether it would fit or whether the water would work properly.

"We got to the site early to wait for it," Upchurch told me, "and around 9:00 A.M. a flatbed truck drove up with this fifteen-ton slab of granite. The driver was a black woman, and her assistant driver was a white woman. We had sent precise instructions on how the granite should be loaded onto the truck so that we would be able to take it off without damaging it—it's only one inch thick at the edge—and right away we saw that they had done it wrong: the lifting device was attached upside down. We sat around for several hours trying to figure out what to do. In the end there was nothing to do but swing it into the air with our crane and turn it over and set it down on the base.

"The bolt holes had also been put in the wrong place, so we had to drill new ones and get everything braced, and by then it was almost ten o'clock at night and the crowds that had been there all day long had gone home, including Morris Dees and the people from the center. Only my men were left. Someone said, 'Should we turn on the water?' We thought maybe we should wait until Monday. But someone else said, 'We've been working for two years to get to this point—let's turn it on!' So we did, and the water worked *perfectly*. And just at that moment Morris Dees came back. He had been too fidgety to wait at home. I'll never forget the look on his face when he saw the water flowing over those names."

Two weeks later, almost 600 members of the families of the men, women and children named on the memorial assembled to take part in the dedication. They came from all over the country—grandparents and parents, sons and daughters, brothers and sisters, uncles and aunts, cousins and babes in arms. Except in a few cases, none of them had ever met, but they shared the same piece of American history. Trying to reconstruct that weekend, I talked to the black van driver at the Madison Hotel who brought many of them from the airport.

"It was sad the way they talked about what had happened," Leroy Terrell told me, "and when you think about it, it *was* sad. There was a lot of crying. I realized that quite a few of those men and women had been very young children when their father or mother died. One white lady from Michigan said she had only been four or five years old when her mother was killed near Selma." That white lady would have been Viola Liuzzo's daughter, Sally Liuzzo Prado.

Later, I watched videotapes of the weekend's two main events. One was a banquet on Saturday night. The other was the dedication on Sunday afternoon, November 5, 1989, when the families were joined by several thousand spectators, packed along the street, to hear songs, prayers, speeches by survivors like Rosa Parks, and brief recollections of the long-lost children by white-haired parents. What struck me about all the speakers was the natural eloquence of their language.

Mamie Till Mobley, mother of Emmett Till: "We are men and women of sorrow, and we are acquainted with grief. But we sorrow not as those who have no hope. We know that we were chosen to be burden-bearers. Emmett's death was not a personal experience for me to hug to myself and weep. It was a worldwide awakening that would change the course of history. With these hurts have come additional responsibilities. We cannot afford the luxury of self-pity."

Chris McNair, father of Denise McNair, one of the four young girls who were bombed in church: "Our daughter Denise, if she had lived, would be celebrating her thirty-eighth birthday next month. When Denise was in seventh grade and everybody in Birmingham was marching and going to jail, Denise said to her mother and her cousin one evening, '*I* want to march!' They both admonished her, saying, 'Denise, you're too little.' Denise, being very fiery, turned to them and said, 'If I'm too little, *you're* not too little and *you're* not free. Why aren't *you* marching?' She never got an answer."

Samuel Younge, Sr.: "Our son Sammy Younge, Jr., is on the Civil Rights Memorial because he gave his life to demand equal rights for blacks. Thus he became the first black college student slain in the civil rights movement of the 1960s. Sammy's desire for equality was evident. He resented using separate water fountains, toilets and eating places. Being of light skin, he drank at whites-only fountains and ate at white lunch counters, while I stood back in awe. On motor trips he said we would not buy gas unless he could use the white rest room. . . . He led pickets to force banks and stores to have blacks in jobs other than that of janitor. To Sammy, his big joy, however, was getting hundreds of blacks registered to vote. It was his voter registration work and his desire to integrate public facilities that led to his death. Nevertheless, our son Sammy Younge, Jr., led a successful civil rights life, and for this my wife, Ereen, my son, Stephen, my entire family, and all of us appreciate Sammy Younge, Jr.'s short and active civil rights life."

As an outdoor monument, the Civil Rights Memorial never closes, and for two days and evenings I watched people stopping by to see it. Adults came in tour buses, children came in school buses, and the rest came by car or on foot. "The memorial has greatly increased tourist interest in Montgomery," I was told by Katie Ufford, director of the city's visitors center. "We're getting many tourists from the North and from the West, and the black population in the South all want to see it.

They also want to visit Dr. King's church, and sometimes they tie it all in with a trip to Selma and Tuskegee." Foreign tourists have also started to come, mostly from England, France and Germany.

Up to now Montgomery has been a tourist site primarily for Southerners and historians, as the first capital of the Confederacy and the place where the Civil War began—the order to "reduce" Fort Sumter was sent from a telegraph office on Dexter Avenue—and as the site of the first White House of the Confederacy, a white Italianate house where Jefferson Davis, the president of the Confederate States, lived with his family, starting in 1861. Its location, when I went around to see it, struck me as piquant: it's just two blocks up Washington Street from the Civil Rights Memorial and just up the hill from King's Dexter Avenue Baptist Church. All three coexist in the shadow of the state capitol, an august white-domed edifice that has on its flagpole, in descending order of pertinence, the American flag, the Alabama flag and the Confederate flag. I recognized Dexter Avenue from newsreels of the '60s: a broad thoroughfare that terminates at the capitol steps. The Selma-to-Montgomery march ended there. So did Jefferson Davis's inaugural parade.

I went into the Dexter Avenue Church, a modest red-brick structure not unlike Baptist churches in many Southern towns, and introduced myself to its presiding deacon, Addre Bryant. The church, which was established in 1885, is now a National Historic Landmark, and Bryant told me it gets a large number of visitors every Sunday from all over the world—"they want to be part of the worship service." On weekdays, tourists enter through the basement and are shown a mural depicting memorable events in Martin Luther King's 14-year odyssey from Montgomery to Memphis. From there visitors go upstairs to the church itself, a sunny interior with pale-blue walls and stained-glass windows in a pattern of bright checkerboard squares. "That's always a silent, solemn period," Deacon Bryant said. "They sit in the pews and meditate. The Civil Rights Memorial has brought far more visitors to the church. There's sort of an unwritten partnership between the two—the memorial has sanctioned what the church did during the movement. Younger people especially don't understand the hardships that American blacks endured at that time."

We were joined by Dr. Zelia Evans, who, though not an elder of the church, is surely its elder stateswoman, having written its history in 1977 at the age of 75. Evans first attended the church as a high school girl in Montgomery, and in the second half of her 44-year teaching career she was a professor of education at Alabama State University, the local college whose black presidents, faculty and students, along with other black professionals, have traditionally given the Dexter Avenue Church its reputation as a "silk stocking" congregation, intellectually rigorous and impatient with emotional religion.

"It was good that Martin Luther King came to a church that was trained to accept his kind of work and that could give him the endorsement he needed," Evans said, although, she recalled, one parishioner asked, "Why did they bring that *boy* here?" (King was 25 at the time.) "Dr. King took the Bible and made it so that you could just *see* it, because of the clarity and the depth of his teaching, and then he always *charged* you to apply it. Teaching was his work just as much as preaching was. Of course that was also true of Jesus. I guess it was the movement of the Lord to call the congregation to call him here."

Walking back up to the Civil Rights Memorial, I thought of how often the words "teaching" and "education" had been woven through my visit. Earlier I had asked Maya Lin whether anything about the memorial—perhaps the stillness, perhaps the water—reflected her heritage as a Chinese-American woman. "If it's Eastern in any way," she said, "it's not because it's Zen, or Buddhist, but because it's a teaching device. It presents information and lets the viewer interpret it, unlike Western art, which tends to be didactic and self-righteous.

"I remember that I designed the Vietnam Memorial for two different clients. First, it was for all the people who had been involved in the war. But it also had to work a hundred years from now. It had to tell anyone who saw it that the losses were immense, the price was too high. The Civil Rights Memorial has that same historical purpose. It's a very educational piece. Viewers are moved less by the stories of the individual men and women than by what was done to them: a boy killed for using a whites-only bathroom, countless people randomly lynched. The memorial touches the surface; *then* you go and find out more about the period."

But what I saw when I got back to the memorial was something that went beyond teaching and learning. Because of the monument's circularity, tourists were having an experience that was both private and shared. Moving around the black granite table, pausing to read and touch the names of the dead, they were also in touch with each other—literally, or in fragments of conversation, or in silent witness. Sometimes there were so many tourists that they formed an almost complete circle. Often nobody was there. The memorial moved to its own found rhythms.

Late in the day I saw a black woman with a videocamera filming three people who were standing over the table. One was a black man, evidently her husband; the other two were an older white couple. The white man walked with two canes and pulled himself laboriously around the table, reading every entry. All three had the ease of old friends, and I asked the black woman if they were traveling together. "No, we just met," she said. "We got out of our cars at the same time."

After a while she and the black man went back to their car. The day had turned cold, and only the white man and his wife were left. I asked them where they were from. He said that they were Sam and Hyla Offen, from West Bloomfield, Michigan, and that they knew about the memorial because of Viola Liuzzo, who was from the same area. Normally when they drive to Florida, he said, they take Route 75 and go by way of Atlanta, but this time they were so eager to see the memorial that they made a detour.

"I'm a Holocaust survivor," Sam Offen told me, "so naturally I empathize with this monument. I was born in Poland, and I never saw a black person until after the war. Right away I saw that they're just people, like everybody else, and Hyla and I have supported the cause ever since we came to America."

"What cause?" I asked, though I knew the answer.

"Liberty for all," he said. "I was deprived of liberty for five and a half years, so I know exactly what it's like to lose it."

Around dusk, when everyone else had left, a young black man drove up in his car, got out, and spent about 15 minutes at the memorial, reading the names and taking photographs of the Biblical words behind the falling water in the failing light. When he had finished I asked if he was from Montgomery. He said he was from Atlanta and that he was a field engineer for a telephone company.

"I told my boss that if a project ever came along in the Montgomery area I hoped he would send me, because I've really wanted to see this monument," he said. "A job came up this morning, and I've just finished. As a young black man, this place makes me realize the sacrifices that all those people made so that I could have a good job today. Back in the '60s a job like mine would have been totally impossible."

9

Mount Vernon

The Civil War I saw ending at Appomattox and the residual hatred of blacks I saw reflected in Maya Lin's tabletop at Montgomery took me into the darkest side of the American story. I also continued to be nagged by the dark myth of the Alamo and to find it troubling. On the simple level of frontier patriotism I was glad enough to salute the courage of 189 men who chose to die for the idea of freedom. But as a macho exercise sanctified into a symbol of American strength it was an early portent, I felt, of the strain of violence that would come to contaminate American life in the decades after World War II—our leaders assassinated, our people routinely shot in the streets—and of a foreign policy based on imperial bluster, love of weapons, military adventurism and enemy-bashing. I hated the trail of American death that circles the world from Central America to Vietnam to Iraq.

Suddenly I felt the need for an older myth, a purifying myth, a founding myth. I needed to go back to George Washington. I needed to go to Mount Vernon, Washington's home on the Potomac River in Virginia, 17 miles south of the capital city that carries his name. I had last seen him on Mount Rushmore, radiating assurance, even in stone. Gutzon Borglum, whose own hero was Abraham Lincoln and who named his son Lincoln, nevertheless knew what billing and what visage to give the four Presidents. Jefferson and Theodore Roosevelt both face inward, one looking contemplative, the other stern, and Lincoln, looking grave, gazes down. But Washington is first among equals, out in front of his fellow Presidents and slightly removed from them—a god—and he looks out across the nation, confident and untroubled. He even seems to have a faint smile.

But who *was* this god?

Of all the iconic places in America, none has been visited by tourists for so long or with such worshipful curiosity as Mount Vernon. Proof of that fact—which I learned soon after I got there—was that on the afternoon of July 31, 1797, Washington told his secretary, Tobias Lear, "Unless someone pops in, unexpectedly, Mrs. Washington and myself will do what I believe has not been [done] within the last twenty years by us, that is to set down to dinner by ourselves."

Washington inherited Mount Vernon in 1754 and died and was buried there in 1799. His 45-year ownership was interrupted by two eight-year periods when he was famously absent: as commander in chief of the Continental Army, which won the Revolutionary War, from 1775 to 1783, and as the country's first President, from 1789 to 1797. The godlike aura that those two roles conferred on him turned his home into a shrine well within his lifetime. He once compared Mount Vernon to "a well-resorted tavern," noting that "scarcely any strangers who are going from north to south or from south to north do not spend a day or two at it."

What attracted all those strangers was not only George Washington as the most exalted of American heroes. It was also the house. For a nation that didn't yet have a permanent capital or a presidential mansion, Mount Vernon filled a deep need, and the flood of visitors, once loosed, never stopped. Rummaging in Mount Vernon's research library, I found many notebooks filled with early travelers' impressions of the house and its squire, recorded—both while he lived there and for several decades after his death—in letters, diaries and journals. One that I particularly liked was written by Andrew Jackson in November of 1815:

> The scite [*sic*] is really a delightful one. By a gentle ascent you reach the summit of an eminence which commands, on the one side, an extensive country prospect, and overlooks, on the other, the majestic Potwamac [*sic*] on the smooth bosom of which vessels of various descriptions are seen perpetually gliding. On that, stands the venera-

ble dwelling of the patriarch of our Liberties, corresponding in its style, with the plain and simple taste of him who planned it. A neat little flower garden, laid out and trimmed with the utmost exactness, ornamented with green and hot houses in which flourish the most beautiful of the Tropical plants affords a happy relief to the solemn impressions produced by a view of the antique structure it adjoins, and leads you insensibly into the most delightful reverie, in which you review in imagination the manner in which the greatest and the best of men after the most busy and eventful life, retired into privacy and amused the evening of his days.

If Andrew Jackson found the house antique in 1815, what would I make of it today? I had almost no feeling for what George Washington was like; gods tend to be aloof. Yet he was a man who lived in one home for almost half a century and thought of himself as a farmer. Like the Roman general Cincinnatus, to whom he is so often compared, he was happiest when he was on his land and left it only because he was called to serve his country. His friend and neighbor Henry ("Lighthorse Harry") Lee, who summed him up for posterity with the deathless half-sentence, "First in war, first in peace and first in the hearts of his countrymen," completed the sentence with a phrase that posterity has preferred to forget: "he was second to none in the humble and endearing scenes of private life."

The image that I brought to Mount Vernon was of a formal white mansion, classical in its lines, with a row of tall columns running its entire length. But that wasn't what I saw when I got there. The columns are on the rear, facing the Potomac, and most visitors approach from the front, arriving by car or bus or taxi and walking up a long driveway. (Some take an excursion boat from Washington.) From the front, the house struck me as less formal than I expected— almost boxlike, or even barnlike, with a bright red roof that was a little too cheerful to be elegant. There was also something slightly askew about the facade: the windows and doors weren't quite in symmetry. But I had to take a second look to notice the imbalance—my eye had been fooled into an illusion of symmetry by the careful placement of two matching dormers, a central portico and a cupola.

Later, I learned that Washington had twice enlarged what had been a modest house when he inherited it, making the most ambitious additions—creating the mansion as we know it today—after 1775. He also added outbuildings for the several hundred servants, workers and slaves who lived there: a plantation community that raised its own food, spun its own wool, made its own clothes and supported itself by selling tobacco, fish and other crops. Overseeing the plantation was Washington's consuming love, and even when he was away winning the Revolutionary War and running the country, he wrote weekly letters to his managers and expected detailed letters back.

"He has about 8,000 acres, well cultivated, and superintends the whole himself," wrote a traveler named Robert Hunter, Jr., who visited Mount Vernon in 1785, two years after Washington got home from the war. "Indeed, his greatest pride now is to be thought the first farmer in America. He often works with the men himself: strips off his coat and labors like a common man. . . . I was struck with his noble and venerable appearance. . . . The General is six foot high, perfectly straight and well made, rather inclined to be lusty. His eyes are full and blue and seem to express an air of gravity."

I joined the line of tourists entering the house, and we were pleasantly shepherded through the successive rooms by members of the Mount Vernon Ladies' Association, the oldest national preservation organization in the country, which rescued the mansion in 1858. Roughly one quarter of the furnishings are original; the rest, assembled over the decades, are true to how the mansion looked the year Washington died. I was startled by the colors in the formal rooms downstairs. Both the large and the small dining room had walls of verdigris green, a translucent glaze that was more Day-Glo than colonial, and the Prussian blue of the West Parlor was equally vibrant. It turned out that a major research project of the past decade has been to analyze and replicate the original paints—a feat of scientific detection that involved grinding the pigments by hand and using 18th-century brushes to apply them with fidelity. Washington chose the electric colors to give the candlelit rooms more brightness after dark.

The mansion struck me as gracious but not grandiose; it had the feeling of an old country house that the new owners have periodically added to and fixed up for company. Its finest object, in the large dining room, was a marble mantelpiece, a gift to the general from an English friend, Samuel Vaughan. Thanking Vaughan, Washington wrote that it was "too elegant and costly by far I fear for my room, and my republican stile [sic] of living." I noticed, however, that he didn't send it back.

Where I first began to feel Washington's personality was in his downstairs study, a room that he built below his bedroom, with a connecting private staircase that made it a sanctuary from the bustle of the household and its incessant visitors when he came back to Mount Vernon after the war, as he thought, to retire. A man of methodical habits, Washington went down to the study every morning between four and five o'clock, shaved and dressed there, and worked on his correspondence, his diary and his estate records until breakfast, after which he toured the plantation on horseback. The letters that went forth from that study, written to James Madison, Alexander Hamilton and other founding fathers, gave shape and momentum to the idea of a strong federal government and to the creation of the Constitution. As one observer said, the room was "the focus of political intelligence for the new world."

It was very much a man's room, with pine-paneled walls and bookcases—no verdigris green or Prussian blue at this end of the house. Every object reflected an energetic and practical mind: a commodious desk; a handsome globe that Washington had ordered made in London; a library that emphasized history, politics, law, agriculture, literature and travel; a hand press for making copies of letters; a barometer and a telescope; some surveying instruments; a few swords and guns, and a reading chair with a pedal that activated a wooden fan that stirred the humid summer air and kept the flies away.

Our tour of the house continued with a glimpse of the upstairs bedrooms, including the one in which Washington died, and then we were free to walk around the grounds. I began by sitting out on the rear piazza under the famous columns and looking at the view. That lofty porch, evidently Washington's own creation—architecture was his favorite art—was a highly enjoyable idea. The general kept a row of Windsor chairs out there, a perfect spot for talking with visitors and keeping cool, and it was in one of their modern replacements that I sat and gazed across the wide Potomac—a tranquil vista, unaltered since Washington's day. Afterward I stretched out on the grass and admired the house, which, seen with its eight columns, now looked like a proper colonial mansion, grand and aristocratic. Around me, fellow tourists strolled or sprawled and children played on the grass, as tourists have since the 18th century. We all felt that the house, like Yellowstone Park, belonged to us. If going to Mount Vernon wasn't quite the same thing as going back to some family homestead of our own, it was part of the same need.

"It's interesting to me how possessive Americans are about Mount Vernon," its curator, Christine Meadows, told me. "After we restored the original paint in the downstairs rooms, people were not only horrified by the color; they were angry that we had messed around with George Washington's home."

Mount Vernon gets almost a million tourists a year and is the most visited historic house in America after the White House. Two types of tourists are on an unusually serious quest. "A great many people continue to come here as if it's a pilgrimage," Meadows said. "The shrine aspect of Washington's home has been important to visitors since the 19th century. That's an especially powerful force at houses where the grave is on the grounds, like Mount Vernon and Jefferson's Monticello. We've also begun to get a large segment of people who are quite knowledgeable and sophisticated about restoration and furniture and the decorative arts. They've been to Colonial Williamsburg and Winterthur and Historic Deerfield, and they're caught up in the intellectual content of the field.

"During the 19th century the room that evoked the most moving expressions was Washington's bedroom, because that was the death chamber, and the 19th century was preoccupied by death—there was that Victorian gloominess that descended on people. Today, visitors are more interested in the dailiness of Washington's life. They want to know: 'Did he own that?' or 'Did he sit in that chair?' People desperately want heroes and models, and there's a reaching out to connect with objects that Washington used."

Leaving the mansion, I followed a path leading to the Potomac. Halfway down the hill I came to the tomb where George and Martha Washington are buried—a simple red-brick vault containing two marble sarcophagi. "Within this Enclosure Rest the remains of Genl. George Washington," says the inscription on a stone tablet over the entrance. (Naval ships toll their bell when they pass.) Next I toured the small service buildings adjacent to the mansion: kitchen, smokehouse, washhouse, coachhouse, stable, storehouse, spinning house and icehouse. Then I strolled around the two large gardens that form part of the main approach to Mount Vernon, giving it the well-groomed look and sumptuous boxwood smell that have long been the signature of estates belonging to the Eastern rich. One garden has plants that were common in the 18th century, and it adjoins a small botanical garden where Washington experimented with rare plants and shrubs that he sent away for.

At every step I felt the presiding intelligence of a landowner who was endlessly curious about his land: how it looked and what could be coaxed out of it. His eye was obviously exceptional; as one visiting European nobleman remarked, the plantation proves "that a man born with natural taste may guess a beauty without ever having seen its model." The man was also a compulsive fiddler and fixer. When I later examined the letters Washington wrote throughout the war to his steward, a distant cousin named Lund Washington, I didn't envy Lund having a boss so obsessed with the minutiae of his house and grounds. Writing from New York on August 19, 1776, the General begins with a reminder that "the New Chimneys are not to smoke," and continues:

> I mean to have groves of Trees at each end of the dwelling House, that in the South end to range in a line from the South East Corner to Colo. Fairfax's, extending as low as another line from the Stable to the dry Well, and towards the Coach House, Hen House, and Smoak House as far as it can go for a Lane to be left for Carriages to pass to, and from the Stable and Wharf from the No. Et. Corner of the other end of the House to range so as to shew the Barn &ca. in the Neck; from the point where the old Barn used to stand to the No. Et. corner of the Smiths Shop, and from thence to the Servants Hall, leaving a passage between the Quarter and Shop, and so East of the Spinning and Weaving House (as they used to be called) up to a Wood pile, and so into the yard between the Servts. Hall and the House newly erected; these Trees to be Planted without any order or regularity (but pretty thick, as they can at any time be thin'd) and to consist that at the North end, of locusts altogether, and that at the South, of all the clever kind of Trees (especially flowering ones) that can be got, such as Crab apple, Poplar, Dogwood, Sasafras, Laurel, Willow (especially yellow and Weeping Willow) twigs of which may be got from Philadelphia) and many others that I do not recollect at present, these to be interspersed here and there with ever greens such as Holly, Pine and Cedar, also Ivy; to these may be added the Wild flowering Shrubs of the larger kind, such as the fringe Tree and several other kinds that might be mentioned. It will not do to plant the Locust Trees at the North end of the House till the Framing is

up, cover'd in, and the Chimney Built; otherwise it will be labour lost as they will get broke down, defaced and spoil'd. But nothing need prevent planting the Shrubery at the other end of the House. . . .

Planting was only one of the multitudinous odds and ends of home maintenance that were on the absent General's mind. Lund must have dreaded the arrival of the postman. Writing from New Windsor on March 28, 1781, Washington asks:

How many Lambs have you had this Spring? How many Colts are you like to have? Is your covered ways done? What are you going about next? Have you any prospect of getting paint and Oyl? are you going to repair the pavement of the Piazza? is anything doing, or like to be done with respect to the Wall at the edge of the Hill in front of the House? Have you made good the decayed Trees at the ends of the House, in the Hedges, &ca. Have you made any attempts to reclaim more land for Meadow? &ca. &ca. An acct. of these things would be satisfactory to me, and infinitely amusing in the recital, as I have these kind of improvements very much at heart.

Even the moral tenor of Mount Vernon wasn't left to chance—or to Lund. Writing from Cambridge, Massachusetts, on November 26, 1775, at the beginning of his service as commander in chief, Washington tells Lund:

Let the Hospitality of the House, with respect to the poor, be kept up; Let no one go hungry away. If any of these kind of People should be in want of Corn, supply their necessities, provided it does not encourage them in idleness, and I have no objection to your giving my Money in Charity to the Amount of forty or fifty Pounds a Year, when you think it well bestowed. What I mean, by having no objection is, that it is my desire that it should be done. You are to consider that neither myself or Wife are now in the way to do these good Offices. In all other respects, I recommend it to you, and have no doubts, of your observing the greatest Oeconomy and frugality; as I suppose you know that I do not get a farthing for my services here more than my Expenses.

I thought historic preservation was a fairly modern idea in America, dating as a discipline from the years following World War II. But then

I heard the intertwined story of Ann Pamela Cunningham and Mount Vernon, and it cranked my thinking back a whole century. If she isn't the movement's patron saint, who could have beaten her to sainthood?

A South Carolina lady who had long been a semi-invalid, the result of a fall from a horse when she was 16, Miss Cunningham was being treated by a doctor in Philadelphia when her mother came for a visit in 1853. Later, returning home by steamer down the Potomac, on a night when the moon was full, Louisa Dalton Bird Cunningham came out on deck and saw the spectral shape of Mount Vernon. It was far gone in decay—its roof was sagging, one of its columns had fallen, and the lawn was high in weeds. Its owner was John Augustine Washington III, the last of four family members who inherited the estate after the death of George Washington but didn't get his agricultural gene; the land had steadily lost fertility. No longer able to maintain Mount Vernon or to deal with the growing crowds of tourists who regarded it as a sacred site, John offered the house and 200 acres to the federal government in 1851 for $200,000. Congress, however, refused to authorize the funds. Two years later he offered it to the state of Virginia and was again rejected. Commendably, he turned down some speculators who offered $300,000 and wanted to make it a commercial attraction.

It was at this point that Mrs. Cunningham saw Mount Vernon in the moonlight. Dismayed by the ruin of the first President's home, she wrote to her daughter and suggested that perhaps Mount Vernon could be saved by the collective efforts of the women of the South. For Ann Pamela Cunningham, who had been a high-spirited girl before her accident, the letter was an elixir. Signing herself "A Southern Matron," she sent letters to newspapers throughout the South, urging Southern women to save Washington's home and burial site.

So fervently was her call answered that she was able to offer John Washington his asking price of $200,000. John was thus placed in the unthinkable position of selling to a group of women, and he put the ladies off. Finally his sense of accounting triumphed over his sense of Southern chivalry. How Ann Pamela Cunningham got John Washington to sell and raised the money to buy is a tale of high persuasion and tenacity, and on April 6, 1858, her Mount Vernon Ladies' Association took title to the house and grounds. By 1860 Miss Cunningham had appointed 31 women from different states to serve as vice-regents, creating the mechanism that has governed the estate ever since.

Once in possession, Ann Cunningham hired a manager to live at Mount Vernon and get started on the repairs. She also intended to stay there herself, but the death of her father called her home to South Carolina to look after the family plantation, and the Civil War kept her there. But she didn't leave Mount Vernon without a guardian angel, installing her secretary as a resident feminine presence. A young woman from New York, hardly less remarkable than her boss, Sarah Tracy elicited a promise from both the Northern and the Confederate armies to treat Mount Vernon as a neutral area—the Civil War's only demilitarized zone—and to allow her to pass through the lines to go about her restoration work. Once, when her pass was countermanded by General George McClellan, she ran the blockade, walked to the White House and put her problem to President Lincoln. "He received me very kindly," she later reported, "and wrote a note to Mr. McClellan requesting him to see me and arrange the matter in the best way possible."

As for Ann Pamela Cunningham, she finally moved to Mount Vernon in 1868, spent six years supervising the structural work on the house and refurnishing it with objects that had once been there or that were historically apt, and retired with a rhetorical flourish, enjoining the Ladies' Association at its annual meeting in 1874 as follows:

> Ladies, the home of Washington is in your charge—see to it that you keep it the home of Washington! Let no irreverent hand change it; let no vandal hands desecrate it with the fingers of "progress"! Those who go to the home in which he lived and died wish to see in what he lived and died. Let one spot, in this grand country of ours, be saved from change. Upon you rests this duty.

Today that is still the mission of the Ladies' Association. "Our emphasis," Christine Meadows told me, "is on Washington as a farmer and on the working life of the plantation. We're getting a lot of scholarly interest in the other populations who lived here, especially the blacks and the indentured white servants."

Afterward I saw some laborers who had the look of college graduates digging near the mansion, and I asked one of them, who turned out to be Dennis Pogue, Mount Vernon's chief archaeologist, what they had found. "Right here," he said, pointing to some trenches outside the kitchen, "we found a pit filled with household trash: everyday items like bottles and ceramics and table glass and buttons and buckles and pipes, plus food remains, such as bones and oyster shells, and floral remains, such as pits and seeds and nuts, which enable us to reconstruct the family's diet. Nobody hauled trash away in those days. It just got thrown out.

"We've also found trash pits under the slave quarters and near the houses where the servants and the craft people lived. They tell us how the living styles of the working families differed from those in the main house. At one time it was suggested that the outbuildings be demolished because they had housed 'menials.' But Ann Cunningham had made it a principle that whatever existed in Washington's time was to be preserved *as it was*. I'm here to support the notion of making Mount Vernon as authentic as possible. That could lead to reconstructing other components of the estate. For instance, we now know where Washington's orchard was: we've found the boundaries and the fence lines and the roots of some of the trees, and we also have Washington's record of what was in it. That orchard was an important part of Mount Vernon's landscape that's been missing, and we'd like to put it back.

"Shrines are dull places by definition—they don't have any people, because the people you want to know about are gone. You feel moved—you're seeing sights you've heard about since fourth grade—but you also want to know: What was really going on here? What was the context for this extraordinary man in American history? Today there's far more to the study of history and social history than the story of the great white fathers. How about Washington's life as a slaveholder—the dark side of the shrine?"

The word "dark" startled me. I had come to Mount Vernon to get away from the darkness and back into the sunlight of America's youth, and I had been refreshed: everything I heard about Washington added up to a man of exemplary character and judgment, almost too good to be true. Yet he was a slave-owner. Nobody told Washington that it was politically incorrect to own slaves in 18th-century America, any more than Columbus understood how much colonial damage he was bringing to the new world in 1492, and although I was glad to see the dark side of Mount Vernon being honestly faced, I was also glad that the work was in the hands of scholars from the nonjudgmental disciplines of anthropology, archaeology and the "new" history—men and women who were literally excavating the truth about the plantation and letting it speak for itself.

"People are drawn to our work because we're really *doing* something," assistant archaeologist Esther White told me. "Very young kids love the fact that we're working in the dirt, digging up George Washington's trash, finding things that are two hundred years old, like old knives and forks that just wore out."

"The level of documentation here is unparalleled," said Michael Quinn, director of education, citing Washington's weekly letters to his managers, their weekly replies, and the precise account books he kept. "Because Washington was away so much, the plantation never left his mind. Until recently Mount Vernon was seen only as a place for inspiration. Now we don't think that's enough. We can't assume that children know so much about George Washington that they're awestruck when they get here. Our job is to help people understand the essence of the man. After all, he lived here for forty-five years. There has to be some insight into his character that you can draw from that."

Of the 200,000 students who visit Mount Vernon every year, Quinn said, "We want to make their visit so provoking that they'll go home and want to know more." One provocation had been to invite 800 schoolchildren every day for four weeks to visit Mount Vernon and lay a carnation on Washington's sarcophagus. "I hope when they're older they'll think, 'Something important happened that day. When I was six or seven I put a flower on that man's grave.'"

I wished I had been similarly provoked at a similar age. Instead I had gone through life lugging a plaster statue of a pious boy who couldn't tell a lie and a prim general who stood up in a boat. My days at Mount Vernon brought the statue to life. When I left, I asked Christine Meadows what George Washington meant to her after 30 years spent in his company.

"He's the man I work for," she said, "He's endlessly fascinating. Physically he was more attractive than portraits would make him appear. He genuinely enjoyed the company of women and was interested in their education. He was a more genuine person than Jefferson and was certainly a more consistent person than Jefferson. During his life there was enormous curiosity about him; in people's minds he was a true hero. Even Jefferson, who became his political enemy, felt that he was the only person who could lead the country. He had the ability to work with men of diverse types and to draw the best out of whoever he worked with. There was such a core of credibility about him. People sense that."

10

Kitty Hawk

With Mount Vernon behind me, I felt that I had been put in touch with many of America's fundamental events and beliefs: the Revolutionary War and the idea of freedom, Washington and the idea of a citizens' republic, Lincoln's Civil War and the idea of a Union, and the idea of nature as a source of nourishment and land as a frontier homestead to die for. I had caught up with the emancipating Thoreau and the mythologizing Mark Twain and the dark legacy of slavery in the South. Now I wanted to get closer to the fabric of life: to look at three places that shaped the American character and ethic. Kitty Hawk, Abilene and Chautauqua were the America that loves machines, the America that takes its strength from small-town values, and the America that has a hunger for education.

I went to Kitty Hawk in late December because that was the time of year—December 17, 1903, to give the date its tremendous historical due—when Wilbur and Orville Wright, two bicycle mechanics from Dayton, Ohio, made the first powered flight in a heavier-than-air machine, and I wanted to get a feeling for the wind and the weather they worked with on that remote strip of sand off the coast of North Carolina, called the Outer Banks, which so ideally suited their needs.

They found the site the way they found everything else, including the knowledge of how to fly: by methodically gathering information. Wilbur initiated the search on May 13, 1900, by writing a letter on the stationery of the Wright Cycle Co. to the aging Octave Chanute, an early believer in powered flight, who lived in Chicago. Wilbur was then 33, the older of the brothers, and his letter began like this:

> For some years I have been afflicted with the belief that flight is possible to man. My disease has increased in severity and I feel that it will soon cost me an increased amount of money if not my life. I have been trying to arrange my affairs in such a way that I can devote my entire time for a few months to experiment in this field.

Explaining that he could only get away from his bicycle business in the slow months from September to January, Wilbur said, "I would be particularly thankful for advice as to a suitable locality where I could depend on winds of about 15 miles per hour without rain or too inclement weather." His plan, he said, was to launch gliders from a tower in order to learn the principles of flight, which he would then apply to a powered machine. Chanute replied that he thought it would be safer to launch gliders from a hill of soft sand, and he suggested two beaches that had steady winds, in California and Florida, adding that others might be found in South Carolina or Georgia.

Soft sand struck Wilbur as a good precaution, but he wanted a site that was nearer and less expensive to reach, and he wrote next to the National Weather Bureau, which sent him a set of its *Monthly Weather Reviews*. Studying these, he saw that winds of the strength he wanted had been reported at Kitty Hawk. That prompted a letter to the Kitty Hawk weather station. What could they tell him about the terrain and about possibly renting a house? The local telegraph operator wrote back that the beach was a mile wide and had no trees, but that houses were sparse and Wilbur should bring a tent. This was followed by a warmly welcoming letter from postmaster William J. Tate, who added the crucial detail that there was an 80-foot-high dune several miles to the south that might lend itself to glider launching. The weather, he said, got a little harsh around November.

Thus began the annual trips that would bestow mythic fame on what had been one of America's most isolated communities, consisting of only a few fishing families and a few men who worked at the weather stations and lifesaving stations along the treacherous beach, which was legendary for its shipwrecks. No bridge connected Kitty Hawk to the rest of the world, and as Wilbur found on September 9, when he got off the train at Elizabeth City, North Carolina, with various glider parts that he and Orville had assembled, "no one seemed to know anything about the place or how to get there." Only after three days did he find someone who would sail him and his gear across the 30 miles of Albemarle Sound to Kitty Hawk, whereupon he sent for Orville.

This conjunction of two men and a place has been fixed in my imagination all my life, partly because the very name of the place—Kitty Hawk!—is so perfect, so suggestive of flight. What happened there is one of the American stories I most enjoy thinking about. Each fall two brothers from Ohio lug their latest contraption to a barren beach by the Atlantic Ocean and expect the thing to fly—*and it does*. Nobody else so symbolizes for me the idea of America as a race of people who can fix anything: all those kids who spent their boyhood out in the shed or down in the basement and ended up inventing our cars and telephones and light bulbs and radios and the whole endless gadgetry of American life.

I've also always assumed that the Wrights were a little odd: absent-minded, antisocial, awkward in conversation, not much fun at a party; that went with being an inventor. But then I did some preliminary reading—most enjoyably, in a biography called *Wilbur and Orville*, by Fred Howard—and I found that their story was even better than I thought, even more solid in its old-fashioned American values.

As boys the Wrights played the usual boys' sports, and they grew up in a family that enjoyed being a family. Birthdays and homecomings were important. Their parents—Milton Wright was a United Brethren bishop, Susan Wright had been a teacher—encouraged them to pursue whatever intellectual notion piqued their curiosity, and their sister, Katharine, tolerated with affection their encroachment on the house and particularly on her sewing machine, which they used to make the muslin wing coverings for their planes. (Two older brothers had married and moved away.) "Will spins the sewing machine around by the hour while Orv squats around marking the places to sew," Katharine wrote in 1902 to Bishop Wright, who was away on church business. "There is no place in the house to live, but I'll be lonesome enough by this time next week"—when Wilbur and Orville would have left for Kitty Hawk—"and wish I could have some of their racket around." The brothers in turn were faithful letter writers when they were at Kitty Hawk, keeping the family informed about their trials and errors, and one of the first satisfactions they expressed after their historic flight on December 17 was that they would be able to get home for Christmas.

Neither of the brothers had more than a high-school education, but between them, as Fred Howard writes, "they were as capable of inventing new shapes and motors as any mechanical engineer. They had all the algebra and trigonometry necessary for calculating the strength and stresses of the necessary materials, and they were practical mechanics capable of constructing the wood and metal parts of a flying machine." In managing their personal affairs, a domain where inventors are famously woolly-headed, they were no less tidy. Determined to finance their flying experiments with their own money from their bicycle business, they proceeded with such frugality that the four-year cost of inventing the airplane—including materials, provisions and transportation to and from Kitty Hawk—came to just over $1,000.

The wonder of mechanical flight was first revealed to Wilbur and Orville when they were young boys, in the form of a present that their father brought home. Unlike most presents, which lie still when they are opened, this one ascended to the ceiling. It was a toy helicopter made by the French inventor Alphonse Pénaud, with twin propellers that were powered by a twisted rubber band. Pénaud's toy got the boys making toy helicopters of their own and, when they were grown men, reading about the work of various flying-machine pioneers, especially a German engineer named Otto Lilienthal, who made more than 2,000 glides near Berlin before crashing to his death in 1896. "Sacrifices must be made," he is reported to have said as he died. It was Lilienthal's death that inspired Wilbur and Orville to think about carrying on his work, to read Octave Chanute's book, *Progress in Flying Machines* and, finally, to write to Chanute himself for advice on a "suitable locality" for testing a machine of their own.

The winds when I arrived at Kitty Hawk obliged me by being of the same velocity as they were on the day of the Wright brothers' first flight: 22 to 27 miles per hour out of the north and gusting. I had no trouble making a connection with the climate that the brothers had to put up with—I could feel in my bones the cold air off the ocean and could hear enormous waves crashing onto the beach; few American places are so naked. But there was no way I could see the Outer Banks as they looked in the Wrights' day, when only an occasional shack added a human touch to the landscape. Today the area is what realtors call prime oceanfront, heavily developed with vacation houses, motels, mini-malls, convenience stores, fast-food outlets and all the other commercial debris of the American highway.

Following signs to the Wright Brothers National Memorial, I was disappointed to find that it wasn't at Kitty Hawk but at Kill Devil Hills, four miles farther south. So potent is the myth of Kitty Hawk that I didn't want the first flight not to have taken place there. Fortunately, it did. In 1903 Kitty Hawk was one of only two towns on the island—Nags Head was the other—and its boundaries included three sand elevations known as Kill Devil Hills. The biggest of those dunes was the 80-foot hill that Bill Tate mentioned in his letter to Wilbur Wright, and when the Wrights saw the hill and its adjacent miles of level sand they knew they had found their laboratory. Later Kill Devil Hills became a town in itself, thereby gaining official possession of the site, if not of the myth.

Today the hill dominates the Wright Memorial, I noticed as I turned in off the highway, especially because it has a commemorative pylon perched on its summit. It was the kind of monument that certifies a site as historic ground—granite is our validating stone—and I assumed that it was trying to tell me that this was where the first flight took off. But that was a false clue, I was soon reminded. The whole point of the first flight was that it *didn't* use a hill. As Orville summed it up, it was the first flight "in the history of the world in which a machine carrying a man had raised itself by its own power into the air in full flight, had sailed forward without reduction of speed, and had finally landed at a point as high as that from which it started."

"They weren't just bicycle mechanics who stumbled into the air," Darrell Collins, the park historian, told me. "Those men were true scientists. Very few tourists who come here realize exactly what they did: that they laid the foundation of aviation as it has been known ever since. Even aviation people are in a state of shock when they grasp the achievement. One of the things I do in my ranger talks is to ask whether anyone in the audience is a commercial pilot, and often there is—someone who flies a big plane like a 747. By then I've used our replica of the Wrights' plane to demonstrate how their controls worked, and I ask the pilot how the Wrights' control system relates to the one on *his* machine. The answer is always, 'Basically it operates on the very same principles.'"

How the Wrights arrived at those principles in four seasons at Kitty Hawk can be briefly summarized.

In 1900 they flew their double-decker glider mainly as a kite, but near the end of their stay they also made some free flights, with Wilbur as pilot. Their premise was that they would never be able to build a motorized plane until they learned how to build and control a glider. What they learned was that they would need far more flying time to give them useful information about wing curvature, control and lift.

In 1901 they were back with a bigger glider, in which they made several hundred glides, finally discovering that the laws and tables of air pressures they had been using, as formulated by Lilienthal and other pioneers, were, as Orville said, "mostly, if not entirely, incorrect." Discouraged over so much wasted effort, they talked about quitting. But Octave Chanute urged them to continue, pointing out that it would be years before anyone came along who knew as much as they knew now. Back in Dayton, they started over. To obtain correct information, they built a wind tunnel in which they tested the effect of air pressure on 200 different surfaces. Those meticulous tests gave them a body of knowledge—previously unknown—that told them the correct shape of a wing that would enable a plane to fly, and they incorporated their new data into the still larger glider they built and took to Kitty Hawk in 1902.

In this 1902 glider, which has been called the world's first true airplane, the Wrights made almost 1,000 flights. Those flights proved that they had mastered roll, pitch and yaw, or lateral, longitudinal and vertical instability—the three fundamentals of flight control, which had eluded earlier scientists, many of whom, like Samuel P. Langley, secretary of the Smithsonian Institution, were well connected and well financed.

That left only the problem of lift and thrust, which would be provided by an engine and propellers. Finding no automobile manufacturer who could build an engine as light as the one they needed—car engines of that era were as heavy as the Wrights' entire plane—they built one themselves, and having no airplane propellers to use as models, since none yet existed, they also figured out how to design and build those. All these elements came together in the Wright Flyer, which they designed in Dayton and spent two months arduously assembling at Kitty Hawk in the fall of 1903. Finally, on December 17, in heavy winds, the Flyer made its four historic flights of 120 feet, 175 feet, 200 feet and 852 feet.

I was glad to see that the visitors center gave the place of honor, at the entrance to its small museum, to a huge blowup of the photograph of the first moment of that first flight, probably the most famous of all aviation photographs. It's a picture that can be looked at for a long time. The Flyer has just lifted off the monorail track that the Wrights laid down for the launch. Orville is at the controls, Wilbur is running alongside the right wing, and the footprints of both men can be seen in the sand where they fussed over last-minute adjustments. Ahead of the rising Flyer is a limitless expanse of sand, and I couldn't help thinking about the limitless reaches of air and space that opened to man at that instant.

The fact that a camera was there to record the ascent was no fluke; photography was still another of the Wrights' interests, and they routinely documented their aerial tests with pictures, just as they kept precise daily diaries. The fluke was that the historic picture was taken by someone who had never seen a camera. John T. Daniels was one of three men from the nearby lifesaving station who came when they saw the Wrights' signal flag notifying them that a flight was going to be attempted. Tagging along with Daniels and Willie S. Dough and Adam D. Etheridge were two other people who happened to be on the beach that morning: William C. Brinkley, a lumber buyer from nearby Manteo, who was hoping to salvage some wood from a shipwreck, and a 16-year-old boy named Johnny Moore. They would be the sole witnesses of the day's momentous events.

Orville placed his camera on a tripod, handed the rubber bulb to Daniels, and told him to squeeze it when the Flyer reached the end of the launching track. How well Daniels did his squeezing the Wrights didn't know until they developed the glass-plate negative when they got back to Dayton. As for the boy Johnny Moore, who died in 1972, having lived long enough to see men fly to the moon, I was told by one of the rangers, Fentrice Davis, that after the day's fourth flight, of 852 feet, "Johnny never stopped running—he ran the eight hundred and fifty-two feet and ran all the way to Bill Tate's house in Kitty Hawk to spread the news."

Actually it would be five years before the world woke up to what the Wrights had done. Partly this was because of their modesty and their prudence in protecting their invention until they got it patented—a long ordeal, as it turned out. But mainly it was because the public had become skeptical after a number of highly ballyhooed flights failed disastrously. Nobody really thought flight was possible, aviators were regarded as crackpots, and if the experimental planes of prominent men like Langley plummeted instantly into the Potomac, why should anyone believe that two unknown brothers on a remote beach had made it into the air?

Of the half-million tourists who come to Kitty Hawk every year, half are what Ann Childress, supervisor of the National Park Service site, calls incidentals—families who are spending a few days at the beach. "The other half come to Kitty Hawk as a destination. They're people who have some tie to aviation—they're pilots, or they've had a pilot in the family, or they're connected with the aeronautics industry, and they're looking for the roots of things. We find that we periodically have to replace photographs of Wilbur and Orville in our exhibits because their faces get rubbed out. Visitors want to touch them."

I asked Childress what she most enjoys about working at Kitty Hawk. "The genius of the Wrights," she said immediately. "They were everyday guys, barely out of high school in their education, and yet they did something extraordinary, in a very short time, with minimal funds. They succeeded wildly—they changed how we all live—and I think, 'Could *I* be so inspired and work so diligently to create something of such magnitude?'"

The lure of Kitty Hawk, according to ranger Fentrice Davis, reaches beyond aviation professionals to touch everyone who has ever been tantalized by the idea of flight. "Visitors tell us, 'We've always wanted to come here, ever since we were kids,' or 'ever since we learned to fly,' and for some old-timers it goes back to the first time they ever saw a plane. Remember, there are still people around who were alive when the Wrights made that flight. This place is also a mecca for tinkerers and machinists. They walk around and look at the Wrights' plane and their engine, and as they talk you get a feeling for their hobbies. They ask you how something works, and all the time they're telling *you* how it works."

The visitors center is no bigger than it has to be, which isn't very big; one marvel of the Wright brothers' story is its compression—two men, a bicycle shop and a beach. Only two rooms are needed to tell the story. One contains photographs, documents and artifacts, including a replica of the Wrights' wind tunnel—a crude wooden box, six feet long, with an electric fan at one end and some suspended strips of metal at the other. "All it is is hacksaw blades," said Darrell Collins, the park historian, showing me the metal strips, which nobody would call a precision instrument. "But the information the Wrights got from this tunnel has been fed into modern computers and found to have an error of less than one percent."

The other room houses a replica of the 1902 glider and a replica of the 1903 Flyer, the crown jewel of the collection. I spent a long time looking at that historic biplane, enjoying its simple beauty. It was bigger than I expected—the wingspan is 40 feet, 4 inches—and it was wonderfully clean in its lines. Every detail was a study in logic, the product of two minds that broke down every problem into small, sequential steps. I was in the presence of two practical spirits—born mechanics who used whatever was at hand in their shop. For one main link I saw that they had used an ordinary bicycle chain. In their attention to detail they reminded me of someone else, and I realized it was George Washington, the methodical author of all those finicky letters to Lund, back at the plantation. Americans are a practical people and their first President was a practical man, father not only of his country but of all its inventors and mechanics and architects, its home-repair experts and computer freaks, its Edisons and Fords and Frank Lloyd Wrights.

If the Wright brothers' plane is Kitty Hawk's sacred icon, the sand just outside the visitors center is its sacred soil. By now it has been partly grassed over to keep it from blowing away, and several generations' worth of trees have sprung up along the beach. I had to keep reminding myself that in 1903 I would have seen nothing there but sand and the two small wooden buildings that the Wrights constructed to serve as their camp: a shack where they lived and a hangar where they kept their plane out of the fierce wind.

Today the two buildings, reconstructed from the brothers' photographs, stand where they stood before, along with a nearby boulder marking the takeoff point on December 17, 1903, and four cement markers with plaques designating the length of the day's four flights. How those markers got put in exactly the right spot is still another story of family efficiency. When the park was opened as a memorial, in 1928, on the 25th anniversary of the flight, all the surviving partici- pants and witnesses assembled for the dedication, including Orville, who would live until 1948, but not Wilbur, who had died of typhoid in 1912. The three men from the lifesaving station were on hand, plus Johnny Moore and the lumber buyer William Brinkley and some old Kitty Hawkers like Bill Tate who from the start had given their friend- ship to the two strangers from Dayton.

"They all had shovels," Darrell Collins told me, "and they dug around and found some pieces of wood from the two buildings buried in the sand. Finally they identified one of the fragments as the corner of the foundation of the hangar. That was what they needed. Orville had brought along his 1903 diary, and he paced off the distance from that corner to where he and Wilbur launched the flights, and that's where they put the big stone. Today I see many visitors go out to that stone. They start there and walk the route of those four flights, trying to savor the moment—to reflect back on how the flights felt."

"There's only one place in the world where the first plane flew," Ann Childress said, "and going out there and walking on that spot is as close as you can get to the real thing. If you're in some other part of the country and you read about Kitty Hawk, you can only imagine what the conditions were like. Somebody once said the National Park Service has the best classrooms in America, because the *essence* of a place can have a tremendous impact. You're learning through all five of your senses." Hearing her, I heard the voices of rangers in other parks, especially George Robinson, who told me that tourists come to Yel- lowstone to renew themselves on a sensory level. "The things we learn best and remember longest are those that we've come in physical con- tact with," he said, and it was true that I now carried somewhere in my senses the chirping of elk in Yellowstone and the rumble of water at Niagara, the smallness of the Alamo and the stillness at Appomattox.

Therefore I was glad to be not just imagining the Wrights' flight but to be bracing myself against those 22-to-27-mile-per-hour winds. I thought about the fact—unthinkable in modern casual-wear Ameri- ca—that Wilbur and Orville always wore a business suit, a starched collar, a necktie and a cap, even when they were flying one of their planes; work clothes were for the working class, not the middle class. The restored interior of their shack was further evidence of Dayton respectability transplanted to the wild. The Wrights' dining table had an oilcloth top, the dining chairs were upholstered, and cups and dishes and pots and pans and tins of food were neatly arrayed on shelves or hung from hooks. In this genteel bivouac, as their diaries tell us, the brothers often waited out ferocious Atlantic storms that lasted for days, never seeming to lose their patience or their good humor. Tenacity is required baggage for anyone who dares to live the American dream.

I went over to the big stone and walked into the same kind of headwind that Orville flew into at 10:35 A.M. on December 17, 1903. His time, as I saw when I reached the first cement marker, was 120 feet in 12 seconds, airspeed 30 miles an hour. Continuing on, I came to the 175-foot marker, denoting Wilbur's distance on the second flight. Like Orville, he was new to the controls of the heavier plane, which responded differently from the controls on the 1902 glider, and he didn't have enough time in the air to compensate for the wind that made the plane lurch back to the ground.

Before the third flight, Orville made some adjustments and then flew a steadier course, staying aloft for 200 feet. Reaching that destination myself, on foot, I looked ahead to the fourth marker. It was impressively far away—a total length of 852 feet, which Wilbur covered in 59 seconds on the last flight of the morning. He didn't want to take the plane higher and try to stay up longer because the winds were so strong. "Those who understand the real significance of the conditions under which we worked," he said afterward, "will be surprised rather at the length than the shortness of the flights made with an unfamiliar machine."

I went back to the big stone and walked Wilbur's 852 feet, taking more time to cover the distance than the man who had gone by air. That was the story I had come to Kitty Hawk to get into my metabolism. Man would never be earthbound again.

11

Abilene

Dwight D. Eisenhower wasn't born in Abilene, Kansas—his parents moved there from Texas when he was a baby—but he might as well have been. "The proudest thing I can claim is that I am from Abilene," said the man whose two separate careers—as supreme commander of the Allied armies that defeated Germany in World War II and as an immensely popular two-term President—won him the friendship of kings and prime ministers and a renown probably unmatched in American public life. He never forgot or let anyone else forget that he was the product of a small town on the prairie. He referred to it often, went home to it regularly, and was buried there in 1969. Almost 100,000 people came to his funeral.

I went to Abilene because it symbolizes for me an idea that is at the heart of the American dream: that no place is too small or too isolated to produce great men and women in every field—and, in fact, that the smallness of the place is often the source of the values that made them great. Harry Truman's Independence, Missouri, was such a place, and there are few Presidents whose small-town values I admire more. But Independence didn't have the remoteness I was looking for; it was a suburb of Kansas City.

It also didn't have the personal tie that I felt to Eisenhower. The man from Abilene has been part of my life since I was an enlisted man in the war that made him famous, stationed at a base not far from his headquarters in Algiers, and over the years I've had a curiosity about that Kansas town that created him. I suspected that behind the million-dollar smile was a man smarter than he chose to let on—smarter, certainly, than most of his White House successors at keeping us out of big and small wars—and considerably less amiable. He seemed to have learned at an early age the lessons that would take him far: to assess his options coldly, to make tough decisions, and to work hard. His apparent luck at always being in the right place at the right time was no fluke; he made his luck by character and by being prepared for the favorable moment. I wanted to see where that character got shaped.

Route 70 is a ribbon that runs across the middle of Kansas, connecting towns that don't come along very often and that look very much alike when they do. Few highways evoke such a strong sense of being at the utmost center of America; the surrounding plains are still so unpopulated that I can't begin to imagine the loneliness of the families who settled them. Driving west from Kansas City, I had plenty of time to think about the strength of those settlers. Sentimentality would not have been one of their traits—life was too harsh. Eisenhower, it occurred to me, had none. Part of his political genius was that the people he fired went to their grave thinking that the ax had been wielded by someone else.

The only major difference between Abilene and the other towns strung along Route 70—Junction City, Salina, Russell, Hays, WaKeeney, Oakley, Colby, Goodland—is that it is famous; in fact, twice famous. It first entered American legend as the king of the Old West cattle towns. When the Kansas Pacific Railroad pushed westward to Abilene in 1867 it gave Texas cattlemen a railhead at the northern end of the 1,000-mile Chisholm Trail, enabling them to reach desperately needed markets in the East by driving their herds to Abilene, as every student of Western movies knows as surely as he knows that Wyatt Earp and Doc Holliday wiped out the Clanton Gang and Johnny Ringo in a gunfight at the O.K. Corral. Suddenly alive with stockyards, saloons and gambling houses, Abilene became such a lawless frontier town that Wild Bill Hickok was hired as marshal in 1870 to restore order, which he did. By 1872 the railroad had pushed south to

Wichita, and Abilene's brief glory was over. Not until an unknown general materialized out of the oblivion of the peacetime army 70 years later did it enter phase two as an iconic American town.

Scanning the horizon from my rented car, I saw a grain elevator far ahead. That would be Abilene; no other edifice was in sight in any direction. I got off Route 70 at the next exit and drove into the town. Abilene (pop. 7,500) was the standard assortment of low, ordinary buildings containing banks, insurance and real estate offices, drugstores, small businesses and a newspaper, the *Abilene Reflector-Chronicle*. Except for an immense flour mill in the middle of town—a marvel of solid geometry, full of crazy angles, looking as if a giant child had hammered it out of tin—it could have been a hundred other Midwestern towns.

I got out and did some walking around and dropping in. The tempo was slow, the people friendly. "One of the good things about growing up in a town like this," said Bill Jeffcoat, a studio photographer whose cluttered shop looked as if it had photographed much of the population of Abilene since his father started it in 1921, "is that you get to know everybody, from high society to the garbage collector. People seem to have a little more time for each other; they stop on the street. It gives you an intimate view of people, and that gives you a little more self-confidence."

Jeffcoat, who is 66, showed me a famous photograph that his father, Paul Jeffcoat, who grew up next door to the Eisenhowers, took of them at a family reunion in 1926. Artistically grouped on the front porch around their parents, David and Ida, the six Eisenhower brothers stand or sit in their best church or business suits, looking like pillars of the Chamber of Commerce: Roy, 34, on a chair; Arthur, 40, and Earl, 28, on a porch swing; Edgar, 37, and Milton, 27, standing; and, perched on the steps in his spruce army uniform, Dwight, a 36-year-old major just out of the Command and General Staff School at Fort Leavenworth. Bill Jeffcoat told me that his father used an Eastman camera that still works and that his father's mother, Lucy Fritz Jeffcoat, touched up the side view, in the improving custom of the day. The negative lay around the Jeffcoat Studio, unloved and uncopyrighted, until Ike rose to acclaim in World War II, whereupon it was widely published, in *Life* and many other magazines. "All through the years, Ike kept in touch with his hometown people," Bill Jeffcoat told me.

"His roots are here. It was fun to be around him when he was back in Abilene. He always had that smile and some kind of joke for anyone who came up to him."

Growing up in an agricultural community also gives people an appreciation for how men and women get on with making a living, Jeffcoat said. "You see the hard work that farmers do—hard, dirty, dusty work—and it gives you great respect for people who work with their hands to get something out of the ground."

A few blocks beyond the Jeffcoat Studio, I passed an establishment called the Texan Café, which had a down-home look and a sign in the window that said GOOSEBERRY PIE, and I went in for a midafternoon bracer. I noticed that some men had begun to come in and go straight to a large room in the rear. I introduced myself to one of them, and he invited me to join them. He was Richard Danner, owner of the Danner Funeral Home, an Abilene family business going back to the early 1930s, and he said that he and the other men were members of the Abilene Coffee Club, which meets for coffee every day at 10 and 3, as it has since 1933. Its informal constitution is framed on the wall. Attendance varies with the press of business; on the day of my visit the group included a retired doctor, a Methodist minister and a newspaper editor, and as I sat at a long table talking with them I felt a pang of envy. I thought that I would give a lot to have a room in mid-Manhattan where I could always find a friend, at 10 and 3 on weekdays, as needed. "I wouldn't want to live in a bigger town than this," Danner said, adding that he once tried it. "Here you're with people who support each other and are always there for you."

Dean Chaffee, an 80-year-old country doctor with the wisdom of that calling written legibly on his face, told me that his father, Spencer Chaffee, also a general practitioner, was brought to Kansas as a baby in a covered wagon in the early 1870s. The family settled in a town called Talmage, 10 miles from Abilene, which, when Dean grew up, had a population of 150. "It wasn't even an incorporated town," he said, "but it wasn't so small that it didn't have a high school. I graduated from that school in a class of seven and went on to college." After medical school he became a doctor in Abilene, retiring in 1979. Between them, father and son practiced medicine in the area for almost 80 years.

"Abilene through its school system has produced many remarkable people," Dr. Chaffee said, mentioning a number of men and women whose names I recognized from the worlds of education and public service. "There has always been an appreciation of education here—not necessarily higher education, but the basics, which inspire people to go on. You could also always find a mentor in these small, friendly towns. Ike grew up on the wrong side of the tracks, but he sought out people who could teach and encourage him. He was inspired by Charley Harger, the editor of the *Reflector-Chronicle*, who was a contemporary of William Allen White." White, a fellow Kansan, was the legendary editor of the *Emporia Gazette*.

Abilene's churches were another shaper of hometown values, said Tal Tittsworth, minister of the First United Methodist Church. "Because this is a town where you know most everybody," he said, "there's a sense of community and a sense of accountability. If you want to couch it in good old American terms, it's love of God and country. The love that the church espouses gets lived out easier in a small town." (I had already glimpsed that accountability from fragments of conversation among the men of the coffee club. "When you're sick, everybody knows about it," one of them remarked.) "America was based on spiritual values," Tittsworth said, "and in the 1990s I've noticed a return to some of those roots. Since the mid-'50s the country has been through literally a hell of a time: wars, drugs, permissiveness, greed. All of that is certainly a part of life. But with the approach of the year 2000 I think people are saying, 'Let's find out just who we are, and what we really need to base our lives on. Let's get back to the important values, where people are connected, where they look out for one another and care for one another in significant ways.'"

Thus initiated into the rhythms of the town, I was ready to go in search of its famous son. I had also been reinitiated into the oldest currents of American character and decency, which up to now I had largely taken for granted, concentrating instead on the big and obvious icons: Presidents' heads and Presidents' homes, majestic parks and mighty rivers, mythic battlefields and a mythic dune. But the hometown values of hometowns like Abilene were everywhere in my story, whether I had put them there or not. The values that Lincoln and Grant brought to Appomattox were first learned in New Salem, Illinois, and Georgetown, Ohio. Grant knew that the defeated Southern soldiers couldn't begin to reconstruct their lives if they couldn't keep their horses and get a summer crop planted. The values that went into

Wilbur and Orville Wright's comment after they invented flight at Kitty Hawk—they were glad they had succeeded as early as December 17 because now they could get home for Christmas—were the values of Dayton, Ohio, and of their parents, a bishop and a schoolteacher. Home was where the brothers used their sister Katharine's sewing machine to make the wing coverings for their planes. At Abilene I even felt reconnected myself, if it's possible for an urban New Yorker to go home to Kansas, for its Christian values were the ones I had also been raised on.

The next day, signs so diffident as to be almost unnoticeable led me to the Eisenhower Center, just south of the railroad tracks. It consisted of five buildings neatly arrayed on a modest piece of land: the white frame house where Ike and his five brothers grew up, a chapel where he and Mamie are buried, a visitors center, the Eisenhower Museum and the Dwight D. Eisenhower Library. The museum and the library announce by their size and sobriety that they are important repositories: one contains memorabilia of Eisenhower's various careers, the other is a vast scholars' archive of papers, books and photographs. But something told me to start with the house.

What amazed me about the house was how small it was, and how minimal. Six boys grew up in it, four went to college, and all of them became successful men. That was worth thinking about. "It reminds me of my grandmother's house," I heard many tourists say when they first stepped inside from the front porch, noticing the wallpaper and the chairs, the upright piano that Ida Eisenhower bought with her wedding dowry and the Bible that was used for family readings every morning and night. But what the tourists could hardly get over was the plainness of the home in which Ida and David Eisenhower raised those six sons. "They admire the fact that the President grew up in a house so simple," I was told by Toby Weishaar, a college student whose summer job—telling tourists about the downstairs rooms—required almost no walking.

"My dad and his brothers were raised in a situation where they were dirt poor but educated," Eisenhower's son John Eisenhower once explained, "and I believe that created a lot of their ambition. Their parents were educated; they even knew Greek. They would argue about the Bible and they'd say, 'Well, all right, we'll settle that—we'll read it in the Greek.'"

Out in back, the family raised cows and pigs and chickens, and the boys each had a small garden where they grew vegetables. Ike made a point of planting vegetables that came up early, and he took them around town in a cart and sold them. Not having any sisters, the boys also did the household chores; there was no such thing as "women's work." (Ike, I remembered, was a President who liked to cook.) After high school Ike took a job for two years at an Abilene creamery, working an 80-hour week for $90 a month, to help put his older brother Edgar through college. Their plan was that Edgar would then finance Ike. "They were determined that they were going to be educated," John Eisenhower said. (I thought of Dr. Chaffee and Abilene's almost holy belief in education.) The problem of Ike's tuition got solved when he was accepted by West Point. He went off in 1911, at the age of 21, with $5.

I wondered whether the poverty of Eisenhower's boyhood had driven him to succeed—as it obsessively drove Lyndon Johnson—and later I asked Mack Teasley, assistant director of the Eisenhower Library, about it.

"There was no sense of that at all," he told me. "Ike always said he had a happy childhood and never felt that they were poor, though, looking back, it's obvious that they weren't very well off. The boys wore their father's long red underwear under their torn blue jeans—they were known around town as the 'red devils.' Still, it was an idyllic world. They were outdoors whenever they could be, and as soon as they finished their chores on Saturday they could play baseball or go fishing. The boyhood and the house are perfect products of their time. If Abilene gave Eisenhower his values, those values were: people weren't afraid of work and you learned to accept responsibility early. As a result, when Eisenhower went to West Point he was two years older than most of the other cadets and was totally self-confident and comfortable with who he was, unlike Lyndon Johnson."

Eisenhower himself, reminiscing for his granddaughter, said: "You know why we had such a happy childhood? Because we all felt that we were needed."

In earlier days of the republic, Presidents at the end of their term just carted their papers home. "Washington pulled up a wagon, and so did Jefferson," said John E. Wickman, who was director of the Eisenhower

Library from 1966 to 1989. "Their papers got scattered, and now they're in more than twenty different depositories. Lincoln's papers are all over the place—some of them didn't turn up for seventy or eighty years. One of the biggest collections is in the Lincoln Insurance Company in Fort Wayne, Indiana."

Today such disregard for the convenience of scholars and the preservation of public records wouldn't be tolerated; as citizens we expect to find a presidential library open for business in towns that our modern Presidents have called home—places like F.D.R.'s Hyde Park, New York, or West Branch, Iowa, site of the Herbert Hoover Library. That was the other idea about Abilene that had made me want to go there: the town that becomes a center of scholarship because of the local boy who grows up to be a Horatio Alger hero. "The collections here in Abilene are as good as they are anywhere in the presidential library system," said Richard Norton Smith, acting director of the Eisenhower Library. "Partly, of course, that's because Ike had two very distinguished careers."

The system was a long time getting born. "A historian in the 1830s and '40s named Peter Force was the first person who said, 'This destruction of records simply has to stop,'" John Wickman told me. "He was seriously committed to preserving presidential papers, and he got that idea into the conscience of the country." But the disarray of the Civil War and the proliferation of government documents that it caused—a flood never since reversed—frustrated every effort to create some kind of national archive. So continuous was the jockeying between historians and legislators that not until 1934 was a National Archives Act finally signed, providing custodianship for official documents. The first presidential library was that of Franklin D. Roosevelt at Hyde Park, which opened in 1941.

I assumed that presidential libraries were monkish places that couldn't touch my own life except through the books that scholars working there would write. But I dropped that notion when I heard about the series of special exhibits, entertainments and conferences that the Eisenhower Library held in 1990 to celebrate the 100th anniversary of Eisenhower's birth. Their purpose was to focus public attention on the 1950s—the decade of Eisenhower's presidency—and on the social and policy issues that those years put into play. The event I most enjoyed hearing about was a conference that brought together for the first time the principal actors in the showdown at Little Rock in 1957 that changed forever the course of American race relations and public education. Even Orval Faubus turned up.

It was Faubus, the long forgotten yet bitterly remembered governor of Arkansas, who provoked the crisis by refusing to integrate the schools in his state, despite the Supreme Court's historic decision, *Brown v. Board of Education*, that decreed the end of segregation in public schools. In response, Eisenhower sent paratroopers of the 101st Airborne Division to escort nine black students—"the Little Rock Nine"—to Little Rock Central High every morning through an ugly mob. The daily courage of those nine children is one of the bright ornaments of the American civil rights movement.

Now, 33 years later in an auditorium in Abilene, before an audience that included the national press, the following people were assembled for a panel discussion: Governor Faubus; four members of the Little Rock Nine—Ernest Green, Carlotta Walls Lanier, Terrence Roberts and Thelma Mothershed Wair; the widow and two daughters of Oliver Brown, whose 1954 Supreme Court challenge to the Topeka board of education resulted in the court's ruling; Herbert Brownell, Jr., Eisenhower's attorney general and most influential voice for integration; and several other members of Eisenhower's administration who were active in securing civil rights.

"I doubt that thirty years ago we could have envisioned the group we have here today," Brownell said. Ernest Green, now a banker in Washington, recalled the arrival of Eisenhower's troops. "That was the first boulder being moved," he said. "That started the avalanche." Before the conference began, according to the *Washington Post*, Faubus, a white-haired man of 80, encountered "a diminutive, middle-aged black woman" in the hall. He didn't recognize her but thought she might remember his name. "I'm Orval Faubus," he said. The woman shook his hand and said she was Thelma Mothershed. Faubus told her, "I never did see you during all that turmoil." She said, "That's because I was so short. You could never see me in any of the pictures because I was below the heads of the crowds."

I liked the thought of that reunion, and of a library that would think of holding it, and I asked Richard Norton Smith whether such highly visible events represent a new emphasis for the National Archives and Records Administration, which runs the system. "One of my heroes," he replied, "is James Bryant Conant, who was not only the last larger-than-life president Harvard will probably ever have but a man who cared passionately about what he called a cohesive civic culture. Maybe that's naive, but he cared about how educational institutions have an opportunity to educate the citizen. My feeling about presidential libraries is that the scholars will come anyway, one way or another. So what we have is a chance to move beyond that core audience—to use major temporary exhibits and conferences and outreach programs to involve the public. Our Little Rock conference was a very emotional event for everyone who was there, but it wasn't the only historic look at the '50s we did that summer. We also had a concert by Chubby Checker, an outdoor sock hop featuring the Coasters, and a science fiction film festival—all those mutant atomic creatures from the '50s that ate Cleveland. Young people have heard about the '50s and are interested in them, but they don't have any sense of what the decade was like."

For many visitors who came to Abilene for the Eisenhower centennial, its emotional climax was a grand reunion of World War II veterans, a vintage U.S.O. show and a display of wartime aircraft and field equipment, all held on his birthday, October 14. "I've been interested to see the reactions of veterans who come to Abilene," Richard Smith told me. "In many ways this is a patriotic shrine. Coming here is obviously a powerful experience for a lot of people; there's a genuine bond with Ike." His comment took me back to Mount Vernon—to all those early Americans who dropped in on George Washington's home because they felt a bond with *their* general.

But the bond with Eisenhower goes beyond the military, and perhaps what finally binds us is a nostalgia for the lost dignity of presidential conduct. Eisenhower was a President who didn't seek the job; the job came seeking him, as it did with General Washington. Today the Oval Office is sought so strenuously and so callously, each candidate mouthing whatever his pollsters and handlers say will get him elected, that a man who didn't covet the White House and who kept his integrity when he got there reminds us that Presidents used to be trusted. Eisenhower was perhaps the last President who had good relations with Congress, perhaps the last one most Americans were willing—before the Bay of Pigs and Vietnam and Watergate—to believe.

Walking around the Eisenhower Center on my last day, I was sorry that the place is so prim and sacerdotal. Both the library and the museum are monolithic limestone blocks with few windows and no joy. Human warmth is provided only by the house where the six boys grew up and by the tourists, many of whom might have grown up in the house themselves. I had a sudden urge to see wheat, or at least sunflowers, growing between the buildings on those acres where the family once raised cows and pigs and chickens. Amid so much lawn and limestone I had lost Abilene.

An optical coincidence came to my rescue. Standing on the steps of the library and looking across to the museum, I saw, rising beyond the museum, a grain elevator—the same one I had seen from Route 70. Thanks to an obliging retina, it seemed to be rising out of the museum. Turning to my right, I saw an alfalfa-drying plant that I hadn't noticed before, not far beyond the edge of the property. From my left I heard the whistle of a freight train. They were restorative sights and sounds; Eisenhower's town was still intact.

I was reminded of something John Wickman had mentioned earlier. "Eisenhower once told me," he said, "that he didn't want a monument—he had seen enough monuments to dead generals in Europe. He hated the word 'memorial' and said he never wanted it to be used around here. He said if anyone ever referred to it as the Eisenhower Memorial he'd pull out of it."

What he wanted visitors to take away from Abilene was a different idea, and as if to make sure nobody missed the point when he spoke at the ground-breaking ceremonies for the library in 1962, he added a sentence that wasn't in his prepared speech. "As you enter these buildings," he said, "think of them as not a memorial to one man, or one family, but rather as a symbol of what America gives to her children— the opportunity to aspire and achieve."

12

Chautauqua

I used to hear older men and women who grew up in the Middle West talk about the week when the chautauqua came to town. It was an eagerly awaited week, bringing speakers, preachers, singers, theatrical artists and other bearers of culture to people starved for the higher ideas of life. Towns visited by those edifying troupes were known as chautauqua towns, or towns on the chautauqua circuit—the word has long been part of the American language, defined by Webster as "an educational and recreational assembly with a program that includes lectures, concerts, etc." More recently, I've heard people talk about Chautauqua itself. Somewhere in upstate New York there was a town by a lake where families have owned cottages for generations and where Americans still flock every summer to be intellectually recharged. Hearing them talk, I could tell that this was no ordinary summer colony. Some deeper current got into the blood of its sons and daughters, almost religious in its zeal, and the name of the religion was self-improvement.

Self-improvement as a vital American force has interested me since the early 1980s, when I worked for the Book-of-the-Month Club. The club had been founded by a man named Harry Scherman, who already knew how strongly the thirst for knowledge beats in the American breast. In 1914 he had persuaded Woolworth's five-and-ten-cent stores to carry 100 tiny leatherbound classics that he called the Little Leather

Library, which included such thorny titles as Dante's *Inferno*, Browning's *Pippa Passes* and Balzac's *Christ in Flanders*, and he wound up selling 40 million of them. The logical next step was to invent the Book-of-the-Month Club, which he did in 1926, and the club has since sent out almost 550 million carefully chosen books. Its historic role, not unlike that of the public library, has been to provide the best books that Americans were willing to read in their increasingly educated pursuit of knowledge.

"One trend that the Book-of-the-Month Club hooked into from the beginning," I was told by Clifton Fadiman, who has been on its board of judges since 1944, "is the serious American interest in self-education. If you look at a list of the books we've sold most of, I'll bet the majority are books that explain. They're all part of a didactic tradition that goes back at least to Emerson and his interest in self-reliance. There were a lot of self-help books in 19th-century America; don't forget, this is where pragmatism arose: Dewey and James and Peirce. Very few people came to this country with a million dollars in their pocket."

Emerson lives! Today Americans are self-improving as never before: going on study tours, listening to instructional tapes, taking lessons in every art and craft, signing up for extension courses and summer courses and correspondence courses and Elderhostel courses. So invisibly has the idea of adult education become woven through American life that it's easy to forget that somebody had to put it there—and that the main impetus came from Chautauqua. I was long overdue to visit that evangelizing village with the odd Indian name, and when its 1991 season rolled around—its 117th summer—I heard the call. First, however, I caught up on its history.

In 1874 an Akron businessman, Lewis Miller, and a Methodist minister, John Heyl Vincent, decided to hold a two-week program of lectures and classes for Sunday-school teachers at an abandoned camp-meeting ground on Lake Chautauqua. The tents and platforms were the only things they kept; Dr. Vincent had no use for the revivalist hysteria of camp meetings, and he gave his first Chautauqua Assembly a strong educational stamp. That session was so popular, drawing teachers from 25 states, that in 1876 it was extended to eight weeks. Illustrious speakers were provided, and large crowds came. With this format

Dr. Vincent was building on the even earlier Lyceum movement, which sent lecturers to many newly settled parts of America.

The Chautauqua model in turn was soon copied; imitation assemblies sprang up in many states, and by 1890 the number of "little chautauquas"—local programs of lectures and concerts—had multiplied to almost 200. To homesteaders the word "chautauqua" became a beacon of hope. "Too frequently, lured by the glowingly optimistic railroad advertisements," Joseph E. Gould writes in *The Chautauqua Movement*, "the settler and his family had been dropped on the vast treeless expanse of the Great Plains and there left to his own devices. The communities were lacking in the most rudimentary amenities, and a cultural link with the East was out of the question; only the mining communities that had 'struck it rich' could afford to underwrite the cost of Eastern 'talent.' . . . The Chautauqua movement offered the discouraged settlers of the new West a link with the heritage they felt they had lost."

Those little chautauquas had no connection with the town that inspired them, but their use of the name gave them instant respectability, and the word entered common usage, borne by the "tent chautauquas" that in the early 1900s began to descend on towns across America, bringing a one-week smorgasbord of lecturers, concert artists and orators such as that hardiest of chautauqua perennials, William Jennings Bryan. Not until the mid-'20s did they end their remarkable run, killed by three social forces which, almost overnight, changed how Americans got their information and spent their leisure time. Radio became the new national forum, movies brought the world to Main Street, and cars put families on the road. Suddenly deserted, tent chautauqua folded its tents.

Meanwhile, however, it had educated millions of Americans on new movements that otherwise might not have received the popular support they needed to take root, including the graduated income tax, slum clearance, juvenile courts, pure-food laws, the school lunch program, free textbooks, a balanced diet, physical fitness, the Camp Fire Girls and the Boy Scouts. These concepts were brought to communities that would have heard of them only if one of their teachers or ministers had gone to Chautauqua and carried back the news.

But the place to be for anyone seeking enlightenment was Chautauqua itself. Theodore Roosevelt, one of many Presidents who wrapped themselves in the cloak of the village, called it "the most American place in America," by which he meant that it embodied the pastoral ideal in a nation that was fast going industrial. Here in a sylvan utopia the common man could still get himself uplifted. By 1881 Chautauqua was the locale where any national leader seeking a platform for his ideas hoped to be invited to speak. To facilitate that process the town built a 6,000-seat auditorium and a hotel called—what else?—the Athenaeum. That's where I reserved a room.

I got to Chautauqua by driving interminably west across New York State until I ran out of state. Erie, Pennsylvania, was just across the border, Pittsburgh not far to the south. Only technically was I still in New York; emotionally I felt that I had arrived in the Midwest—on a small Midwestern island. The insularity was reinforced by a steel fence around the grounds and by a massive gate where an admission charge of $8.25 per person per day was charged—a discovery, as I later learned, that can startle tourists who think all American towns are free. The ticket admits visitors to the day's lectures and concerts and is one of the Chautauqua Institution's methods of paying for its nine-week program: the speakers, the resident symphony orchestra, the opera and theater companies, and the school that holds classes for students of art, music, drama and dance. In summer the town has a population of almost 10,000; after that it dwindles to 200 families.

The gate made me uneasy. I'm an American boy who hated summer camp and will make a mighty effort never to be subjected again to someone else's arcadia in the woods. Entering the grounds, I felt a pang of the old claustrophobia: the tree-shaded cottages and boarding-houses were close to each other, in the manner of a camp meeting ground. But I was saved by the gods of domestic architecture. The houses came in many eclectic styles—gingerbread and shingle style and steamboat Gothic—that were a refreshment in themselves, Victorian relics as fossilized as the woolly mammoth. Beyond that, the stately Athenaeum was airy and high-ceilinged, with a lofty front porch where I could sit in a rocking chair along with other rockers and gaze out at the lake, and the grounds had grassy plazas where people could sit and socialize. I was reminded of a small college campus; the atmosphere was one of purposeful bustle.

Good behavior was expected. "Please do not disrupt Chautauqua's

tranquillity," said a leaflet called "Visitor Guidelines and Responsibilities," which was handed out at the main gate. Because the community
was "family-oriented," it said, there was to be no drinking in public
places and no eating or smoking in the amphitheater; noise should be
kept to a minimum, and cars could be driven only to and from the
main gate. At the Athenaeum, dinner rules called for men to wear a
jacket and a tie and for ladies to be "dressed in their loveliest." Such
written laws were hardly necessary; Chautauqua's ladies were born
knowing them. They looked the way older women used to look, especially older women in the Midwest—comfortable with their age and
their hairdo and their nice dresses; not a pants suit or a blue hair was in
sight. In the evening as I strolled among the cottages, I heard no hint
of television; people sat on their veranda reading a book under an old-
fashioned reading lamp, more yellow than white in its glow. The ambi-
ence was one of white-middle-class Protestantism. These people were
churchgoers—I recognized them as a native son-in-law of Iowa.

So strong was the Protestant veneer—two of the most imposing
buildings were the Hall of Christ and the Hall of Missions—that I
admired John Heyl Vincent's original wisdom in insisting on education
as Chautauqua's purpose, for what has brought people there ever since
is the hunger for knowledge. Each of the nine weeks of summer has a
theme ("Education Week," "Arts and Humanities Week," "Social
Issues Week"), and every morning at 10:45 a leader in that field gives a
lecture in the old auditorium, an amiable wooden structure, open on
three sides, that is the hub of all Chautauqua life. Anybody wandering
by can hear what is being said or prayed or played or sung on the stage,
from the early-morning sermon to the midmorning lecture to the
midafternoon orchestra rehearsal to the evening concert. Much of the
education is ad hoc, catching, among other unsuspecting folk,
teenagers who in a formal setting would howl at being exposed to culture. Whatever is heard is then passionately discussed, back at the
Athenaeum or on walks around the grounds, the residents often beard-
ing the day's lecturers on *their* walk to pursue a scholarly point. I heard
two ladies from Ohio, who didn't look like intellectuals, pushing the
morning's speaker into terrain he said he hadn't reached himself. One
of them mentioned hermeneutics.

"I was brought here as a child by my parents around 1920," said
Alfreda L. Irwin, who, at 79, puts in a full day at the library as town

historian, "and I was very conscious of people who came to Chautauqua having accomplished things—not just the famous lecturers and musicians but the people my parents invited around at night, sitting on our porch. It was an exposure to *educated* people, and that made me want to accomplish things too. I had these pictures in my head. At the end of summer when I got back home I'd go to the piano in the parlor and try to play, or I'd go out in the backyard and give a lecture. Of course I had no talent. But the men who founded Chautauqua believed that 'knowledge is power' and that learning ends only with life.

"People have always found refreshment and renewal here before they go back to their demanding jobs. That's not to say it isn't hard work. Looking back, it's amazing that in the 19th century Chautauqua could get so many people to come every summer to hear speakers lecture on subjects like labor laws and immigration laws and women's rights. But John Vincent and every president since him has emphasized that the most important thing for Chautauqua to do is to stay close to society and its needs."

The present president, Daniel L. Bratton, believes that what draws people to Chautauqua is that it caters to the sum of who they are. "There are places that have better musical facilities, like Tanglewood," he told me, "and there are places that have equally good lecture programs. But none of them does as good a job of serving the totality of a person's being: mind, body and spirit. Chautauqua affirms the importance of having culture in your life, of having a spiritual side in your life, and of having fun."

The word "fun" caught me off guard; if I were looking for laughs I would look somewhere else. Bratton's point was that Chautauquans spend as much time swimming and sailing and playing tennis as they do rushing to and from lectures and seminars with titles such as—to take three from the summer of my visit—"Feeding the Brain to Maximize the Mind and Mood," "Envisioning a Sustainable Society: Learning Our Way Out" and "A Paradigm Shift for Sexuality and Religion?" But they don't act like people who swim and sail and play tennis; they act like people hell-bent, or heaven-bent, on self-improvement. Some of them, in residence all nine weeks, attend all 45 morning lectures. "When they go home, they feel plugged in to the culture of the country," Bratton says. Still, he doesn't want Chautauqua to be too serious, and he reminded me that the symphony orchestra performs only three nights a week, leaving the other evenings to such lesser musical deities as Tony Bennett and Mitch Miller. I noticed, however, that the audiences were just as big and attentive when the fare was Mahler and Hindemith as when they sang along with Mitch.

For me those nightly concerts were a high moment, whether the fare was Lutoslawski's *Livres pour orchestre* or Mr. Jack Daniel's Original Silver Cornet Band, because all of us were caught up in the shared enjoyment that small-town Americans have always taken in listening to outdoor music on a summer night, sitting on a bench next to friendly neighbors. "Chautauqua is one of the few constants in the lives of families who come back year after year," Bratton said. "America today is a rootless society, and when these people drive through the gate every summer they get a powerful feeling of coming home. If you walk around the cemetery you'll see that most of the people buried there are from somewhere else. They've moved around so much that when it comes time to die, they want to be in the one place that has represented stability and continuity for them. This summer we have four families who are in their seventh generation."

It didn't take acute vision to see in all those generations a pattern of white-middle-class values, and I asked Bratton whether he would call Chautauqua elite. "Sure it's elite," he said, "but not in socioeconomic terms. People are simply not going to come here unless they have some intellectual curiosity; there are plenty of easier places to sunbathe and read a book or be entertained. It *is* very white, but I honestly think that's going to change. Back in the 1870s there were very few Jews here; now there are many. My grandfather was an Irish immigrant who came to New York's Lower East Side in 1890, and you didn't see many of *those* here." Bratton, that Irishman's grandson who is now the president, told me that in his career as an educator he has lived in so many parts of America that he doesn't think of any of them as home. Recently he bought a plot in the Chautauqua cemetery.

I was impressed to find that Chautauqua was still such a going concern. Even more impressive was the story of how many forms of adult education it gave to the American people. Today, summer school in America is an assumed right; anyone who wants to take courses during the off months will find plenty of providers. But for most of the 19th century there was almost no way for a nontraditional student to attend college. To fill that need Chautauqua chartered itself as a university in 1887. "It was the first degree-granting university in the United States whose enrollment consisted of part-time students and a high proportion of women," Bratton said. "Otherwise you had to have the money and the determination to be a full-time student somewhere, and not many women could manage that. Higher education was very sexist."

The university found such a grateful constituency that other colleges began to offer summer classes in the 1890s, at which point it went back out of business. "It closed because other colleges finally picked up the ball," Bratton said. Similar borrowings can be found throughout the history of American education. The University of Chicago, which I always assumed had an old and venerable lineage, traces its late-19th-century birth to Chautauqua—specifically, to a $600,000 gift by John D. Rockefeller to build a Baptist "super-university" which, he was told, would "take the wind out of the sails of Yale, Harvard and even Johns Hopkins." Rockefeller had been struck by Chautauqua's energetic president William Rainey Harper and his program of flexible courses for students of all ages, and when the University of Chicago opened in 1891 it had Harper as its president. In Harper's *Official Bulletin No. 1* he outlined a revolutionary plan for a division called University Extension Work, consisting of special lectures, evening classes and correspondence courses.

"The concept of the extension of university resources to everyone, regardless of age or academic preparation, was a Chautauqua idea," Gould writes in *The Chautauqua Movement*, "as was the proposal to allow work toward a degree to be distributed over a long period of time or divided between work in residence and work by correspondence." I later learned that the community college was also Harper's idea, and therefore at least a stepchild of Chautauqua.

But the most influential of Chautauqua's ventures was a book-reading program. In 1878 Vincent realized that far more people would like to take courses at Chautauqua than could get there. His solution was to found the Chautauqua Literary and Scientific Circle. Thus with one stroke he created America's first book club and its first correspondence course. The CLSC would send out the books; members would read them in small discussion groups in their hometown, and those who completed the four-year course would come to Chautauqua for a summer graduation ceremony.

Even Vincent, who was one of the visionary figures in American education, must have been stunned by how richly his faith was rewarded. In the CLSC's first year, 8,400 people signed up; within a decade, enrollment had reached 100,000, and by 1914 the program had enlisted half a million members in 12,000 circles in every state and had graduated almost 49,000. The circles were mainly in Pennsylvania, Ohio, New York, Iowa and Illinois, in towns of 3,500 people or fewer, but lively groups also sprang up in big cities such as New York, Brooklyn, Philadelphia and Chicago. Usually the members met in somebody's home or in a Methodist, Presbyterian, Baptist or Episcopalian church; denominational ties were encouraged. Most of the members were women. They were hungry for the education they hadn't been able to obtain, and some of the most poignant mementos in the club's archives are letters from farm wives explaining that they had been too busy with their chores to finish their assignment on time.

Today all the books ever sent to CLSC members are arrayed on shelves in the Chautauqua library, and I took down some of the early ones. What struck me, through the dust and the cracked bindings, was the earnestness of the effort that went into both the choosing and the reading of the books. Typical titles from the first decade are *A Short History of the English People, Fourteen Weeks in Human Physiology, Merivale's General History of Rome, Cyrus the Great and Alexander the Great, A Short History of Art, The Art of Speech, Walks and Talks in the Geological Field, Steele's Popular Zoology, From Chaucer to Tennyson, An Introduction to Political Economy* and *Recreations in Astronomy*.

What was it like to receive such books in an RFD mailbox a century ago: books that were a window into the world beyond the county seat and into the great civilizations of the past? "A key word to the Chautauqua mission is 'empowerment,'" Bratton had told me, and I imagined that the readers of those books felt more empowered as a result of their immersion in Chaucer, their 14 weeks in human physiology, their recreations in astronomy, and their walks and talks in the geological field. I also imagined that they felt a certain moral superiority—it's hard not to feel the winds of self-righteousness blowing at Chautauqua—and I wondered whether the program had perhaps fostered in its members the notion of a ruling class. I got part of my answer in an excellent Ph.D. dissertation by Charles Robert Kniker, called "The Chautauqua Literary and Scientific Circle, 1878-

1914: An Historical Interpretation of an Educational Piety in Industrial America."

"Members believed themselves to be among the cultured elite of the United States because of their education through CLSC reading," Professor Kniker writes, noting that the Circle appealed mainly to "those who were or who became the prestigious, the professional, the wealthy and the powerful in their communities." After they graduated from the program they rarely became involved in any kind of social reform—"society was to be improved, not restructured," and the means to salvation was knowledge. "In their activities and their attitudes they represented only a segment of American life: evangelical liberal Protestantism," a segment whose tenets then included the belief that "Anglo-Saxons were to hold power over immigrant groups and blacks" and that "the nation was a civilizing agent for the world."

Today the CLSC continues to occupy a central position at Chautauqua, operating out of a bungalow within earshot of the civilizing speeches and concerts that waft out of the auditorium. Its books still go to members all over America, their titles still attuned to the instructional needs of the day: *The Long March*, by Harrison Salisbury; *The Moral Life of Children*, by Robert Coles; *The Making of the Atomic Bomb*, by Richard Rhodes; *Infinite in All Directions*, by Freeman Dyson; *An Urchin in the Storm*, by Stephen Jay Gould; *The End of Nature*, by Bill McKibben. Membership has long since fallen off—again, because somebody else picked up the ball; book clubs are now an American fixture. But the graduates still come back every August for Recognition Day, a ceremony that has never changed. They march past applauding crowds and through golden arches into the Hall of Philosophy, which was my favorite of all of Chautauqua's engaging structures—a temple with Doric columns, modeled on the Parthenon and situated, appropriately, in a grove. The handmade banners of all the classes since 1878 are brought out for the occasion.

After several days at Chautauqua I could feel my time running out. It was that old summer-camp constriction, the feeling of being the captive of grownups who know what's good for me. I realize that I'm a minority crank on this issue; most people find Chautauqua an almost impossible dream come true in modern America—an oasis of intellectual sustenance, sheltered from the bleak realities of everyday life. But old phobias are not easily shed, and on my third night the panicky thought occurred to me that I might not be allowed back *out* of Chautauqua. I knew that in the early 1900s the main gate was locked every Saturday night and 10,000 residents spent the Sabbath in Christian imprisonment on the grounds, safe from such secular temptations as the Sunday paper.

I got up early the next day, retrieved the car that had been taken away from me when I checked in at the hotel, and drove to the main gate. The guard studied me for what seemed like the rest of the morning and finally waved me on. I never looked back, and nine hours later I was inhaling the free, toxic air of Manhattan.

But I wasn't through with the village by the lake. In the days that followed I found pieces of my visit tugging at me: facts I had learned from a lecture, strands of music I had plucked from a concert, ideas I had heard around me. The long arm of self-improvement, reaching out from John Heyl Vincent's Chautauqua of 1874, had plenty of muscle left. Something powerful was still going on there.

13

Disneyland

When I first called Disneyland and was put on hold, the canned music I got was "When You Wish Upon a Star." It made my day, or at least that two minutes of it. Of all the affable songs that ran through the Walt Disney movies I grew up on, none conveyed with such assurance—not even "Some Day My Prince Will Come," from *Snow White and the Seven Dwarfs*—the Disney message of infinite possibility. When you wished upon a star, the song said, it didn't matter who you were; anything your heart desired would come true. Jiminy Cricket sang it in the opening scene of *Pinocchio*, 50 years ago, and in 1991 it was still on the job, epitomizing not only Disneyland but its surrounding homeland of southern California, world capital of make-believe.

It was to that far-off Eldorado that a young man named Cecil B. DeMille came from New York in 1913 on an exploring trip, dispatched by his partners—Jesse L. Lasky and Samuel Goldfish, who later changed his name to Goldwyn—in a newly formed film-producing company. Their first picture was *The Squaw Man*, and they needed a rural site that they could populate with cowboys and Indians. DeMille found an old barn with some fruit trees and chicken coops in a drowsy section of Los Angeles called Hollywood, and he proposed to Lasky that they rent the barn and an acre of land as their production center.

"O.K.," Lasky wired back, "but be careful."

That may have been the last time that restraint was urged on any of the moguls who founded "Hollywood," one of the most famous civilizations that man has built, a synonym in every corner of the world for glamour and wish fulfillment. Goldwyn would become the "G" of M-G-M, the mightiest dream factory of them all, and the second "M," Louis B. Mayer, would impose on the colony an almost religious belief in the happy ending and the punished sin. I was reared on the movies that were spun out of that factory, and when I grew up and toured the studios as a writer in the twilight of their golden age, in the 1950s, I saw the sets that had once transported me to distant lands and dynasties. I saw the Middle Kingdom pylons from *The Egyptian* and the medieval castle from *Prince Valiant* and the Siamese court from *The King and I*. I saw Caligula's Rome and Napoleon's Paris and Disraeli's London and Diamond Jim Brady's New York and Wyatt Earp's Dodge City. I saw the columns of Tara and the train that finished off Greta Garbo in *Anna Karenina*. I saw the Chinese village from *The Good Earth* and the picket-fenced street where Andy Hardy lived. Huddled on the back lot, the ghostly sets waited to be reanimated by the rustle of costumed extras and the director's cry of "Action!"

Instead the sounds that were heard were the sounds of demolition. The founding moguls died, the back lots were sold off to developers, and a new breed of independent producers began to forge a new Hollywood, where agents would be quoted more often than stars, where studios would be bought and sold like junk bonds, and where the movies that did get produced were not made according to the gospel of Louis B. Mayer. Hollywood as the purveyor of happy dreams was shutting down. But 27 miles to the south, in Anaheim, on a rural acreage not unlike the one that DeMille and Lasky and Goldfish bought in 1913 to start it all, another dream merchant was about to take over the franchise.

Walt Disney first talked in the early 1940s about building a "magical little park" next to his movie studio in Burbank. It would cover eight acres and would feature pony rides, train rides, "singing waterfalls" and statues of Mickey Mouse, Donald Duck and other Disney cartoon figures with whom tourists could pose for pictures. He wanted to create something different in entertainment parks, having found as a father trying to entertain his young daughters that existing parks were "dirty, phony places, run by tough-looking people." His plans were halted by World War II, and when they were revived a decade later they had outgrown the small tract in Burbank, reaching a level of aspiration that was unheard of in America and unwelcomed by its banks. Bankers were not persuaded that a family park called Disneyland was what American families were waiting for.

"Dreams offer too little collateral," Walt later said, explaining the banks' aversion, and to raise the money he and his brother Roy did the traditional borrowing against their life insurance and selling of treasured assets that are the stuff of American capitalist legend. They bought 180 acres of orange groves in Anaheim, began "imagineering" the new kind of theme park they had in mind, cleared the land, built their Sleeping Beauty Castle and their Rocket to the Moon and their fantasy villages and rivers and rides, and opened on July 17, 1955. More than 300 million people have since paid their way in.

Thus Disney dreams were proved to be prime collateral after all, and in the 1970s they financed the orgy of land acquisition and construction in Florida that created Walt Disney World and Epcot Center. But Anaheim was where the brothers first tried out their idea on the American people and found that they had struck a deep psychic need. Disneyland, not Walt Disney World, was the true icon—carved, like Mount Rushmore, out of virgin America—and that's where I went next, flying to an airport so aptly named for Orange County, John Wayne Airport, that just landing there made me feel better. Walt and the Duke would watch over me and see that all my endings were happy.

The psychic need that Disneyland fills is the need to be whisked away to any time and place except present-day America. Being transported—on mechanical rides or on the wings of imagination—is the essence of the park. Its central metaphor, anchoring all the other contraptions of escape, is the old-fashioned Main Street that constitutes its entrance. It looks the way we like to think America looked in its late-Victorian age of innocence, or at least the way Disney chose to re-imagine his boyhood town of Marceline, Missouri, and as soon as I saw its genial facades and storefronts—mansard roofs with red-white-and-blue bunting, ice cream parlors and candy palaces and penny arcades—I gladly let myself sink into the warm bath of that turn-of-the-century world. Given a choice of turning centuries, there was no choice; Disney's late 1890s were a far nicer place than my 1990s, which I had left just outside the main gate—a vast tundra of asphalt, parked cars, tourist buses and sightseer hotels. Greater Anaheim was greater nowhere.

I began my visit by taking a ride on the old-fashioned steam train that leaves from an old-fashioned brick station at the head of Main Street. Hanging on the wall of the station was a French barometer in an ornate Victorian frame, and I wasn't surprised to see that its needle was at *très sec*, safely beyond *variable* and well past *grande pluie* and *tempête*. There is no *pluie* in Disneyland. Nor is there a speck of dirt, as I noticed when I got back to Main Street. The pavement is hospital clean, and even the horses that draw the horse-drawn trolleys leave no evidence behind. I stopped to look in the window of the clockmaker and the Blue Ribbon Bakery and the Silhouette Studio and the Market House ("Jellies and Jams") and then went up onto a turn-of-the-century front porch and sat on one of its turn-of-the-century chairs and watched the day's arriving crowds as they hurried by.

Actually they *strolled* by, their gait subliminally set by the music, all of which was in three-quarter time. One after another the gently lilting waltzes came and went—"East Side, West Side," "On a Bicycle Built for Two," "I'm in Love with the Man in the Moon"—and I realized that no other time signature in music is so suggestive of good old summer pleasures, of picnics in a grove and rowboats on a lake. Three-quarter time is an intravenous drip of yesteryear. Sometimes I heard competing music from the coin-operated nickelodeon in the Penny Arcade across the street, but it never violated the emotional codes—it was ragtime piano or steam calliope, ingenuous and jaunty, with no harsh edges, just as the colors of the buildings had no hard tones. They were pastel yellows and greens and gray-blues, or, at the loudest, the pink of a strawberry ice cream soda. The saleswomen in the shops wore peppermint-striped shirtwaists, high at the neck, and tied their hair up in ribbons—definitely not "tough-looking people." The men wore vests and suspenders and boaters, and occasionally four of them came gliding by on a bicycle built for four. It was an old Alice Faye Technicolor musical brought to life, and what it said as an architectural statement was that Main Street circa 1900 was America's lost paradise, recoverable only in facsimile.

I thought about that architecture, that Disney haute nostalgia.

Hadn't I seen it somewhere else? I had. I had seen it replicated in upscale shopping malls in upscale towns across America—towns like Aspen, Colorado, and Naples, Florida. I remembered from a visit to Naples that the twin ideas of "postmodern" (reinventing the past) and "retro" (re-creating the past) have merged there to form the collective taste. Though taste is seldom easy to define, Naples, it's safe to say, is united in the belief that yesterday was wonderful. Proof of that homage was a six-block complex of 110 stores, restaurants and art galleries that were as aggressively charming as the set of *Meet Me in St. Louis*. I also remembered a visit to the Georgetown section of Washington, D.C. Walking along its main street, admiring its authentic Federal facades, I turned through an archway and found myself in a vast turn-of-the-century world. It was a three-story mall called Georgetown Park, with every *faux* gaslight and lamppost and storefront in place—a pure appropriation, I realized, of Disneyland. I wondered whether this influence is taught in architecture schools. Just as America's postwar architects inflicted on our landscape the glass boxes of their revered Bauhaus modernism, their successors have taken their inspiration from Anaheim Victorian, building mini-Disneylands across the country to soothe our worries away. Thus Main Street America comes full circle. Though we have eagerly abandoned our actual Main Streets for the new mall out on the strip, we don't have to give up the *idea* of Main Street. Thanks to Disney, we can still make believe that the good old days never went away.

At the far end of Main Street, Disneyland fans out into other "lands," including Fantasyland, Frontierland, Adventureland, Tomorrowland and New Orleans Square—each of them, like Main Street, a perfect amalgam of preformed ideas and memories. Fantasyland, which I reached by crossing a moat perpetually washed by a dulcet rendition of "When You Wish Upon a Star," was "a timeless land of enchantment," as Walt Disney once called it, invoking two of the park's operative words. Many of its attractions have "enchanted" in their name, and what makes Fantasyland "timeless" is that it is a tapestry of images that go back to the fairy tales of our early childhood, which in turn go back to folk myth. Fantasyland could have been built by Bavarian elves, not Anaheim carpenters. The turreted Sleeping Beauty Castle was every castle from every illustrated storybook about princes, princesses, wicked stepsisters and enchanted toads, and the town that lies at its feet, with its half-timbered stucco houses and weathered beams, was every medieval European village from the tales of Grimm to the opera *Hansel and Gretel.*

No less familiar to me were the neighboring principalities of Adventureland and Frontierland, where I went next. Adventureland was all-purpose exotic: the South Seas of Maugham and Gauguin and Jack London, with an Amazon cruise and appropriate jungle drums thrown in. Every Pacific culture from Melanesia to Maui had been rifled for an identifying artifact—tribal masks and tiki statues, tapa cloth and thatched roofs, Hawaiian music and bamboo porch railings—and the resulting town was the generic "away" of every dreamer who dreams of getting away from it all, just as Frontierland was the generic Old West that Hollywood has planted in our minds as the real Old West, instantly recognizable for its trading posts and cowboy outfitters and wooden sidewalks. The genius of Disneyland is that it has no shocks of nonrecognition; we are safely cushioned against change. Walt Disney wasn't Wilbur Wright, or Gutzon Borglum, or Thoreau; he was at the other end of the American rainbow from those peppery individualists. He was Mr. Mainstream, a boy who never entirely grew up and who intuitively knew that the rest of us haven't entirely grown up either.

I spent my two days at Disneyland taking rides. I took a bobsled through the Matterhorn and a submarine under the Polar Ice Cap and a rocket jet to the Cosmic Vapor Curtain. I took Peter Pan's Flight, Mr. Toad's Wild Ride, Alice's Scary Adventures and Pinocchio's Daring Journey. I took a steamboat and a jungle boat. I took the Big Thunder Mountain railroad to coyote country and the Splash Mountain roller coaster to Critter Country. I took a "Pirates of the Caribbean" ride (black cats and buried treasure) and a "Haunted Mansion" ride (creaking hinges and ghostly laughter). I took monorails and Skyways and Autopias and PeopleMovers. More precisely, those rides took *me*: up and down and around sudden corners and through dark tunnels and over rooftops, and all I had to do was sit back and let whatever conveyance I was sitting in do the driving. I had no desire to be at the wheel myself. In Disneyland that primal American urge—the urge to drive—gets suspended, replaced by the still more primal urge to be eternally transported to timeless lands of enchantment.

I didn't even mind waiting for the rides. The lines had been shrewdly configured in bends and loops to look shorter than they were, and the crowds moved along without impatience, the children cheerful and well behaved. Parents with very small children had dutifully left their strollers in one of the areas designated for "Stroller Parking": ultimate tidiness. The crowds were also very white. Although I noticed a number of Mexican-American and Asian tourists, I saw only one black family in two days. American blacks, I suspect, know that it will take more than wishing upon a star to make their hearts' desires come true.

How the Disney people view their park—what dreams and needs they think their millions of visitors bring to Disneyland to be fulfilled—I never found out; they weren't allowed to talk to me. When I first called to introduce myself, I was told that if I were writing an article there would be no problem—I could interview anybody. But books were another matter: anything connected with a book had to be cleared by the Disney legal department.

On one level that was good news. At a time when writing and reading are increasingly devalued, books were still important enough for lawyers to worry about. Books got into libraries. Magazines and newspapers were mere visitors in our midst, leaving no imprint on the culture; as a young reporter I was often told that the morning newspaper is what fish get wrapped in at night. But now, because I was working on a book, I would have to write Disneyland a formal letter of request. I did, and word came back that the legal department would process my letter soon. That "soon" never arrived. When I got to Disneyland the publicity staff refused to see me, or give me any publicity material, or even let me cross their doorstep. "Our hands are tied," they told me on the phone—the closest I came to meeting them—and no untying was ever done.

I couldn't help thinking about the American values I had seen certified and glorified on Disneyland's turn-of-the-century Main Street — such things as neighborliness and trust. At all my previous stops I had been replenished by hearing men and women talk about the place where they work and what it means to them. Their sense of work as useful and satisfying was an old-fashioned value that I found alive and well, especially in the National Park Service. In towns like Abilene, I was reminded that the people who traditionally lubricated small-town America in Disney's beloved yesteryear, helping people to get on with their lives, were the bankers and the doctors and the lawyers. None of them could have imagined that with the turn of another century Americans would be so protective of their image that they would cede to lawyers much of their freedom to act. Half the country, it often seemed, was waiting for legal clearance.

Because Disneyland is a collage of many cherished American myths, I found myself encountering in its synthetic "lands" many of the folk heroes I had met earlier on their authentic turf. The Mississippi steamboat I took in Frontierland was the *Mark Twain*, and the island it circumnavigated was Tom Sawyer Island. Davy Crockett, late of the Alamo, appeared to me three times. In Critter Country I rode in a Davy Crockett Explorer Canoe; in Frontierland I shopped in a store called Davy Crockett's Pioneer Mercantile; and at a nearby log stockade I saw a sign informing me that a string of such forts, like Fort Pitt and Fort Duquesne, once linked the American frontier. "Davy Crockett and other famous scouts," it said, "spent much time in and around such wilderness outposts acting as 'eyes and ears' of the woods."

Therefore I should have known that I hadn't seen the last of Abraham Lincoln. Earlier I had seen him in granite at Mount Rushmore and had felt his healing presence at Appomattox. Now, as I was about to leave, I noticed a building called the Disneyland Opera House. GREAT MOMENTS WITH MR. LINCOLN, its marquee said. That was for me—I'm always up for great moments with Mr. Lincoln. Inside, I watched a brief film in which Walt Disney explains his process of Audio-Animatronics, the technology that has become a trademark of his parks, enabling all manner of seemingly real people, animals, birds, fish and other critters to hail us as we come riding by. "Ever since I was a small boy I've had a great personal admiration for Abraham Lincoln," Disney says, recalling that he first Audio-Animated Mr. Lincoln for the New York World's Fair of 1964, using a life mask of the 16th President that was taken in 1860, before he grew a beard. "The final result is so lifelike you may find it hard to believe," the narrator of the film said, and we were duly ushered into a theater to try to believe it.

After a brief slide show recapitulating the Civil War, the curtain went up and I saw on the stage a tall man in a black suit who somewhat resembled Abraham Lincoln. He was sitting in a chair, with a diorama of the Capitol behind him, and something in me kept hoping he wouldn't try to get up. But he did, struggling arthritically to his feet and moving a few steps forward. He wanted to talk to us about liberty, he said, and he began to expatiate on respect for duty, the law, faith in divine Providence, and dangers facing the nation. They sounded like disconnected homilies, and as I later learned, they were: snippets plucked from five speeches delivered during the mainly beardless years of 1838 to 1864. This was not my writer's Lincoln. In fact, was it any-body's Lincoln? As the tall man rambled on, emphasizing his points with hand and arm gestures that were angular and spasmodic, his long legs just a little unsteady—would he *fall*?—I was reminded of another tall figure from the dim recesses of Hollywood make-believe who moved with the same mechanical vulnerability, the same endearing wish to be human. It was Boris Karloff in *Frankenstein*.

With mingled joy and regret, as they said in the old Hollywood travelogues, I bade farewell to Disneyland and stole out into the parking lot. There I caught a shuttle bus that took me to my modern hotel across a landscape that was not spotless and not beautiful; I didn't see a single orange tree. But it was real, and I was glad to get back to my America. Two days in Disneyland had been a welcome release from the stressful present into an America as long gone and as deeply longed for as the boyhood of Tom Sawyer. I could only tell myself that Walt Disney's turn-of-the-century Main Street and Mark Twain's mid-19th-century Hannibal—the handiwork of two masters of make-believe—were also not as ideal as they made themselves believe.

14

Rockefeller Center

In his classic book *Here Is New York*, E. B. White said that there are roughly three New Yorks, the first being the New York of the man or woman who was born there and who takes for granted its size and its turbulence. The second is the New York of the commuter—"the city that is devoured by locusts each day and spat out each night. Third, there is the New York of the person who was born somewhere else and came to New York in quest of something. Of these three trembling cities the greatest is the last. . . . It is this third city that accounts for New York's high-strung disposition, its poetical deportment, its dedication to the arts, and its incomparable achievements. Commuters give the city its tidal restlessness; natives give it solidity and continuity; but the settlers give it passion."

That's as true and as lyrical as when it was written, in 1949. Passionate settlers from places like Abilene continue to enrich the city for those of us who were born here. But there's a fourth New York, which White didn't mention: the city of tourists. Those multitudes are equally a part of my life. They often come up to me to ask directions—NATIVE SON is evidently printed on my face—and what most of them ask is, "Where's Rockefeller Center?" or "Where's the skating rink?" or "Where's the Christmas tree?" There's no need to say, "What rink?" or "What tree?" America has only one skating rink and one Christmas tree, and one Radio City Music Hall and one Rainbow Room. They are four icons wrapped in a super-icon, one that has the further iconic stature of being the ultimate symbol of American capitalism.

Of all the landmarks in New York, Rockefeller Center, which gets an estimated 175,000 visitors a day, is the one that tourists feel most possessive about. No other Japanese purchase of American property—movie studios, golf courses, hotels, ski resorts—raised such an outcry as the news in 1991 that the Mitsubishi Estate Company had "bought" Rockefeller Center. "Say it ain't so!"—the national wail of disbelief—echoed across the land. What Mitsubishi actually acquired was 80 percent of the Rockefeller Group, a private corporation that owns 28.5 percent of the Center's original buildings, the ones built between 1931 and 1940; the remaining 71.5 percent is held by a real estate trust that is traded on the New York Stock Exchange. The Group also owns the Time & Life Building and 55 percent of the McGraw-Hill Building, two of the edifices that went up after the war when the Center expanded, mainly across the Avenue of the Americas, bringing the total to 19. Arithmetically, therefore, Mitsubishi didn't buy Rockefeller Center. Symbolically, however, it did; the purchase had an arithmetic of its own, deeply upsetting to Americans.

That phenomenon—the fact that a capitalist corporation had crossed over into a semipublic state of grace—was one that I saw strongly at work when I went to Rockefeller Center as my next-to-last stop. I realized that I knew almost nothing about its origins as an experiment in humane urban space. I thought I remembered from my childhood—when my three older sisters and I were expediently taken to stores like Best & Co. and DePinna's, which sold both girls' and boys' clothes—that Fifth Avenue was the heart of New York, a vibrant business district. But at that time the three core blocks of what is now Rockefeller Center consisted of low, nondescript residential brownstones, boardinghouses, bistros, nightclubs, speakeasies and other marginal establishments. The blocks belonged to Columbia University, which had received them from New York State as part of the disposition of the Elgin Botanic Gardens, which stood there in the early 18th century. From those three midtown blocks Columbia collected rent of only $300,000 a year.

John D. Rockefeller, Jr., was enticed into the situation in 1928 by the directors of the Metropolitan Opera, who wanted to quit their old opera house at Broadway and 39th Street and build a new one on the

Columbia property, where most of the leases were about to expire. As they negotiated for one block, they felt the need for an adjacent block to give their opera house a gracious public square, and they went to Rockefeller for help. "The plan commended itself to me as a highly important civic improvement," he later recalled, and he ended up leasing all three of Columbia's blocks. Grandiose plans were drawn for an opera complex, and the Met inched closer to its dream of moving "uptown." With the stock market crash of October 1929, that dream abruptly died, along with the roaring optimism of the roaring twenties. The Opera dropped the plan it had initiated, leaving Rockefeller, its recruited angel, who wasn't even an opera devotee, holding three blocks of unloved real estate as the Depression settled over America and chilled the very idea of financial adventure.

That Rockefeller decided not to simply sit tight but, instead, assembled a team of visionary architects and planners who built a city-within-a-city during the worst years of the Depression, giving employment to 75,000 construction workers and hope to a despondent metropolis, is a story of high collective nerve, which I found told in warm scholarly detail by Carol Herselle Krinsky in her book *Rockefeller Center*. A cultural center had to be hastily reinvented as an integrated business, retail, entertainment and dining complex unlike anything that then existed. Even for Rockefeller it was a race against disaster, for after he had bought up all the remaining leases and torn down 229 brownstones, he would get no more income from the property until a new family of buildings had been erected there and a new family of business tenants persuaded to move in.

The odds were poor. The area wasn't identified with business or served by rapid transit: the Sixth Avenue subway hadn't yet been built. There was also a sudden glut of vacant office space in New York—most dramatically, in the brand-new 102-story Empire State Building. But one big piece fell into place. The Radio Corporation of America, an emerging giant of popular culture, agreed to replace the Metropolitan Opera as the property's central tenant and occupant of its showcase building. Radio was America's booming new medium, and RCA, which owned or controlled the National Broadcasting Company, RKO Pictures and RCA Victor Records, needed big new RCA and RKO office buildings and big new studio space for NBC. Thus the Center's early nucleus, together with Radio City Music Hall, came to be known as

Radio City—a perfect name for the dawning decade, when "modern" was the ascendant god and radio would enter every American home and heart. (The decade would have its perfect apotheosis in the wonderful New York World's Fair of 1939, the futuristic "world of tomorrow.")

Public reaction to the planners' first model—a cluster of frankly commercial buildings—was hostile, bordering on savage. "The crux," said the *New York Herald Tribune*, "is that Radio City is ugly. Its exterior is revoltingly dull and dreary." The *New York Times* spoke of "aberrations and monstrosities." Reeling back to the drawing board, the designers softened their plan, giving it the breathing room and human scale that have endeared it to visitors ever since, and a new rendering of the RCA Building, by the architect John Wenrich, projected a surprisingly slender 70-story limestone shaft rising from a sunken garden at its base. But the animosity didn't die away. As construction began, the Center continued to be the object of derisive letters, jokes, cartoons and comedy skits, and realtors unanimously predicted its failure, especially when RKO went broke, bequeathing to Rockefeller the last thing he needed just then—a bankrupt partner. His only choice, he said, was to "keep sawing wood."

One form that the wood sawing took was an intensive search for tenants abroad, few American corporations being willing or solvent enough to sign up. British and French interests were induced to lease the low twin buildings on Fifth Avenue that they have occupied ever since, and other foreign governments were wooed and won for smaller tenancies. Thereby John D. Rockefeller, Jr., brought to Rockefeller Center, as it was officially named in 1932, an international presence, consistent with the family's long internationalist bent, which set it apart from other urban complexes. The foreign flags around his sunken court anticipated the United Nations buildings—which Rockefeller also made possible, by donating the land—that would truly internationalize the city after World War II.

By the end of 1933 the jokes were no longer funny. Irving Berlin's Broadway revue, *As Thousands Cheer*, dropped a skit that lampooned the Center, and pedestrians began to explore the mini-city that was materializing in their midst, especially the private street, Rockefeller Plaza, that so unexpectedly bisected it, varying the urban grid. New Yorkers began to realize that the much-mocked millionaire was giving them something special. *Architectural Forum* certified the shift; the Center, it said, was "an inspiring spectacle to New Yorkers." Commercially, another three years would pass before the project stopped losing money. The certifying bard was Ira Gershwin, who, in his lyric for "They All Laughed," wrote:

They all laughed at Rockefeller Center,
Now they're fighting to get in....

Rockefeller Center has been an intimate part of the landscape of my adult life. I walk past it almost every day, and at one time or another I've been a writer for some of its oldest tenants, including *Life* and NBC and Simon & Schuster. But I seldom walk *through* it, and I had never paused to analyze it as designed space. Now what struck me was how inviting it was: it literally invited me to step into its garden and partake of its beauty and civility. Unlike the massive recent buildings that have been crammed into mid-Manhattan, including Rockefeller Center's own new buildings on the Avenue of the Americas—ice-cold, monolithic slabs perched on a windblown plaza—these three original blocks were woven into the fabric of city life, ready to welcome me whenever I might want to drop in and whatever I might want to do: work, eat, shop, skate, see a show, look at flowers, or just sit. I wouldn't feel lonely: thousands of other people would have accepted the same invitation.

I stopped to notice all the art that had been routinely placed over doorways and in lobbies: sculptures, friezes, reliefs, gold-leaf panels, bronze panels, limestone panels, painted murals, leather murals, photomurals, plaques, cartouches, wood carvings, mobiles, mosaics, pylons, portals, screens, maps, ornamental grillwork, carpets, tapestries, wall decorations, wallpaper and Art Deco fixtures—the work of more than 50 artists, from Josef Albers to William Zorach. I particularly admired Isamu Noguchi's stainless-steel sculpture, *News*, over the entrance of the Associated Press building—a tightly composed arrangement of five journalists wielding the tools of their craft: telephone, teletype, camera, wirephoto, and pad and pencil. It had that '30s earnestness about industrial progress and about work as noble toil that characterized so much of the Center's heroic statuary and allegorical art, often invoking figures of mythology as symbols of strength and creativity—sturdy Atlas and soaring Prometheus—and giving its works such titles as "Wisdom," "Radio" and "Intelligence Awakening Mankind." Just as Christian saints and angels are tucked into countless crannies of medieval cathedrals to assert the faith, the bright promise of the machine age is stamped all over Rockefeller Center.

I noticed that there were no delivery trucks clogging my path. The planners had deflected them onto a ramp leading underground—this was a *people's* center—and that in turn reminded me of what else was underground: more than 200 shops in a honeycomb of connected arcades. Many of the stores that I walked past in Rockefeller Center had the familiarity of old friends—Acme Passport Photo, Librairie Française—and so did the *art moderne* block capitals that spelled out their names. Nothing had changed! I was in an intact tribal village, and everyone walking around the village looked placid and at ease. I had seen the same look in the national parks.

"When I first came to work here I thought tourists were asking the most bizarre questions," said Lisa Lane, who works the main information desk, in the lobby of 30 Rockefeller Plaza, from nine to five. "Now I don't. No request seems unusual, because I've learned that whatever they want, they can get it here. 'I broke a tooth,' they tell me, or 'Where can I get perfume?' or a passport, or a facial, or a foreign-language newspaper. We have consulates and a post office and specialty bookstores and thirty-six restaurants and every other kind of service. Many old people come in regularly to visit Radio City Music Hall, and they stop by to ask when the show starts. A lot of people telephone to ask about the Christmas tree; they plan their whole trip to New York around it and want to be here when the switch is thrown. It's a tradition, a specific thing that's been done for years and years, something their grandfather did, which you don't find much anymore. People enjoy that continuity. They feel that the Center belongs to them. After they ask me what to do, they often say, 'I guess we'll just go out and watch the skaters for a while.'"

I also went out to watch the skaters. They were making their guileless circles around the small rink, past Paul Manship's shiny gold *Prometheus*, and I was soon lulled into a contentment that took me back to watching Niagara Falls and drifting down the Mississippi River at Hannibal; watching people skate was another one of those old simple pleasures that don't need any enhancing. The rink was so obviously the animating heart of Rockefeller Center that anyone would assume it was there from the start. But it was a latecomer, born of desperation. The sunken plaza that had been planned as a refreshing change of level turned out to be a dud; pedestrians didn't want to venture down there, and several shops around its rim had failed. Nobody could think of anything that might bring it to life. Finally someone mentioned that a Cleveland inventor had found a way to keep outdoor skating rinks from melting. In the spirit of "we'll try anything," a skating rink was temporarily tried. The rink opened on Christmas Day, 1936, and it has been credited ever since as the single biggest factor in the popularity of Rockefeller Center as a goal for tourists and a show for New Yorkers.

"In winter the spectators are packed wall-to-wall up there," said Carol Olsen, manager of the rink. "They hoot and holler for certain skaters and really get into it. They cheer for the skater who wipes out, and the skaters are good sports about it; they get up and wave back. People love to watch the ones who struggle to maintain their balance. Some of them can really go into contortions trying to stay up; it would be better for them to fall. Ninety percent of the skaters are from out of town. They say, 'It's the one place we had to come.' In every group there's always one person who doesn't want to skate. 'I'm not doing that in front of all those people,' they tell me. I say, 'I guarantee you'll never see those people again.'"

But for most skaters the rink is an outlet. "It's their release from whatever is going on in their lives," Olsen said. "They go into their own dreamland. Their faces express oblivion—they're having that one moment of fantasy. When you were a child there was always something you didn't get to do, and skating is one way of living out that dream. Young boys go out on the ice and you can tell that they're envisioning themselves playing hockey in an NHL game. Girls imagine that they're Dorothy Hamill—they'll go out in the middle and do their little spins. Parents and grandparents tell me, 'I haven't been here since I was eight—I can't believe I haven't been back in all this time.' They feel that it's their rink, and they're trying to repeat with their children what they remember doing long ago."

That ritual repetition took me back to Yellowstone Park and all those parents who first came there as children and were now back with kids of their own, "making a pilgrimage to the memory of their childhood experience." I also thought of the families I had seen stretched out around me on George Washington's lawn—*our* lawn—at Mount Vernon; many of those parents were reenacting an old memory. But somehow I hadn't expected to find the urge to recover the past as potent in midtown Manhattan. I thought such yearnings needed a more tranquil setting, a Hannibal or a Yellowstone. Now I saw that place per se was not as important as the memory of what happened in that place. I saw that the search for memory—personal memory or historical memory—was what much of my journey had been about.

Carol Olsen told me to look up at the sky over the rink. "That sky is a Colorado blue," she said, "which is strange, because you never see that blue anywhere else in Manhattan." I looked up past the RCA Building, which I still think of as the RCA Building even though it's now the GE Building, and felt an intimation of Denver. "This rink is a little oasis in the middle of a drab and unsettled city," Olsen said. "When I first came here from Lake Placid, I was a little scared, but now I think it's nice. My husband says, 'Get out of your little bubble and see what the city is all about.'"

I stood at the railing, massaged by Viennese waltzes and Broadway show tunes, and watched the skaters come and go. During the Christmas season, when the tree is up, the rink stays open until midnight and gets at least 1,500 skaters a day. Some skaters, I noticed, don't stay long—"their ankles hurt," Olsen said—but quite a few looked like regulars, and I stopped one old man in a beret as he came gliding by. His name, he said, was Fritz Chandler, and he was 94 years old. He said that he was a former ice-show entrepreneur, that he had met his wife on the rink, and that he still skates for several hours every day. I asked him why he does it. "Why else would I be here," he said, "if it wasn't important?"

Unlike the late-arriving ice, planting was part of Rockefeller Center from the start, and probably no botanical displays in America are as widely known and enjoyed as the ones that adorn the promenade that slopes from Fifth Avenue down to the rink. Because the exhibit changes as often as 14 times a year, it keeps taking pedestrians by surprise as they hurry along the avenue; overnight, something botanically unexpected has appeared in our midst. Only Christmas with its trum-

peting angels and Easter with its lilies and tulips and daffodils are pre-
dictable. While I was there the display consisted of 200 blueberry
bushes with real blueberries that anyone could pick, and an earlier
cycle had featured 40 orange trees with real oranges that anyone could
smell and squeeze.

"I brought those trees up here with the *hope* that people would
touch the oranges," said David P. Murbach, manager of the garden
division, who has a graduate degree in public horticulture. "Not everyone has the luxury of going to Florida or the Caribbean. People
couldn't believe those were real oranges and real blueberries. I just
love plants, and I really want people-plant interaction. Though Rockefeller Center is private space, I took this job because I felt that it was
public-spirited space, and, in fact, people comment on our work as if it
came out of their taxes or was part of the Parks Department. They say,
'Gee, I really like geraniums—why aren't you using geraniums?' But
most of their comments are rare and wonderful. When we're putting
in a new installation they say, 'Why are you doing this? Is something
extraordinary happening today?' I tell them, 'No, we're doing this
for you.'"

The pride that Rockefeller Center's employees feel at being part of
"something larger," Murbach said, hit him on his first morning at
work, in December of 1985. "I got there at 7:00 A.M.," he recalled,
"and just then the Christmas tree arrived and around the corner came
three camels from the Nativity pageant at Radio City Music Hall.
They were being walked around the block for exercise." The displays
that Murbach has since mounted, which range from tropical jungles to
Oriental gardens to topiary dinosaurs, get installed in less than a day,
and it doesn't bother him that the labor of his gardeners is also on display.

"A lot of people like change and process," he said. "Our best audience is the working population of this area. They like to see us plant
and they like to watch us garden, and it's good that they notice us and
ask questions. When I did a children's garden with fanciful shrubbery
based on *Alice in Wonderland*, people said, 'I haven't seen that since my
mother's garden.' It made them think of their childhood. They look at
our gardens and think other thoughts." Today Murbach's future
exhibits are being cultivated far from New York on a schedule that he

keeps on a Rolodex in his head—a rare species of rhododendron, for instance, that is being grown for him in Vancouver for a display seven years from now.

But the show that requires the most coordination is the Christmas tree, the hardest requirement being to find one that is perfect. "Most trees don't come perfect," Murbach said. "You know how you bring home a Christmas tree and the kids say, 'Dad, why did you get that tree? It's got a crooked branch.' So you put the bad side against the wall. But our tree has to be perfect on *every* side, and it has to be thick on every side, which means that it has to grow in full sun. That eliminates getting it from a forest; those trees would be too narrow, like a pencil. This year's tree, which grew all by itself, is huge—it's the maximum object that anyone can move. But trees like that are getting harder and harder to find as the Northeast gets more developed."

The Center's first tree was a scrawny specimen that the workers stuck up in 1931 in the rubble of a block they had just demolished, where the British Empire Building now stands. A contemporary photograph shows them bunched near the tree in depths-of-the-Depression patience to get their pay on Christmas Eve. The first formal tree was erected in its present location two years later, and its annual lighting, around 5:00 P.M. in early December, is one of the events most beloved by American tourists, who, to qualify as tourists, don't have to come from any farther away than New Jersey or Westchester or even outer Queens.

"Thousands and thousands of people start arriving around two o'clock," I was told by Bob Fugowski, supervisor of carpenters, painters and plasterers, whose men have the job of constructing the l00-foot-high scaffolding around the tree, after which 25 electricians spend five days attaching the 25,000-odd lights. On the appointed afternoon, Rockefeller Center's blocks are closed to traffic, and the crowds awaiting the instant of illumination are densely jammed around and near the rink. "It's amazing," Fugowski said, "that so many people are mesmerized for such a small second. All the years I've been here, it still never fails to reignite a little spirit of something."

In 1932 the 6,200-seat Radio City Music Hall, which had been created by the legendary impresario Samuel L. Rothafel, known to the world as "Roxy," had a grand opening so grand as an announcement of its cultural pretensions that the curtain didn't come down until 2:30 A.M., by which time much of the glittering audience was home in bed. The show's 19 acts had something for everybody, including a ballet, excerpts from *Carmen*, symphonic interludes by Ferde Grofé, the Flying Wallendas, Fraülein Vera Schwarz of the Berlin Staats-Oper, the "outstanding young American dancing comedian" Ray Bolger, the Roxyettes (later the Rockettes), the Tuskegee Choir, and Martha Graham and her Dance Group, who performed "a choric dance for an antique Greek tragedy."

Like so many of Rockefeller Center's early launches, it bombed. "Gigantism was the fatal flaw of the Radio City Music Hall," Carol Krinsky writes in *Rockefeller Center*. "The tremendous dimensions of the auditorium and of the 100-foot-wide proscenium arch make performers look like dolls. The personalities of the people on stage do not project well to people in the orchestra, let alone to those 180 feet away in the upper mezzanine," she says, noting that 180 feet is just 20 feet shorter than a New York city block. Roxy's idea of filling a vast house with continuous "variety" entertainment was seen to have been a vast blunder, and after the show's disastrous first weeks he quit in disgrace, leaving the Rockefeller interests, once again, derided and compelled to reinvent the format. Their solution was to feature a good first-run movie, combined with elements of live entertainment, such as the Rockettes, and they reinforced the elegance of their theater by treating their customers, who were always called "guests," with elegant courtesy.

It was somewhere in those early years that I was first taken to the Music Hall as a boy, and I still remember the awe I felt when I walked through the 60-foot-high Grand Foyer and was led by a uniformed usher to my seat in the great auditorium and saw its firmament of golden semicircles rising out of the proscenium arch. The discredited Roxy had at least built well—I wasn't in a theater; I was in a palace. I can still picture Dick Leibert playing the multi-keyboard organ, Erno Rapee conducting the symphony orchestra as it rose—rose!—into view, and the Rockettes kicking with a precision that was a miracle. I don't remember what the movie was, but I'm sure it was wholesome, for the secret of the theater's subsequent success, together with its annual Christmas and Easter spectacles, was that families would never be unpleasantly surprised by anything that wasn't family entertainment.

By the mid-1970s, when the Music Hall fell on hard times, partly because movies were no longer fit for children or even for families, 250 million people had come through the doors, often after waiting patiently in long lines—one of the Center's familiar sights—that snaked back and forth in the street. In 1978 the losses were so heavy that the theater announced that it would close and perhaps be torn down. Such was the public clamor, much of it orchestrated by placard-wielding Rockettes, that the Music Hall was saved and given landmark status. To pay its bills it changed direction once more, embarking on its present policy of forgoing movies and booking short-term gigs by pop groups and pop stars like Liza Minnelli.

Now, in 1991, I took a guided tour of the Music Hall, along with a dozen other pilgrims. The house was between shows, and our guide led us upstairs and downstairs and backstage, giving me a close look not only at Dick Leibert's mighty Wurlitzer but at a real Rockette, clad in a silver-sequined costume that mercifully didn't hide her legs. She answered our questions about that famous sorority, telling us, among other things, that the 36 seemingly identical Rockettes range in height from 5 feet 8 1/2 inches to 5 feet 5 1/2 inches, the illusion of parity being achieved by placing the shorter ones at the ends. But what most struck me was the beauty of the public spaces, especially the lofty Grand Foyer and its related lounges, mezzanines and rest rooms, each a time warp of '30s murals, sculpture, banisters, fixtures and Art Deco ornamentation. Today the rooms are regularly used by fashion photographers as settings to evoke the period's ocean-liner high style.

"Nothing was considered too mundane to be rendered beautiful," said Sandra Manley, the Music Hall's director of public relations. "Everything was made for a patron's ease and comfort—there's a sense of time enough and space enough. These areas are a living museum, and that excites people." I marveled at the ladies' lounges and powder rooms—mirrored and wallpapered salons reminiscent of a Ginger Rogers movie. The one on the second mezzanine had chrome and leather furniture set against a floral mural by Yasuo Kuniyoshi, who got the job after Georgia O'Keeffe backed out.

"Our guided tour includes the rest rooms by popular demarid," Manley told me. "Older women remember the ladies' room. It was as much a part of their experience as anything they saw on the stage, because kids always have to go to the bathroom, and in this case parents were glad to take them there. It does something for me to know that there was a culture that treated a necessity of life as if it was a luxury. The building is still exactly the way it was, and we all get a sense of beauty from it, even young people who have never been here before. When we first started holding rock concerts, we didn't know how the audiences would behave. But we've found that if you put people in a beautiful place and surround them with beautiful things they'll take care of it."

On my last day of hanging around, I was approached by a tourist couple. They were holding hands, as tourists do in Rockefeller Center; it's one of the few parts of New York where that quaint custom can be observed. "Can you tell us where the Rainbow Room is?" they said. I pointed straight up, to the summit of the RCA Building. The building never fails to please me with the purity of its lines, especially after dark, when it is bathed in white light and looks even purer. Along with the Chrysler Building, it is still the champ; those two sexagenarians outclass every corporate office, except the Seagram Building, that has been erected in New York since.

"We've always heard about the Rainbow Room," the two tourists said, explaining why they wanted to see it, and I was reminded of something that James V. Reed, assistant vice-president of the Rockefeller Group, had told me. "Rockefeller Center," he said, "is probably the most preintroduced place in the world. So many people know about it even before they see it." In almost the same words, Sandra Manley of the Music Hall had said, "People think they've been here even if they haven't." What had mainly preintroduced Rockefeller Center, most of the people who worked there felt, was Hollywood. Hundreds of movies have used it as a backdrop to catch the urbanity of New York. Most of them, I assumed, were romantic comedies; the Center is not associated with the darker emotions.

"I see an old movie on TV—and there's Rockefeller Center," the carpentry supervisor Bob Fugowski told me, "and I see a *new* movie—

and there's Rockefeller Center. When I go away on vacation and the same thing happens, I get a little annoyed. My wife finds it hilarious. She says, 'You can never get away from that place.'"

Like the out-of-town couple, I had heard the Rainbow Room calling down to me, and I went up to check it out. In 1987 the room emerged from the cocoon of a project that lovingly restored it to the way it looked on October 3, 1934, when it opened as a chic supper club suspended high above Manhattan, where big bands would play for couples dancing on a revolving floor—glamour incarnate—and aspiring new performers like Mary Martin, Judy Holliday and Edgar Bergen (and Charlie McCarthy) would be introduced. Reading about that opening night and its featured star, the French diseuse Lucienne Boyer, in a 1934 society magazine, I was transported back to an era and a journalistic language as frozen in aspic as an old Cole Porter song:

> "Oh, you're just in time," everybody cried when we got off the elevator at the 65th floor. "She's going to sing any moment."
>
> We knew who they meant by "she." Who but Boyer, whose voice we had all been listening to on foreign gramophone records, especially the one of "Parlez-Moi d'Amour"?
>
> Tossing our wraps hither and yon to attendants, we began moving toward the Rainbow Room proper, through whose windows we could see the whole of uptown New York laid out like a pattern of diamonds.
>
> Everybody we ever knew was there. We passed young S____, with a table full of visiting Britishers, one of whom had just landed the week before on the same boat with Boyer and was practically light-headed from this, his first view of New York night life.
>
> "But I say," he kept exclaiming, "it's surely not all as utterly utter as this?"
>
> "No," we answered him, "it isn't. This is special."

The man who supervised the restoration of the Rainbow Room and now manages it, Joseph H. Baum, remembers his initial glimpse. A veteran restaurateur, Baum was a young student of hotel management at Cornell when his class was brought to New York to see the Rainbow Room's kitchen, and it was from there, through the kitchen door, that he got his first look at the room itself. "I was bowled over," he told me. "It was so grand!"

Today Baum gets requests for reservations from all over America, many of them accompanied by letters recalling an early visit to the Rainbow Room and even what the letter writer wore. "We feel we have the affection of the world," Baum told me. "It has something to do with mortality—the belief in something that's been here a long time and that will outlive us." Cole Porter's songs, it occurred to me, were one of those mortality-defying links across the decades. In 1991 they were being played in the Rainbow Room with the same rhythmic zest as when they and the room were new, in 1934, when the patrons might have just come from hearing "You're the Top" and "I Get a Kick Out of You" in Porter's *Anything Goes* on Broadway.

"Whenever people are conscious of time," Baum said, "it's always time past—time that has come and gone. This place is a reaffirmation that time goes on, and people want to be part of that. The true New Yorker is loyal and proud of New York—he wants to be thought of as enjoying the pace and standards of the city—and our customers are people who want to be New Yorkers for a short time. It has to do with participation. There are very few things that there's a common feeling for and that express what you're proud of."

Baum asked me what other American places I had visited, and as I mentioned them I realized that they were all places that Americans have a common feeling for and are proud of. "We have an advantage over Mount Rushmore," Baum said, "in that we have an energy that is current. We're alive. We have an opportunity to entertain you, to express the excitement and beauty of the city, to say to young people that New York is a place of endless possibility."

15

Pearl Harbor

Like every American old enough to remember Pearl Harbor, I remember where I was on December 7, 1941, when I heard about the Japanese attack that pulled the United States into World War II and would send me and my generation off to fight it. But what I remember most vividly is the first thought that popped into my head: Where's Pearl Harbor? I had never heard of it and had no idea why it was a place worth bombing. I was a typical pre–World War II American, a product of the cultures that had come across the Atlantic; my upbringing and my schooling had been pointed toward England and Europe, Greece and Rome. Asia was "the inscrutable East," and it could stay that way.

Soon enough after that December day we found out where Pearl Harbor was and never again forgot it. For four years the cry "Remember Pearl Harbor!" rallied and sustained a military effort of immense scale and complexity, one that brought the geography of Asia and the Pacific crashing into our lives—Bataan, Guadalcanal, Eniwetok, Tarawa, Truk, Iwo Jima—and that was ended only by an even more cataclysmic event. The atomic bomb that fell on Hiroshima in 1945 was hatched from the bombs that fell on Hawaii in 1941. A drowsing and divided America was united overnight, and the two nations have been psychically linked ever since by the two air raids that framed their war.

Today the words "Pearl Harbor" still echo somewhere in my head, as they do for all Americans of a certain age. December 7, 1941, is our great dividing line, not only because it brought the nuclear age but because the United States was never the same country again. In hundreds of ways as irreversible as the splitting of the atom, American life was altered by World War II. Yet I never had any particular urge to visit the place where it all began. My Pearl Harbor was well preserved in the form of old newsreels, still playing in my head, of crippled battleships and billowing black smoke.

But suddenly it was 50 years later, and I wanted to know: What did that harbor really look like? How was it set among the hills that the Japanese planes came roaring over? What kind of monument had been built there to commemorate the day? I decided to go and find out. The last leg of my journey would take me, appropriately, to America's westernmost—and most Asian—frontier.

I got to Honolulu on a Sunday afternoon, checked into a hotel, hailed a cab, and asked the driver to take me to Pearl Harbor.

"Where in Pearl Harbor?" he said.

"I want to go where the tourists go."

He said, "You want the Arizona Memorial?" I said I didn't think so. Why would I want an Arizona memorial?

"So where should I take you?" he asked.

I told him to take me where he takes all the other tourists.

"That's the Arizona Memorial."

I said O.K. Whatever it meant would be revealed. We drove across the verdant island of Oahu, out past the airport, until I saw a large, almost enclosed bay on my left. The taxi stopped at the visitors center, next to the bay. "Is that Pearl Harbor?" I asked the driver. He said it was. It was a peaceful body of water; I couldn't see a single vessel on it. *This* was Pearl Harbor? Bastion of naval might? I could have been looking out over Shiloh or Saratoga or any other long-asleep battlefield.

A large crowd of tourists was waiting for the next showing of an orientation film, and I joined the line filing into the theater. Inside, a National Park Service ranger told us that our program would last an hour. First we would see the film and then we would go by boat to see the sunken remains of the *Arizona*, where a memorial had been built honoring the 1,177 men who died when that battleship, her ammunition exploding after direct hits by Japanese bombs, sank in nine minutes. "They died before they even knew who they were fighting, or why," the ranger said. Fewer than 100 bodies were ever recovered; the rest are still in the ship. Of the day's 2,407 dead on Hawaii, including servicemen and civilians at airfields where 350 army and navy planes were also destroyed or damaged, almost half went down with the *Arizona*. The ship still leaks some oil every day.

I had forgotten all about the *Arizona*—if in fact I had ever focused on her as a separate navy tragedy in the larger ruin of the day. I had lumped her with all the other ships that were damaged in Pearl Harbor, most of which eventually got salvaged and sent back to sea. Now I understood why the monument that I expected to find, marking the events I think of collectively as "Pearl Harbor," was largely a memorial to one ship; Pearl Harbor was, after all, a navy base. Even so, the shrine had been a long time getting approved and built. Only after a decade of fund-raising, lobbying and legislative maneuvering was it finally dedicated in 1962. As specified by the navy, it took the form large enough to hold 200 people, of a platform suspended over but not touching the barely submerged *Arizona*.

Our orientation film quickly came and went. It was a pastiche of newsreel clips that reviewed the events leading up to World War II in Asia: Japan's seizure of Manchuria in 1931, its brutal invasion of China in 1937, its subsequent occupation of Indochina, and the months of polite diplomatic talks with the United States while Japan was preparing for war. It explained that the American government had broken the Japanese code but failed through repeated bungling to warn the commanders at Pearl Harbor. It showed the Japanese carriers launching their planes and then showed the attack itself and its terrible swift rain of death and destruction. It quoted the statement of Admiral Husband E. Kimmel, commander in chief of the Pacific Fleet, who told Congress that the raid was "one of the most brilliantly planned and executed attacks ever achieved at the start of a war." It hailed the navy's glorious recovery—"like the mythical phoenix the fleet would rise"— and it ended by saying that "the lesson of Pearl Harbor is that we must never be unprepared again." The film was just long enough to remind me of the newsreels of Japanese atrocities in Peking, Tientsin, Shanghai and other Chinese cities that ran like a nightmare through my generation's growing up at the movies, especially the 1937 rape of Nanking, where more than 100,000 men, women and children were bayoneted, burned alive and otherwise slaughtered.

After the film we were herded onto a launch. As we bobbed across the water I noticed an elongated, odd-shaped white structure at the far side of the harbor, which I guessed was the memorial. Many of my fellow passengers were boys and girls in their late teens and early twenties—kids the same age as the sailors who had been sleeping on the *Arizona*, and as carefree. Many were older men and women whom I took to be World War II veterans and their wives. Many were Japanese and Chinese tourists. None of us seemed to know quite what we were being taken to see. We were given no details of the Japanese attack: there were 130 ships in the harbor, the raid began at 7:55 A.M., the first planes came over those hills. We were only asked to be respectful when we got to the memorial, and we were, staring silently down at the submerged skeleton of the *Arizona* and at the two gun turrets that still jutted above the water, and then staring silently up at the wall where 1,177 names—including 34 sets of brothers—were carved. Then, just as abruptly, we were back on the launch.

Out on the water again, I tried to imagine the horror and chaos of that long-ago December morning. Half a century hadn't dimmed the tactical brilliance of the Japanese attack; it was, as Admiral Kimmel said, a military masterpiece. The Japan of 1941 was a poor, overpopulated nation crammed into a space half the size of California. Over the previous half decade it had become a military state ambitious to expand onto the Asian mainland to obtain the territory and resources it didn't have at home. Now, with important portions of China and Indochina already in its hands, it was poised to strike at the Philippines and Thailand and at the British and Dutch colonies—rich in oil and tin and rubber—of Malaya and the Netherlands East Indies. Toward the United States its feelings had long festered, and the recent American embargo on exports of oil and steel to Japan had brought that hostility close to desperation. While the diplomatic talks and ultimatums eddied around them, the Japanese generals and admirals dreamed their dreams. A knockout punch of the American fleet would enable them to conquer the Philippines and the coveted countries of Southeast Asia with little opposition.

"If you want the tiger's cubs you must go into the tiger's lair," said

Admiral Isoroku Yamamoto, who conceived the astonishing idea of bombing Pearl Harbor. At first his idea was opposed by the entire Japanese high command because the necessary secrecy would be impossible to maintain over so many months of preparation and so many miles of sea. But Yamamoto pursued his plan, gradually refining it in such meticulous detail that the doubters agreed that it might just work. His strike force of aircraft carriers would take a northern route across the Pacific that was off the main shipping lanes, turning south to their target from a point 1,000 miles north of Oahu. To test the emptiness of those waters he sent an ocean liner to Honolulu and back over the same route, with two naval officers aboard as observers. Scrutinizing the horizon through binoculars, they saw no other ships and only sparse air patrols north of Oahu.

That news—the fact that American patrol planes seldom flew north—had already been provided by Yamamoto's secret agent in Hawaii, a young officer named Takeo Yoshikawa, who, in the protective coloring of an aloha shirt, had been monitoring daily life at Pearl Harbor since March and looking for patterns. One pattern he noticed was that American ships that went to sea during the week invariably returned to Pearl Harbor by Friday afternoon and stayed there until Monday or Tuesday. Another was that on Sunday mornings Pearl Harbor was, as Richard M. Ketchum writes in *The Borrowed Years, 1938-1941: America on the Way to War*, "a lazy, relaxed base under peacetime conditions, where many of the men slept late and many were on liberty, while those on duty appeared to be doing little more than killing time." Yamamoto selected Sunday morning, December 7, for his surprise.

On November 26, in Hitokappu Bay, off the northeastern tip of Hokkaido, an armada of 30 ships—including two battleships, three cruisers, an array of destroyers and six carriers carrying 430 planes—set out under a blanket of silence. The radio operators' sending keys had been removed, and in the village of Hitokappu all outgoing mail and telegrams had been halted and all fishermen stopped from leaving port. Sixteen days later, just before 8:00 A.M., Lieutenant Commander Mitsuo Fuchido, who had been training his flight crews relentlessly since May, led the first wave of bombers down over Pearl Harbor, where, as he was relieved to see, nobody in America's Pacific fleet, densely berthed in its landlocked anchorage, was expecting him.

I felt let down by my brief trip out to the *Arizona*—the experience had been so meager—but I also felt that more was going on than I could discern. At the visitors center, big new crowds were waiting for the next film and browsing in the small museum and souvenir shop. They average, I was told, between 3,500 and 4,500 people a day, or, annually, well over a million and a half. But who were they, and why did they come? Who were the kids? Who were the Japanese? I decided to return in the morning and get some answers.

On my way out, I saw an older man standing by the information desk. He had a name tag, ART CRITCHETT, and a helpful look, and I asked him if he worked there. He said he was one of eight or nine Pearl Harbor survivors who volunteer at the center, giving informal talks about what they saw on December 7 and just being available. Many of the tourists who gravitate to him are World War II veterans, eager to make a living connection with their past. "If they were at Pearl Harbor on that day they always want to tell their story," Critchett said. I asked him to tell me his story.

"I was on the destroyer U.S.S. *Dewey*," he said. "The *Dewey* was in Pearl Harbor for its annual overhaul. We were in a nest of destroyers at the north end of Ford Island, and we were moored next to the U.S.S. *Dobbin*, a destroyer tender. It was a very quiet morning—part of the crew was ashore for the weekend—and after breakfast I was sitting on the fantail reading the Sunday paper. All of a sudden there appeared in the area a large concentration of aircraft, which was very unusual on a Sunday morning in Pearl Harbor. Generally there was just an occasional flight from Hickam Air Base.

"It wasn't long before we knew that something was amiss, because we could see large columns of smoke coming from Battleship Row. We could also see planes bombing air stations directly behind us—hangars and runways and planes sitting on the runways. So we went immediately to 'general quarters.' My station was the number three five-inch gun on the aft portion of the *Dewey*, and from there I saw the *Arizona* blow up. I also saw the target ship *Utah* capsize, with many of its crew members sliding down her bottom into the water, trying to escape. The *Dewey* didn't have any damage or casualties, but the *Dobbin* wasn't as lucky—it had three men killed and seven injured by a bomb. Afterward, we were the last ship to leave Pearl Harbor, and hundreds of servicemen came swarming onto our ship, eager to go out and fight. They wanted to get into it. We had captains and we had commanders and all kinds of people."

Quite a few widows also seek out the survivors like Art Critchett. "There's one lady who lost her husband on the *Arizona* who comes here every two or three years," he told me. "She gets very upset, but she says she just can't help coming every so often." Time doesn't soften the memory of the Japanese attack for those who were touched by it. "Even today," Critchett said, "any trip out to the memorial is very emotional for me. It still seems like yesterday."

That night at my hotel I bought a copy of Walter Lord's *Day of Infamy* and settled down to read it. "Monica Conter, a young Army nurse, and Second Lieutenant Barney Benning of the Coast Artillery," it began, "strolled out of the Pearl Harbor Officers' Club, down the path near the ironwood trees, and stood by the club landing, watching the launches take men back to the warships riding at anchor. They were engaged, and the setting was perfect. . . . For the first time since July 4 all the battleships were in port at once."

Nurse Conter and Lieutenant Benning were no more naive, no more frozen in a reverie of America the unassailable, than the service-men on the ships riding at anchor, or than I was back East in college, or than most Americans were in the 48 slumbering states. One recur-ring theme that struck me in Walter Lord's sequential account of December 7 was the refusal of people all over Oahu to believe that what they were seeing—unidentified planes, falling bombs, rising smoke—was an enemy attack. It was just the army fooling around, it was just this, it was just that—anything but the unbelievable truth.

Day of Infamy brought the day back to me in all its helplessness and humanity, stirring emotions I thought had long since ebbed away. Remember Pearl Harbor! The old cry still had some life in it. Once again I felt the fear and paranoia of that early wartime period, deepen-ing as we got news from the Philippines of the Bataan death march and other Japanese army atrocities committed against American soldiers. Surely an attack as cunningly planned as the Pearl Harbor raid was only a prelude. Hawaii was about to be invaded! California was about to be invaded! If hundreds of Japanese planes could materialize out of nowhere, so could some Japanese divisions. Spies were imagined everywhere. Lights went out and blackout curtains went up and air raid wardens patrolled the beaches. Sabotage was the new goblin in our midst, its power so frightening that the United States would massively betray—by uprooting and interning more than 143,000 American citizens of Japanese descent—the democratic freedoms it was at war to defend. Remember Pearl Harbor!

Yet something else had happened in those 50 years that nobody foresaw and that greatly complicates the experience of visiting Pearl Harbor today. To feel it I just had to walk out into the streets of Honolulu. It wasn't only that I was in a predominantly Asian city, its white population a minority outnumbered by native Hawaiians and families of Chinese, Japanese, Filipino, Korean and Vietnamese descent. Much of the city was now Japanese-owned, including the hotel I was staying in and most of the other Waikiki Beach hotels. The inscrutable East had become part of the fabric of American life. The enemy was our landlord.

"We're dealing with a swirl of emotions here," said Gary Warshefski, chief ranger of the site, when I went back to Pearl Harbor the next morning. "Before I took this job I visited the Arizona Memorial as a tourist, and while we were out there I saw an older American man shove an Oriental visitor and remove his hat and tell him to have respect. There were Americans who also had hats on, but he didn't approach them. I realized that at any site where feelings are that strong we have to be very careful, not only about what we say but about how we say it. We get protests every day, for instance, about the fact that Admiral Kimmel's remark to Congress is used in the orientation film and on a caption in the museum. People think we're being pro-Japanese or justifying the raid."

I had come to Pearl Harbor, Warshefski told me, at a turning point in the life of the memorial and in the idea of what kind of site it should be. "To many people," he explained, "it's a national cemetery, strictly a monument to the dead, like the Vietnam Memorial, with a list of names and very little interpretation. But as that generation passes on, visitors are looking at it less as a memorial and more as a national historic area where they can learn about the history of the United States. To these generations coming along, the names of the dead will be meaningless unless they have some perspective on the events that led up to December 7—that whole history of ultimatums and oil embargoes and failed negotiations. One of the main reasons why tourists from Japan come here is that Japanese education doesn't deal greatly with World War II, and they want to learn about the context of Pearl Harbor."

Feelings, however, still run deep, and the Park Service, which took over administering the site from the navy in 1980, urges tourists to express what they feel. "Those older men who are Pearl Harbor survivors have filled a big need," Warshefski told me. "Unfortunately, that resource is slowly leaving us. But our rangers make an effort to provide the same kind of help, and we also put a box for comments in a very obvious place at the front desk. 'Say anything you want,' we tell visitors, and they do. Their opinions are very well reasoned and thought out. They range from 'Being prepared is no longer an appropriate theme—the memorial should be talking about peace' to 'Don't let the Japs buy any more of Hawaii.'"

"Japanese tourists here are very quiet and reserved," Donald E. Magee, superintendent of the site, told me. "There's a strong Japanese tradition of honoring the dead, and they're the ones who throw a lei on the water out at the memorial and say a little prayer. What causes much of the friction is that we've been getting a large number of Oriental people who are here from Singapore, Hong Kong and Taiwan on group tours—Pearl Harbor is a free stop for the local tour operators. But most of their tourists don't know the language or anything about the site. If they get restless or a little boisterous, many Americans assume that they're Japanese and get hostile. They're the same ones who complain about the signs in Chinese characters on the rest rooms. They're looking for any opportunity for Japan-bashing."

One recent basher left a note in the comment box that said, "How can you have a Japanese ranger?" The ranger being asked about, Stanley E. Igawa, is a third-generation American who was a high school student in Los Angeles at the time of Pearl Harbor. Interned in a camp for almost three years, he enlisted in the army in 1944, served in World War II, and was later called up again for the Korea war and the Vietnam war. "I get both the positive and the negative," he told me when I asked him about the note, blaming much of the negative on the "annoying" Chinese tour groups and on the fact that most white Americans "don't know from Adam whether a person with an Oriental face is Chinese or Japanese or Korean or Thai or Indonesian." Positive reaction comes from World War II veterans who tell him how proud they were to have fought alongside the much-decorated Japanese-American 100th Battalion and 442nd Regimental Combat Team in Europe, or who were with the 141st Infantry Regiment, the "lost battalion" that was rescued from German encirclement by the 442nd with heavy loss of life. Stan Igawa would like to see American tourists at Pearl Harbor made aware of the role that Japanese-Americans played in many areas of the war effort, including the fact that they constituted the largest group of civilians killed on Hawaii on December 7, 1941, by Japanese bombs. "I'd like people from the mainland to know: Hey, we were caught in it too!"

Superintendent Donald Magee's last post was at Stones River National Battlefield, in Tennessee, the site of a Union victory that, as he can now appreciate, took place conveniently long ago. Pearl Harbor offers no such refuge from living memory. It also carries different meanings for different visitors, depending on their age. "For older veterans it's a place they feel they have to see," Magee said, "and the lesson really is that America must never be unprepared again. Younger Americans see it as a peace memorial. Because of Vietnam, they believe that war is not the answer to international disputes—that there have to be other lessons."

Such had been the funerary nature of the site that when Magee arrived, in 1989, he inherited a regulation prohibiting children from going out to the Arizona Memorial if they were under 45 inches high. Wondering how the policy originated, he found in the files a letter written by a previous administrator to a congressman who had protested on behalf of the parents of a child who was insufficiently tall. "The Arizona Memorial is a place for quiet reflection," the letter explained. "Its meaning is difficult for young children to appreciate. In addition, inappropriate behavior on the part of young children can negatively impact the experience. The height restriction is an attempt to address the problem." Magee soon lifted the ban. "I don't think children are too young to appreciate what that sunken ship represents," he told me. "They'll remember it if they see the leaking oil—if they see that the ship is still bleeding."

His own view is that the site should be informative and nonjudgmental. "The National Park Service does two things very well," he said. "We preserve history and we teach history. The appropriate ground for us educationally is straight historical perspective. We don't take sides at Civil War battlefields or at any other sites where controversial decisions were made, like the Custer battlefield, and here at Pearl Harbor we don't condemn the Japanese. We want to find a more humanistic approach." In this spirit, several new exhibits are being prepared, and a new film will replace the present one. One point it won't make is that eternal preparedness is the lesson of Pearl Harbor.

"We're going to have to be more creative in showing that this was a war that changed America forever," said park historian Daniel A. Martinez. "Militarily, Pearl Harbor was a defeat, but socially it altered the country in many fundamental ways. It ended a depression. It gave government huge new social responsibilities. It reshaped the family unit: women went into the work force, and children went to day care. It brought major demographic shifts—poor people who had never had opportunities came north to the big cities. It paved the way for civil rights and other realizations of the American dream, and it brought huge advances in science and medicine—the most powerful one, of course, being the birth of the nuclear age."

Older tourists understand this. "They see Pearl Harbor as a touchstone," Martinez said, "and they come here to fulfill a patriotic duty. Young people think it's a tourist attraction and expect to be entertained. But then the reality of what this place means hits them between the eyes. Suddenly they see that the freedoms they take for granted and the vacation they're enjoying were bought and paid for by the previous generation. It's not just palm trees and hula skirts. The waters here are sacred. The blood of thousands is in that water."

The biggest loss that America suffered at Pearl Harbor, Martinez believes, was the loss of innocence—the belief that the nation could never be attacked. "That loss led to a certain wariness, which in turn led to an arms race: America would never be caught off guard again. Much of the smoke that still surrounds defense rhetoric in American politics comes from Pearl Harbor. Any time you bring up the subject of arms reductions, Americans are going to look for a very simplistic reference point: 'We'll have another Pearl Harbor!' But the historic reasons for what happened at Pearl Harbor—the social, political and economic forces behind Japan's drift toward war and why she attacked us—are almost unknown to the general public. The absence of that knowledge is a serious deficiency in understanding the Arizona Memorial. Most visitors think the Japanese attack was just an aberration—some kind of spasm. How many of them understand the risk Japan took that day: that Japan in fact committed suicide that day? The Japanese themselves don't see Pearl Harbor as a victory site. To them it's the symbol of Japan's greatest mistake.

"We can never explain to tourists who are only here for an hour the complexity of the causes of the attack. But we can try to show the public that, as misguided and misled as Japan was at that time, she too was human—that the Japanese also were people who had sons and daughters who went to war. And there's another story we should tell. After the war Japan rose out of the ashes of defeat. But helping her in her struggle was the very country she had attacked, and that American benevolence was what enabled her to prosper. How many conquering nations have extended the hand of recovery? Here at Pearl Harbor I think we can appeal to the qualities that made America great: fair play, understanding and forgiveness."

Looking Back

When I look back on my journey I'm struck by how many assumptions I took along that turned out to be not true. The words "I assumed" recur in this book with sobering frequency. I assumed that Mount Rushmore was slightly hokey. I assumed that Mount Vernon was an elegant mansion and that George Washington was too lofty to care about mundane details. I assumed that Grant and Lee met in a courthouse and that the Civil War ended at Appomattox. I assumed that the Wright brothers were oddballs and that everyone in Hannibal loved Mark Twain. I assumed that the Alamo was out in the country and that Walden Pond was a woodland jewel. I assumed that Yellowstone Park was no bigger than any other big park and that Old Faithful went off every 57 minutes. I assumed that presidential libraries were inert repositories and that book clubs began with the Book-of-the-Month Club. I assumed that Rockefeller Center was a success from the start and that Pearl Harbor was a major World War II memorial. I assumed that lynchings in America stopped in the 1950s. No piece of information so stunned me as the fact that a 19-year-old black boy was hanged from a tree in Mobile in 1981.

With that one exception I was glad to be so constantly surprised. I thought Mount Rushmore was wonderful. I thought the Wright brothers were wonderful. I thought George Washington was wonderful. I thought the whole trip was wonderful. I enjoyed my country and

I enjoyed my countrymen—not only the famous Presidents and generals, but all the mavericks and dreamers who kept bobbing up in my path and who also were messengers of an American idea: Ann Pamela Cunningham at Mount Vernon and Louisa May Alcott in Concord, William Travis at the Alamo and Joshua Chamberlain at Appomattox, Nathaniel Langford in Yellowstone Park and John Heyl Vincent at Chautauqua, Gutzon Borglum at Mount Rushmore and Morris Dees at Montgomery. They were vivid to me because I went to them and didn't just read about them in a book. I felt the wind at Kitty Hawk and the early morning chill at Lexington; I saw the river at Hannibal and the tavern in Appomattox where 28,231 Confederate soldiers got their paroles. What I saw was that America is its own best classroom. The country I had gone looking for was waiting for me—or for anyone else—to find it.

What I also saw was why we all go. I don't mean that I know the story behind every family trip; people bring different needs to sacred places and take different meanings away. It's also true—another fact that caught me by surprise—that these places aren't static; they keep being reshaped by new events and social currents. Operation Desert Storm hit America when I was midway through my journey, hyping the national thyroid overnight, and I felt the new patriotism everywhere, especially at the Alamo; it wasn't the same place for me in 1991 that it would have been in 1990. I also had plenty of occasions to ponder the mortal truth that the perception of history varies with the age of the perceiver. My Pearl Harbor, which started my war, is not the Pearl Harbor of middle-aged men and women who only heard about it from their parents, and *their* children, teenagers gazing down at a long-sunken battleship, think of it as a relic from a battle almost as distant as Gettysburg. It wouldn't occur to them how strange it was for me to spend an afternoon at that watery cemetery and then to go back to a Japanese-owned hotel.

But on a deeper level all of us are on the same quest. We are looking for continuity. The most powerful theme I found running through my trip was the need to make a connection. Most often it was a connection with greatness: great natural wonders or great natural leaders. At Mount Vernon I was told that there is "a reaching out to connect with objects that George Washington used—people desperately want heroes and models." At Kitty Hawk I was told that it's necessary to keep replacing photographs of Wilbur and Orville Wright "because their faces get rubbed out—visitors want to touch them." At Abilene I was told that there is "a genuine bond with Ike." Connecting also took the form of a sense of belonging. At sites as different as Yellowstone Park and Rockefeller Center, tourists were nourished by the idea that the place was a family possession. They had first been brought there as children and were now back with children of their own, pilgrims to the memory of what they once did with their parents. Old Faithful and the Skating Rink were twins in their ability to link the past and the present and the future across the generations and to reaffirm the pleasure of bringing up a family in America.

As I traveled I often found myself wondering what America's countless new immigrants from all over the world would make of our iconic places. Yellowstone and Niagara would work for them—places above culture and language, conveying the American idea of land set aside "for the benefit and enjoyment of the people." So would certain shrines that I didn't visit, instantly accessible in their imagery, such as the Lincoln Memorial and the Liberty Bell and the White House. I would also bet on Montgomery's Civil Rights Memorial to speak to any fugitive from injustice, and I wouldn't write off Mark Twain's Hannibal; his books have been translated into more than 60 languages, including Czech, Korean, Latvian, Ukrainian and Urdu. But when I tried to picture a family of Cambodians peering up at the Anglo-Saxon gods on Mount Rushmore, or at Daniel Chester French's Minute Man standing with his rifle ready for the British, or at the genteel living room where Lee surrendered to Grant, I didn't know if they would be able to use those totems—like blue jeans and baseball caps—to ease their assimilation as new Americans. I hoped they would.

If I'm hopeful it's because what all of us finally want to be connected with—old or young, native-born or newly-arrived—is the best of America. The voices that echo loudest for me at the end of my journey are the voices of American decency and compassion: the "fair play, understanding and forgiveness" that I heard invoked at Pearl Harbor; the clemency of Grant toward the defeated South at Appomattox ("it will do much to conciliate our people"); the generosity of George Washington at Mount Vernon ("let no one go hungry away"); the kindness of Abilene ("you could always find a mentor in these small, friendly towns"). Even Maya Lin's Civil Rights Memorial, an epitaph to victims of hate, is an act of grace. Just as her Vietnam Memorial broke the conventions of patriotic statuary and thereby enabled Americans to begin to heal through their fingertips the wounds of a war that had torn them apart, her tabletop at Montgomery says to all who touch the names of the dead through the water, "This is not how we meant it to be. We can do better."

Speaking to us across the years with stone and symbol, narrative and myth, America's iconic places remind us of our anchoring principles and our best ideals and intentions. "This is where we started and what we believed and who we hoped to become," these places say. At least that's what they said to me.

Acknowledgments

I set out across America with full confidence that people would be willing to talk to me about their work, and that assumption about American friendliness was amply repaid. I warmly thank all the men and women who gave me their time and their trust when I dropped in on them, a stranger from New York. Six of the sites were administered by the National Park Service, and I greatly admired its rangers of every rank and length of service. America is lucky in the commitment and the intelligence of these guardians of its sacred places.

Besides those dozens of helpful men and women, who figure in the book and are quoted by name, the following people gave me information, guidance or hospitality that I gratefully accepted: Bruce Hopkins and Bob Grogg of the National Park Service in Harpers Ferry; Rex Alan Smith in Rapid City; Scott Meyer in Hannibal; Don Graham and Maxine Hairston at the University of Texas; Barbara McMillan at Mount Vernon; Donald R. McCoy at the University of Kansas; Nately Ronsheim in Chautauqua; Bevin Maguire at Rockefeller Center; Cynthia Barrett and Buz Wyeth at HarperCollins; and Caroline Zinsser in New York.

Two editors in particular sustained me. Maggie Simmons was the first editor to encourage my interest in this project, and her continuing support, as editor of *Travel Holiday* magazine, where many of these chapters first appeared, was important to me. John S. Rosenberg once again generously provided from start to finish the wise editorial advice and emotional nourishment that I have by now come to depend on.

Sources

The books, journals and articles that have been written about these 15 places and the events connected with them would fill a large library. What follows is an informal bibliography of the works cited in the text and of other books, booklets and articles that I found helpful and enjoyable. I'm grateful to the authors for their scholarship and for the pleasure of their company. At most National Park Service sites and at historic shrines such as the Alamo and Mount Vernon, the visitors center or souvenir shop carries a broad range of books, pamphlets and other educational materials for adults and children. For scholars on special quests, the town library (e.g., in Niagara Falls and Chautauaqua) and the town's bookstores (e.g., in Concord and Rapid City) are often a rich source of local and regional historical lore.

MOUNT RUSHMORE

Mount Rushmore, by Gilbert C. Fite. University of Oklahoma Press, Norman, 1952; paperback. A definitive and warmly written history of Mount Rushmore and the innumerable people who brought it into being. Interesting photographs.

The Carving of Mount Rushmore, by Rex Alan Smith. Abbeville

Press, 1985. A local historian's thorough and pleasant account of how the actual work was done and of the men who did it. Striking photographs.

LEXINGTON & CONCORD

The Thoreau Lyceum, 156 Belknap Street, Concord, MA 01742, headquarters of the Thoreau Society, has a good collection of Thoreau-related books and research materials.

"Resistance to Civil Government," an essay by Henry David Thoreau. *Reform Papers*, edited by Wendell Glick. Princeton University Press, 1973.

NIAGARA FALLS

Niagara Falls: Icon of the American Sublime, by Elizabeth McKinsey. Cambridge University Press, 1985. Professor McKinsey's book, handsomely written and printed, with more than 100 contemporary paintings, prints and sketches, traces the changing images and interpretations of the falls in literature and in the visual arts, from the early explorations into the 20th century.

Niagara: Two Centuries of Changing Attitudes, 1697–1901, by Jeremy Elwell Adamson, with essays by Elizabeth McKinsey, Alfred Runte and John F. Sears. Corcoran Gallery of Art, Washington, D.C., 1985. A spacious and informative catalogue of the exhibition "Niagara," held in 1985–86 by the Corcoran Gallery, the Albright-Knox Museum and the New York Historical Society.

Niagara and the Daredevils, by Philip Mason. "The Story of the Niagara River and the Men and Women Who Defied It." Published by the Niagara Daredevil Gallery, 1969. An entertaining booklet with period photographs.

YELLOWSTONE PARK

The Yellowstone Story: A History of Our First National Park, by Aubrey L. Haines. Yellowstone Library and Museum Association (Yellowstone National Park, WY 82190), in cooperation with Colorado

Associated University Press, 1977. A wonderful two-volume history of the park, written with narrative vigor and scholarly detail. Full bibliography, notes, appendixes, etc.

The Discovery of Yellowstone Park, by Nathaniel Pitt Langford. University of Nebraska Press, Lincoln, 1972. Langford's observant and highly personal journal of the 1870 Washburn Expedition, which was influential in the establishment of Yellowstone as the first national park.

Roadside History of Yellowstone Park, by Winfred Blevins. Mountain Press Publishing Co., Missoula, MT 59806; 1989; paperback. An amiable guide and brief history for tourists driving through the park today.

Old Yellowstone Days, edited by Paul Schullery. Colorado Associated University Press, Boulder, CO 80302; 1979. Eleven accounts of visits to Yellowstone Park, by Owen Wister, Rudyard Kipling, Theodore Roosevelt, Frederic Remington, John Burroughs and other early travelers—most memorably, Mrs. George Cowan, whose story of her encounter with Chief Joseph is the gem of this pleasant collection.

The Yellowstone National Park, by John Muir. Outbooks, Inc., Golden, CO 80401; 1986. Originally published in the *Atlantic* in 1898, this article by the eloquent naturalist describing the park's wonders has been reprinted as a small booklet with contemporary illustrations.

The Geologic Story of Yellowstone National Park, by William R. Keefer. U.S. Geological Survey Bulletin 1347, reprinted by the Yellowstone Library and Museum Association. A 92-page illustrated booklet explaining in plain language the geological history of the park and the processes still at work there.

Yellowstone on Fire! by the staff of the *Billings Gazette*. Billings, MT 59107; 1989. The story of the Yellowstone Park fires of 1988, vividly told in words and color pictures by reporter Robert Ekey and four staff photographers of the Montana newspaper.

The American West as Living Space, by Wallace Stegner. University of Michigan Press, Ann Arbor, 1987; paperback. A wise and graceful meditation on the West as a region and as a state of mind—both of which, the author says, are his native habitat.

HANNIBAL

The Adventures of Tom Sawyer, by Mark Twain. Afterword by Alfred Kazin. Bantam Books, 1981; paperback. First published in 1876. Hannibal (here called St. Petersburg) as Mark Twain reimagined and pre-served it.

THE ALAMO

A Time to Stand: The Epic of the Alamo, by Walter Lord. Harper & Row, 1961. University of Nebraska Press, 1978; paperback. A charac-teristically solid Walter Lord re-creation, based on contemporary sources, of the Alamo's final days and of the lives of the men who were part of the saga.

"Remembering the Alamo: The Story of the Texas Revolution in Popular Culture," by Don Graham. *Southwestern Historical Quarterly*, July 1985. A trenchant analysis of the repeated uses of the Alamo to perpetuate racial stereotypes and Anglo-Saxon worthiness.

"Fabled Facade," by Brian Huberman and Ed Hugetz. *Southwest Media Review*, Spring 1985. A study of 10 Alamo movies from 1911 to 1979, demonstrating that each was made "in response to a specific threat to American democracy."

Alamo Movies, by Frank Thompson. Old Mill Books, Box 100, East Berlin, PA 17316. An Alamo buff's encyclopedic survey of 80 years of Alamo movies, including stills and production credits for them all.

APPOMATTOX

Appomattox Court House. Handbook 109, Division of Publications, National Park Service, Department of the Interior, Washington, D.C., 1980. Typical of the excellent interpretive materials prepared by the National Park Service for visitors to its sites, this 112-page handbook is a model of its kind: a history, a multiple biography and a guide, with many fine past and present photographs.

Battle Cry of Freedom: The Civil War Era, by James M. McPherson. Oxford University Press, 1988; Ballantine Books, 1989; paperback. Deservedly, this superb study of the Civil War won the Pulitzer Prize for history.

Abraham Lincoln and the Second American Revolution, by James M. McPherson. Oxford University Press, 1991. Essays that develop the point made in the epilogue of *Battle Cry of Freedom*. Professor McPherson also analyzes the President's extraordinary use of language, especially in the chapter "How Lincoln Won the War with Metaphors." For further evidence, see "A Forever Amazing Writer," by Alfred Kazin, *New York Times Book Review*, December 10, 1989.

The Passing of the Armies: An Account of the Final Campaign of the Army of the Potomac, Based Upon Personal Reminiscences of the Fifth Army Corps, by Joshua Lawrence Chamberlain, Brevet Major-General, U.S. Volunteers. G. P. Putnam's Sons, 1915; Press of the Morningside Bookshop, Dayton, OH 45401; 1974.

Abraham Lincoln: A Biography, by Benjamin P. Thomas. Alfred A. Knopf, 1952. Still, I think, the best one-volume biography of Lincoln.

MONTGOMERY

Free at Last: A History of the Civil Rights Movement and Those Who Died in the Struggle, Sara Bullard, executive editor. Civil Rights Education Project, Southern Poverty Law Center, 400 Washington Ave., Montgomery, AL 36104. The center's chronicle—distributed to 55,000 American public schools—of the lives and deaths of the 40 men, women and children named on the Civil Rights Memorial.

Parting the Waters: America in the King Years, 1954–63, by Taylor Branch. Simon & Schuster, 1988. Exceptionally good Pulitzer Prize-winning narrative of the life of Martin Luther King, Jr., and of the civil rights movement. See especially Chapter 5, "The Montgomery Bus Boycott."

MOUNT VERNON

Mount Vernon: A Handbook. Mount Vernon Ladies' Association, Mount Vernon, VA 22121. A useful handbook and guide to the mansion, the outbuildings and the grounds, with color photographs.

Antiques, February 1989. A special issue of the magazine, devoted to the recent restoration of Mount Vernon, particularly the restoring of the original painted finishes in the downstairs rooms.

Mount Vernon: The Story of a Shrine. "An Account of the Rescue and Rehabilitation of Washington's Home by the Mount Vernon Ladies' Association," by Gerald W. Johnson, together with "Pertinent

Extracts from the Diaries and Letters of George Washington Concerning the Development of Mount Vernon," selected and annotated by Charles Cecil Wall. Mount Vernon Ladies' Association, Mount Vernon, VA 22121. A small paperback volume describing Ann Pamela Cunningham's rescue of the mansion, plus a selection of Washington's letters about the house and plantation.

The Genius of George Washington, by Edmund S. Morgan. W. W. Norton, 1980. A concise analysis of the nature of Washington's genius: "an understanding of the uses of power unmatched by that of any of his contemporaries."

KITTY HAWK

Wilbur and Orville: A Biography of the Wright Brothers, by Fred Howard. Alfred A. Knopf, 1987. A thorough and highly enjoyable biography.

Wright Brothers National Memorial, by Omega G. East. National Park Service, 1961. A helpful 64-page booklet that describes what happened at Kitty Hawk and Kill Devil Hills, with contemporary photographs of the brothers' flying experiments and entries from their diaries and logs.

How We Invented the Airplane: An Illustrated History, by Orville Wright. Edited by Fred C. Kelly. Dover Publications, 1988; paperback. Lively contemporary photographs accompany Orville's memoir of the steps that led to the invention of flight at Kitty Hawk.

"The Wright Brothers' Flight-Control System," by Frederick J. Hooven. From *Scientific American*, November 1978. A lucid scientific explanation.

ABILENE

We Like Ike: The Eisenhower Presidency and 1950s America. Wichita Art Museum, Wichita, KS 67203. The catalogue of a 1990 exhibition celebrating the centennial of Eisenhower's birth. Photographs.

"The Underestimation of Dwight D. Eisenhower," by Murray Kempton, *Esquire*, September 1967. Kempton pierces the "habitual veils" in which Eisenhower cloaked himself, noting that Ike succeeded because "he had concealed his marvelous intelligence from admirer and critic alike."

"The Struggle to Establish a National Archives in the United States," by Donald R. McCoy. *Prologue*, the Journal of the National Archives, National Archives and Records Administration, Washington, D.C. 20408, Summer 1984. Professor McCoy's scholarly account of the long and tortuous effort to establish a system for the safekeeping of our government records.

CHAUTAUQUA

The Chautauqua Movement: An Episode in the Continuing American Revolution, by Joseph E. Gould. State University of New York Press, Albany, NY 12201; 1961. An informal short history of Chautauqua and the educational and social changes that it set in motion, including several chapters on the founding of the University of Chicago.

"Utopia by the Lake," by Jeffery Simpson. *American Heritage*, August 1972. A fond history of Chautauqua by a longtime summer native, with photographs from across the decades that capture its distinctive architecture and its seasonal bustle.

Three Taps of the Gavel: Pledge to the Future, by Alfreda L. Irwin. Chautauqua Institution, Chautauqua, N.Y., 1977. An extensive history by the town historian.

DISNEYLAND

I saw only two works about Disneyland on sale in the park: the Official Guide, *Steve Birnbaum Brings You the Best of Disneyland*, and *Disneyland: The First Thirty-Five Years*, © 1984 by The Walt Disney Company, which tells the story of how Disneyland was conceived and built. Unofficially, the literature of Disneyland turns up in biographies of the founder, notably, *The Disney Version: The Life, Times, Art and Commerce of Walt Disney*, by Richard Schickel. Simon & Schuster, 1968.

ROCKEFELLER CENTER

Here Is New York, by E. B. White. Harper & Brothers, 1949. This slender volume is still the best book about what New York means to New Yorkers.

Rockefeller Center, by Carol Herselle Krinsky. Oxford University Press, 1978. An exemplary history of the Center, with an emphasis on architecture, city planning and urban design. The 126 illustrations include many architects' renderings of buildings and plazas, some of which, like the Metropolitan Opera complex, were never built.

The Center: A History and Guide to Rockefeller Center, by Walter Karp. American Heritage Publishing Co., 1982. A magazine-size popular history, with many photographs from the early years.

The Story of Rockefeller Center, From Facts to Fine Arts. Rockefeller Group, 1230 Avenue of the Americas, New York, N.Y. 10020. An official brochure, notable for its guided tour of the Center's many works of art and brief biographies of the artists.

The W.P.A. Guide to New York City: The Federal Writers Project Guide to 1930s New York. Random House, 1939, 1982. Like an old Baedeker, this classic has never been outclassed for style and charm. The section on Rockefeller Center is as fresh as it was a half century ago.

PEARL HARBOR

Day of Infamy, by Walter Lord. Henry Holt & Co., 1957. A vivid sequential reconstruction of the events of December 7, 1941, at Pearl Harbor, in Honolulu, and at other navy and army bases and airfields in Hawaii.

The Borrowed Years, 1938–1941: America on the Way to War, by Richard M. Ketchum. Random House, 1989. This fine book's concluding section, "Pearl Harbor: Day of Infamy," is an admirable history of the diplomatic and political events that led to Pearl Harbor, of the preparations and voyage of the Japanese attack force, and of the disaster in Hawaii on the day of the raid.

Remembering Pearl Harbor: The Story of the USS Arizona Memorial, by Michael Slackman, National Park Service. Arizona Memorial Museum Association, Honolulu, HI 96818. The official story of the memorial, with photographs.